Cover graphic by Thomas Nackid, The Oxford Associates.

Printed in the United States of America

Library of Congress Cataloging-in-Publication Data

The practice of technical and scientific communication: writing in
    professional contexts/edited by Jean A. Lutz, C. Gilbert Storms.
         p.   cm.—(ATTW contemporary studies in technical
    communication)
    Includes bibliographical references and index.
    ISBN 1-56750-361-6 (cloth).—ISBN 1-56750-362-4 (paper)
    1.   Technical writing.   I.   Lutz, Jean A.   II.   Storms, C. Gilbert.
    III.   Series.
    T11.P73 1997
    808' .0666—dc21   97-30772
                                          CIP

Ablex Publishing, 88 Post Road West, Westport, CT 06881
An imprint of Greenwood Publishing Group, Inc.
www.ablexbooks.com

The Practice of Technical and Scientific Communication

Writing in Professional Contexts

Edited by

Jean A. Lutz and C. Gilbert Storms
Miami University
Oxford, Ohio

Volume 4 in ATTW Contemporary Studies in
Technical Communication

ABLEX PUBLISHING
Westport, Connecticut • London

The Practice of Technical and Scientific Communication

Writing in Professional Contexts

Edited by

Jean A. Lutz and C. Gilbert Storms
Miami University
Oxford, Ohio

Volume 4 in ATTW Contemporary Studies in
Technical Communication

ABLEX PUBLISHING
Westport, Connecticut • London

Cover graphic by Thomas Nackid, The Oxford Associates.

Copyright © 1998 by Ablex Publishing Corporation

Printed in the United States of America

Library of Congress Cataloging-in-Publication Data

The practice of technical and scientific communication: writing in
    professional contexts/edited by Jean A. Lutz, C. Gilbert Storms.
            p.   cm.—(ATTW contemporary studies in technical
    communication)
    Includes bibliographical references and index.
    ISBN 1-56750-361-6 (cloth).—ISBN 1-56750-362-4 (paper)
    1.   Technical writing.   I.   Lutz, Jean A.   II.   Storms, C. Gilbert.
    III.   Series.
    T11.P73 1997
    808' .0666—dc21   97-30772
                                                             CIP

Ablex Publishing, 88 Post Road West, Westport, CT 06881
An imprint of Greenwood Publishing Group, Inc.
www.ablexbooks.com

Contents

Introduction

Jean Ann Lutz and C. Gilbert Storms
Miami University
Oxford, OH

ABOUT THIS BOOK

By picking up this book—*The Practice of Technical and Scientific Communication: Writing in Professional Contexts*—you have shown yourself to be a person interested in knowing more about one of the fastest growing professions in the industrialized world. In fact, an article in the March 1994 issue of *Money* ("The Best Jobs in America") ranked "technical writer" as number 18 among its top "100 widely held jobs." Furthermore, *Money* forecast that this career will show a 23 percent employment gain by 2005. Our book invites you to explore this profession for its career potential.

If you are just beginning to find out more about this profession, you may want to know what technical and scientific communicators do. In general, they create communications that enable users to take action, make decisions, or learn new information. More specifically, as a communicator, you might create manuals that tell users how to operate household appliances, computer software, or lasers for delicate eye surgeries; you might assist others in writing articles about new scientific research, creating posters for presentations, or explaining difficult concepts to lay or specialized audiences. You might edit, write, and design many other kinds of communications—proposals, reports, and marketing materials, for example. And you might do so in print or online, as multi-media communications or information on the World Wide Web. Since technical communication today often merges with training, you might design training materials, deliver that training in a classroom or online, or test the effectiveness of training to help your company better satisfy its customers or clients.

As you read this book, you may be a student choosing a college curriculum that will lead you to an interesting job, you may be an adviser who counsels students about courses and careers, or you may be a manager in industry wondering how a professional communicator could help you achieve your company's goals. In any of these cases, this book will help you understand how communicators can add value to a particular business.

The chapters of this book describe what technical and scientific communicators do in 12 different professional areas. We invited our authors to contribute to this book based upon their expertise as practitioners or teachers—or both—in one of these areas. Eleven of the areas—business and manufacturing, engineering, aerospace, computer science, environmental science, hazardous waste management, medicine, pharmaceuticals, general science, government and social services, and technical advertising—either are closely connected to an academic discipline or represent knowledge that can be acquired through training in several related disciplines. Two chapters (engineering and environmental science) provide a general introduction to more specific information contained in the aerospace and hazardous waste management chapters. The twelfth area, freelancing and consulting, might include working with subject matter in any of the 11 areas mentioned above or in a totally different one.

As you might have guessed, the field of technical and scientific communication is so broad that although communicators certainly work in other areas than those we've included, we selected the ones we did because they are the ones in which technical and scientific communicators are most likely to work. They also emphasize the important relationship technical and scientific communicators have with the subject matter about which they write.

Within the book, individual chapters are structured similarly to each other. Each is based on our desire for authors to answer fundamental questions that people entering the profession might have: What's it like to be a writer in a particular professional area? Where might I work? What am I most likely to do or to write? What special skills might I need? And how, exactly, should I prepare if I want to be a technical or scientific communicator? Our authors also answer three other pressing questions: What's the job outlook? What might I expect to earn? Where can I get more information?

Additionally, our authors provide the answer to a different kind of question: What's it like to work on a day-to-day basis in this professional area? We asked our authors to interview two additional practitioners about the details of their work and to present these to you in profiles at the end of each chapter.

Finally, our authors, too, have interesting stories to tell, as you'll see when you read their biographies at the end of this book. They have found their way into technical and scientific communication through many different and exciting routes.

ABOUT THE PROFESSION

Since our primary goal in this book is for you to understand what being a technical or scientific communicator is like, the chapters necessarily highlight the differences among these areas. But our book has a secondary purpose as well. Besides showing you what differences exist in the contexts where technical and scientific communication is practiced, we also want to explain some of the similarities that cut across these areas and distinguish technical and scientific communication from other professions. The remainder of this chapter will be devoted to this task. Its purpose is to identify some unifying principles for all of the contexts we address in the book—to show you, in fact, what all technical and scientific communication has in common. These principles are as follows:

1. The profession of technical and scientific communication is very diverse and is growing even more varied. We demonstrate this diversity by describing, briefly, the origins of the modern profession of technical and scientific communication and by explaining how the profession has changed dramatically in recent years. Today, technical and scientific communication is practiced wherever experts need to communicate technical information to nonexperts or to each other.

2. Technical and scientific communicators do not simply learn information from subject matter experts and convey it to others. In fact, communicators often help create the information that they provide for users. To explain this principle, we address how changes in the way we think about language have affected how communicators create publications.

3. Technical and scientific communicators do not work in isolation but perform their work among different professional communities. We explain what some of these communities are and how writers must

evaluate the voices of community members in creating their communications.

Finally, at the end of this chapter, we discuss how these three principles have affected the role of today's technical and scientific communicators.

Diversity and Growth in the Profession

To begin our brief history, we focus on the roots of scientific and medical writing in 17th century America. According to Connaughton (1981), scientists wrote detailed treatises (in a personal tone and with vocabulary acceptable to their European counterparts) to explain what they observed, share information, and add to existing scientific knowledge. Physicians wrote to the public to share knowledge about diseases, and they wrote to physicians and clergy to build a network of existing medical information. In the late 18th century (c. 1769–1809), the American Philosophical Society (APS), an influential organization modeled upon the transactions of its parent organization, The Royal Society in England, began setting standards for scientific publications chiefly by imposing the standard of objectivity in articles about scientific or medical observations and research. Under APS standards, scientific and medical papers began to be refereed, and scientists turned to editors to help them make their publications more readable and acceptable to reviewers (Connaughton, 1981, pp. 19–22). Popular science writing in the United States, as done by professional science writers, appeared with the 1845 birth of *Scientific American* and later, in 1930, with the publication of the *New York Times* science section (Novozhilov & Richardson, 1976, pp. 89–96). Today, professional scientific and medical writers not only help scientists publish their work but also create communications of their own.

The modern profession of technical writing was born during World War II (Lytel, 1959, in Alred, Reep, & Limaye, 1981, p. 4), when writers were hired to write manuals for the construction, operation, and maintenance of equipment used by the military. After the war, writers documented systems for the electronics and aerospace industries and, later, the computer industry. As in the development of scientific writing, many of these early technical writers were themselves scientists and engineers.

Given these histories, it's not surprising that early definitions of technical and scientific communication portrayed it almost exclusively as writing about the hard sciences or engineering and as occurring in a relatively few, fixed forms—for example, technical manufacturing and repair manuals, engineering proposals, technical reports, and articles in scientific journals.

However, as this book's chapters show, in recent years technical and scientific communication has diversified into many fields and includes not only writing about engineering and scientific research, but computer systems, pharmaceuticals, the environmental sciences, technical advertising, and other "hard" and "soft" technologies. This diversity is reflected in David Dobrin's 1983 definition of technical writing as "writing that accommodates technology to the user," in which technology is "more than an array of tools or procedures. It extends to the way human beings deploy themselves in the use and production of material goods and services" (Dobrin, 1983, p. 242–243). Thus, not only might engineering or medicine be a technology, but so, too, might accounting, investment counseling, or management consulting.

The Creative Role of Technical and Scientific Communicators

Early definitions of technical communication tended to portray it as an extension of pure or applied science, characterized not only by particular forms and subject matter but also by a certain style. That style was supposed to be "objective," and technical and scientific writing were supposed to give an "objective presentation of facts" in keeping with the plain style advocated by the American Philosophical Society. This perspective encouraged thinking of both technical and scientific writing simply as clear language used to convey a knowable and fixed truth. All writers needed to do was discern or learn the truth, choose the right words, and arrange them in clear, grammatical sentences, and the message would be unmistakable to readers—a "windowpane" through which they could see reality (Miller, 1979). Readers were implicitly characterized as vessels into which messages were poured, wholly intact.

As an illustration of this view, we were reminded in writing this chapter that one of us had a student several years ago who was documenting a potentially dangerous piece of machinery for a local manufacturing business. When her instructor tried to make sure that the company would provide her with liability coverage if anyone were injured using the student's documentation, the company's CEO replied, "I don't understand what the issue is. We told her everything. She just wrote it down." This view suggests that the CEO perceived technical writing to be that perfect transfer of knowledge from technical expert to reader. The communicator's role was simply to act as a scribe—to write down the information as it was told to her. The reader, in turn, would receive and understand the information exactly as the writer had written it.

However, communication theorists and practitioners today are far more likely to believe that humans know through language, that there is no uninterpreted knowledge on either the writer's or reader's part, and that technical and scientific communications are "socially constructed"—that is, that they are created through a "dialogue" among persons who construct a shared view of reality.

For example, in preparing communications, technical writers often gather information from subject matter experts, whose language reflects the experts' own perceptions of experience. However, this information isn't just transmitted, unchanged, from expert to writer. The two discuss it, and in the process, both expert and writer come to a shared understanding of the information. Writers, too, interpret information for themselves and act as advocates for their readers. As part of the writing process, writers select what information to emphasize or play down based upon their unique experience and understanding of their subject. Finally, users also interpret information in light of their understanding and use for it.

Thus, the communicator's job is not simply to minimize ambiguity by gathering and writing the "correct" information about, say, a piece of industrial machinery. It is to enter into a dialogue with engineers and others involved in creating, marketing, and using the machinery. Only together can subject matter experts, users, and the writer formulate knowledge about the machinery that will be truly user-centered. The truth, then, is not fixed and known only by a few select people. It is social—arrived at in a group of involved individuals. And the communicator's role is not simply that of a scribe. It is to arrive at and articulate a shared discovery of a communication's content.

To look at technical and scientific communication in this way is to adopt a "social perspective" on the profession. Such a perspective recognizes the value of communicators in shaping the discourses they produce. And since technical and scientific communicators often work with experts in disciplines other than their own, they have an opportunity to influence not only their audiences' views of experience, but also ways of thinking in the technical disciplines and organizations where they work. To understand this idea, it helps to think of technical and scientific communicators as participating in different professional "communities."

Professional Communicators and "Communities"

One of us has theorized (Lutz, 1989) that technical and scientific communication takes place at the intersection of writers with several important groups to which they belong. In this respect, you might think of communicators as belonging to what have been called "discourse communities" (Faigley, 1985; Killingsworth & Gilbertson, 1995), groups in which people arrive at a view of experience by negotiating it through language.

Think, for a moment, of various groups to which you belong—a club, a department at work, a sports team, a group of peers with the same major. You have goals common to your group, and you and the other members understand each other through language that expresses these goals. You use this language to signal that you belong; you use "in" words to participate in the group and to have others understand and respect you. It is often through language that you are perceived as an insider or outsider.

There are at least four such groups that you might belong to as a technical or scientific communicator: the community of writers; the technical or scientific discipline from which the content of your writing comes—medicine, computer science, environmental science, and so forth; the organization for which you work; and those people invested in any particular communication—its audiences and "stakeholders." Let's look at each of these groups in turn.

One obvious community to which communicators belong is that of the writers and teachers from whom they learn writing theory and strategies, such as how to define objectives and audiences for a communication, how to review and test communications, or how to revise, and from whom they draw knowledge about document design, organization, style, grammar, and usage. Today, writers also learn from each other about such things as desktop publishing, Web page design, creating online documentation, communicating across cultural boundaries, and how communication problems are solved in specific contexts.

Second, from the scientific or technical discipline about which they write, communicators gain information about the vocabulary, subject matter, and arguments of that discipline. To learn biotechnology is to learn the language of those who participate in its practice. And communicators must speak this language in order to be respected by members of the discipline and to understand important issues in the discipline.

This is a view that some contemporary philosophers have long held about scientific activity. Thomas Kuhn, a philosopher of science (1970), has argued that each branch of science has a body of knowledge, called a "paradigm," comprising the prevailing and accepted beliefs in that area of science. When new ideas are accepted, the paradigm "shifts." For example, think of the geocentric configuration of the universe as a paradigm. Kuhn would contend that this paradigm changed because other scientists argued against it, their arguments were accepted, and, as a result, the heliocentric configuration of the universe became the prevailing paradigm.

Those who write about science, medicine, and technology must know not only what the prevailing paradigm in their professional area is but also the problems and questions related to that paradigm. They must

learn what topics are worth questioning, what arguments are acceptable, and what kinds of emotional and ethical appeals will be most effective. They must, in a limited sense, learn the discipline about which
they'll communicate so that they can engage knowledgeably with its
members in dialogues about issues in that discipline.

A third community from which communicators draw knowledge is that
of the organizations in which they work. They must absorb and sometimes promote or argue against their employers' goals and values. These
are part of what is termed "corporate culture," the unique, identifying
features that distinguish one organization from another. Think, for a
minute, about the different corporate images portrayed by Saab as
opposed to Ford, by Gateway as opposed to IBM, by Penney's as
opposed to Neiman-Marcus. Every corporate culture is unique and is, as
one of our authors says, "tied up with the corporation's organization, its
self-image, its decisions about what is acceptable behavior, its valuations
of judgment and knowledge, and so on" (Dobrin, 1983, p. 248).

Beyond these communities, good writers also seek out a fourth community: the audiences and stakeholders of their communications. It is
vital that communicators know their audiences, not just to ensure the
success of their communications but also to be genuine advocates for the
communications' users. Moreover, as we learn more about how effective
communications are designed, we learn that understanding one's audience requires rigorous information gathering about the audience and
careful interpretation of that information. It also means replacing ste-
reotyped audience descriptions ("college-educated readers," "the general public," "programmers") with more concrete understandings of how
specific audience members will use communications. We've all been the
victims of the user manual whose writer didn't take us specifically into
account when organizing or developing information.

A communication's stakeholders generally are not audience members,
but those tangentially affected by a communication. Think, for example,
of all those who might be affected by an environmental impact statement concerning the effects of riverboat casino gambling on a small
town where the casino will be docked. Even though the town's residents
might not be the audience for such a communication, their lives could
be changed significantly by its outcome.

Your Role as a Technical or Scientific Communicator

In practical terms, your task as a technical or scientific communicator is
to fulfill your obligations to all of these communities as honestly and
competently as you can. As a communicator, you must be responsive to
the practices of "good writers," you must represent the experts about

whose work you write, you must promote an appropriate organizational image, and you must be an advocate for readers and others affected by your communications.

However, taking a social perspective isn't easy. Even when imperatives from all of these communities agree, you may still find yourself having to sort out and select the information from different community "voices." For example, guidelines for style in an organization may be different from the guidelines you've learned about "good writing." The "facts" conveyed by environmentally concerned citizens affected by the riverboat gambling we mentioned earlier may not agree with the "facts" offered by the corporation building the casino. Or you may find yourself trying to create online documentation for a software program under deadlines or budgetary constraints that don't permit thorough analysis of the users' needs for information or their preferences in how that information should be presented. Karis and Doheny-Farina (1991, p. 513) have pointed out that sometimes performing careful audience and task analysis or user testing can actually be a hindrance to efficient writing.

Nevertheless, even in these kinds of difficulties, listening to community voices is important, whether or not it is possible to take them all into account or expediently deal with them. For it is in taking a social perspective on communication that technical and scientific communicators are able to see problems that might be overlooked by others.

Indeed, the centrality of the professional communicator's position means that you'll need to understand your role as a "boundary spanner" (Harrison & Debs, 1988, p. 5–21). Being a boundary spanner means that you serve as a bridge among groups of individuals inside and outside of organizations. Boundary spanning requires you to consider not just a single audience, but issues such as your own and others' social roles, group purposes, and interaction. It requires understanding how people think about the issues that surround a particular communication.

We hope that this chapter will influence how you think about your role as a technical or scientific communicator. In the past, technical and scientific communicators have been thought of merely as conduits of information. Others had the knowledge, communicators wrote it down, and readers received it, as packaged. Now, however, we tend to see communications as resulting from a dialogue among subject matter experts, communicators, users, and others. It is the "conversation" that surrounds communication that builds responsible scientific and technical knowledge. Thus, technical and scientific communicators must provide not just clearly written documents but communications responsive to all the contexts in which they occur. For these and other reasons, being a technical and scientific communicator is an exciting job and one in which we hope you will become involved.

REFERENCES

Alred, G. J., Reep, D. C., & Limaye, M. R. (1981). Introduction. In *Business and technical writing: An annotated bibliography of books, 1880–1980* (pp. 1–9). Metuchen, NJ: Scarecrow Press.

Connaughton, M. E. (1981). Technical writing in America: A historical perspective. In J. C. Mathes & T. E. Pinelli (Eds.), *Technical communication: Perspectives for the eighties: Proceedings of the technical communication sessions at the 32nd annual meeting of the Conference on College Composition and Communication* (pp. 15–25). Washington, DC: NASA Conference Publication 11.55:2203. [For sale by the National Technical Information Service, Springfield, VA]

Dobrin, D. (1983). What's technical about technical writing? In P. V. Anderson, R. J. Brockmann, & C. R. Miller (Eds.), *New essays in technical and scientific communication: Research, theory, practice* (pp. 227–250). Farmingdale, NY: Baywood Publishing.

Faigley, L. (1985). Nonacademic writing: The social perspective. In L. Odell & D. Goswami (Eds.), *Writing in nonacademic settings* (pp. 231–249). New York: The Guilford Press.

Gilbert, J. (1994, March). The best jobs in America. *Money*, 70–73.

Harrison, T. M., & Debs, M. B. (1988). Conceptualizing the organizational role of technical communicators: A systems approach. *Journal of Business and Technical Communication, 2*, 5–21.

Karis, W., & Doheny-Farina, S. (1991). Collaborating with readers: Empower them and take the consequences. *Technical Communication, 38*, 513–519.

Killingsworth, M. J., & Gilbertson, J. (1992). *Signs, genres, and communities in technical communication*. Amityville, NY: Baywood Publishing.

Kuhn, T. S. (1970) *The structure of scientific revolutions*. Chicago: The University of Chicago Press.

Lutz, J. (1989). Writers in organizations and how they learn the image: Theory, research, and implications. In C. Matalene (ed.), *Worlds of writing: Teaching and learning in discourse communities of work* (pp. 113–135). Carbondale: Southern Illinois University Press.

Miller, C. (1979). A humanistic rationale for technical writing. *College English, 40*, 610–617.

Novozhilov, Y. V., & Richardson, J. G. (1976). Fifty years after the death of Flammarion, the science popularizer. *Journal of Technical Writing and Communication, 6*,(2), 89–96.

chapter 1

Writing in Business and Manufacturing

William J. Buchholz
Bentley College
Waltham, Massachusetts

Jobs

- *Corporate communicator:* public affairs, financial relations, corporate training programs.
- *Marketing communicator:* copywriter, copy editor, promotional writer, publication assistant, marketing communicator.
- *Corporate-based documentation writer:* technical writer, technical editor, documentation specialist.

Responsibilities

To communicate, through written, oral, and visual media, important financial, technical, marketing, and public relations information. With experience, responsibilities may become managerial.

Employment Outlook

Research indicates that employment opportunities will probably remain healthy. The Bureau of Labor Statistics notes an increasing demand for technical writers "through the year 2000."

Salary Range

Entry-level salaries may range anywhere from $22,000 to $43,000, depending upon training, experience, and location; mid-career salaries range from $29,000 to $52,000; senior-level managerial salaries may range from $35,000 to $78,000.

INTRODUCTION

As the economic foundation of modern American civilization, business and manufacturing affect us directly or indirectly every moment of our lives. Call to mind any city's business district, shopping malls, or industrial parks, and you have a good picture of the extent and diversity of our economy. The clothing boutique, stationery store, hardware outlet, computer franchise, record shop, appliance store, automobile dealer, florist—all are engaged in the business of moving goods from suppliers to you, as expeditiously and profitably as possible. On a larger scale, the huge chain stores, franchises, factory outlets, and department stores all fulfill the same profit-seeking function. They simply expand their business activity into regional, national, or global markets.

So where do these millions of goods for all these consumers come from? Nearly every item you see on the market, from a television set to an automobile, from a lawn mower to a CD player, from watches and cameras to computer hardware and software, originates in the manufacturing sector of the economy. Light manufacturers produce smaller, easily movable items, such as clothing, electronics components, consumer products, and paper goods. Heavy manufacturers produce automobiles, steel products, building supplies, ships, airplanes, and machinery. Manufacturers typically sell their goods in huge lots to wholesalers, who in turn sell smaller quantities to contractors and retailers, who ultimately sell the products to the general public. This wholesale and retail transfer of manufactured goods to consumers constitutes fully two thirds of American economic activity.

But American business consists of more than simply producing, distributing, and selling goods. It includes performing services as well. Because they do not produce, package, and display tangible items in stores, members of the service industry are sometimes not recognized as significant business entities. However, they play a vital role in our economy. A computer, for example, once manufactured and sold, must eventually be serviced—its hardware when it breaks down and its software when it is revised or updated. Service businesses perform these maintenance functions. Furthermore, whereas a single company may oversee the manufacturing, sale, and service of its products, such a company, because of a diversity of business needs, must seek help from other organizations that specialize in various support services. Banks, insurance companies, credit corporations, health care institutions, investment services, public accounting firms, hospitals, financial services, engineering consultants, market analysts, trade show vendors, architects, and contractors perform these vital support functions.

What do all these areas of manufacturing, sales, and service have in common? Communication. Throughout the entire economy, hundreds of thousands of people are employed as communicators. They document operations, draft illustrations, write technical reports and manuals, prepare speeches, produce films and videos, photograph products, and create advertising. They communicate important financial, technical, marketing, and public relations information. They plan extensive campaigns to persuade various publics of the beneficial relationship between the corporation and the community. And they advise top management and corporate policy makers about the needs, opinions, and desires of the public, to ensure that the corporation is socially responsible. In short, because products, services, markets, and people must all be linked through human relationships, business and manufacturing simply cannot exist without communication: written, visual, multimedia, and oral.

YOUR LIFE COMMUNICATING IN BUSINESS

Most entry-level positions in corporate communication are devoted almost exclusively to creating written communication or, more likely, editing the writing of others. For example, as an entry-level editor, you would read copy or manuscript drafts very carefully to correct errors in punctuation, grammar, and usage. Most likely you would be aided by a style guide to make sure that the phrasing and mechanics were consistent throughout the piece. Additional duties might involve working with writers on their unfinished manuscripts, helping a senior editor to track projects, and act as a liaison with graphics and production people.

Other companies emphasize writing rather than editing. In these companies, as an entry-level writer, you would write (or help to write) the copy or manuscript drafts for manuals, brochures, video scripts, articles, procedures, and the like. You might be part of a development team, meeting at times with engineers, editors, production people, other writers, or quality assurance people to help guide the written product through all its phases.

With five or more years' experience, you would advance in rank and write a wide variety of material for various readers, from somewhat mundane (though critical) internal corporate memos, letters, and reports to rather sophisticated pieces for public consumption, such as glossy and colorful annual reports.

As you acquire more experience and assume greater responsibilities, you also might become increasingly involved in the visual aspects of communication. More and more, corporate communicators will have to understand the principles, application, and management of visual rhetoric, from publication design to video production.

In publication design, for example, even the seemingly mundane corporate report and product brochure must be carefully conceived, integrating visual and textual elements for greater readability. Understanding basic principles of visual rhetoric will help you to make intelligent design decisions. At minimum, you should know how to integrate text with an illustration, chart, table, or photograph; how to run text around graphic elements; how to select text and display typefaces; and how to choose paper weight, color, and texture. Ultimately, you may be responsible for thousands (or millions) of dollars worth of offset, black-and-white, two-color, and four-color print production.

In addition to print publication, many corporations now release their annual reports, internal employee communications, instructional and training materials, and product or service messages on videotape. Economy of scale (low cost achieved through mass dissemination), ease of use, and immediacy of dramatic impact all make video an effective medium. As a communication manager using video, you might someday be in charge of budgeting, scheduling, storyboarding, and script writing. Though you probably would not function as a video technician, you would need to be familiar with the important technical aspects of production, such as editing, mixing, lighting, sound, and camera work. Finally, you would probably be responsible for evaluating and distributing the finished video product, assuring your corporate clients that the video satisfactorily meets their communication needs.

The computer's versatility also extends the print medium. As a technical communicator, you could expect to create documents in hypertext and online; to employ CD-ROM both as a storage and a publication medium; to design corporate sites on the World Wide Web; and to plan, produce, and manage interactive video for documentation and training purposes. Computer-aided design and production, in print, film, and video, will become common in even the smallest facilities.

Your job would also likely demand oral communication skills. For example, you might be called upon to speak to individuals and large groups of fellow employees about products and project team efforts. You might address department, committee, task force, product development, and sales meetings. And as your expertise became recognized, you might be invited to make recommendations to your superiors.

Outside your company, you might need to pitch campaign ideas to prospective clients or present research findings to a gathering of concerned citizens. In addition, the local and national media might seek you out as a spokesperson, to respond to an industrial accident or corporate crisis.

Notable examples of such crises include the Tylenol poisonings and the nuclear accident at Three-Mile Island in the 1980s, as well as the Exxon Valdez oil spill and cancer-causing silicon-gel implants in the 1990s.

As a speaker, no matter what the circumstance, you would need to adapt information to your audience's needs, clearly presenting sometimes highly technical product, planning, and financial details. The ability to think on your feet, to frame reasonable arguments, to select motivational appeals, and to handle the occasional obstreperous or hostile questioner are important presentation skills that will serve you well in any of these situations. Though you might not be the actual corporate spokesperson, you might have to run a press conference, arrange a photo opportunity, or act as a media liaison for your company, to make sure that your executives could address public concerns. In addition, you might function as an internal consultant, offering your own presentation skills in the form of speechwriting advice (even coaching) to those in your corporation who must appear before the public.

As you can see, the term "communicator" encompasses written, visual, and oral exchanges of meaning through various media. Nevertheless, this chapter concentrates primarily upon communication based on writing, which can be classified, according to the audiences they address, into internal and external communication, and, according to the purposes they fulfill, as corporate communication, marketing communication, and corporate-based documentation.

INTERNAL AND EXTERNAL WRITTEN COMMUNICATION

Internal written communication functions as a managerial, administrative, and informative vehicle inside the organization. External communication serves people outside the organization, providing information to publics beyond the corporate walls, from the general population to vendors, clients, and consumers.

Internal Written Communication

Internal writing often has two functions: Primarily, it informs employees about the ongoing business of the organization, but at the same time, it serves as the corporate memory for purposes of design, production, quality control, implementation, transportation, and litigation. It is thus the history of the corporation.

At the entry level, you might work as an internal publications specialist, writing chiefly for employee publications such as newsletters, quarterly or monthly magazines, and weekly house organs (internal newspapers), or preparing operational handbooks, procedures manuals, training materials, and the like to be used by individuals inside the organization. You'll find that internal corporate writing can be addressed to superiors, subordinates, or peers. The most challenging types of communication to write are those that must simultaneously be addressed to all three audiences.

External Written Communication

External writing is intended for people outside the corporation, from local to international readers. These readers include customers, clients, and the public at large—anyone who may affect, or be affected by, the company's activities, products, or services. In addition, external written communication is an organization's lifeline to the public. Written material sometimes helps a company to establish and maintain its good name within the community—especially if the local attitude toward the corporation is likely to be hostile because of potential operating hazards or environmentally dangerous products (e.g., chemicals, paints, petroleum, and nuclear energy). In these threatening or rapidly changing environments, an open letter in the local paper, a pamphlet mailed to concerned citizens, a radio news release, and a magazine advertorial (a paid advertisement that looks and sounds like an editorial) may all be necessary to keep the corporate/community relationship viable. With the growing interdependence of businesses, local economies, and national and international markets, as well as the growing concern for the environment, corporations increasingly must recognize their accountability as responsible members of the community. The professional writer plays a central role in fulfilling this corporate social responsibility.

Tables 1.1 and 1.2 list selected internal and external communications.

CORPORATE COMMUNICATION, MARKETING COMMUNICATION, AND CORPORATE–BASED DOCUMENTATION

The internal and external communications you prepare as you serve different audiences can fulfill at least three different purposes: those of corporate communication, marketing communication, and corporate-based documentation.

TABLE 1.1.
Three Categories of Selected Internal Communications

Employee	Operational (continued)
Announcements	Specifications
Audio/visual scripts	Style guides
Briefings	Technical references
Bulletin board notices	Training guides
Course/seminar catalogs	User manuals
Departmental updates	
Educational literature	
Emergency warning notices	**Planning**
Envelope stuffers	Advisory studies
Executive announcements	Briefings
Handbooks	Curriculum guides
Manuals	Feasibility studies
Newsletters	Marketing reports
Personnel information	Meeting minutes
Position papers	Needs analyses
Safety guidelines	Outlines
Schedules	Performance reports
Seminar booklets	Position papers
Training literature	Problem analyses
	Production briefs
	Progress reports
Operational	Proposals
Briefings	Research reports
Budgets	Sales reports
Departmental annual reports	Seminar plans
Design disclosure manuals	Status updates
Life cycle support	Storyboards
Operating manuals	Strategic plans
Position papers	Style guides
Procedures	Testing reports
Reference manuals	Trip reports

Corporate Communication

The main purpose of corporate communication is to forge links (using written, visual, and spoken channels) between a business and its internal and external publics. To fulfill its obligation to these publics, corporate communication must be open and receptive. This means that a company takes into account information from various publics before it makes decisions, communicates them, and takes action. Corporate writers, therefore, do not simply produce brochures, pamphlets, magazines, and newsletters that tout the organization. Instead, they function as the company's ears and voice, listening to, informing, and influenc-

TABLE 1.2.
Three Categories of Selected External Communications

Corporate Communications	Marketing/Media Communications (continued)
Annual reports	Public service announcements
Corporate identity pieces	Radio scripts
Corporate backgrounders	Sales letters and brochures
Directories	Telemarketing materials
Executive speeches	Television scripts
Financial reports	Third-party endorsements
Investor reports	Trade show literature
Letters	Video scripts
Position papers	World Wide Web pages
Proposals	
	Corporate-Based Documentation
Marketing/Media Communications	**Course/Seminar Materials**
Advertising copy	Data sheets
Audio scripts	Handbooks
Brochures	Installation manuals
Catalogs	Instruction manuals
Customer release notes	Maintenance manuals
Direct mail pieces	Online documentation
Feature stories	Operating manuals
Media kits	Position papers
New-product releases	Proposals
News releases	Reference manuals
Pamphlets	Research papers, articles
Pitch letters	Specifications
Points-of-purchase materials	Style guides
Press releases	Systems manuals
Product or service case histories	Technical articles
Product specification sheets	Technical manuals
Product status bulletins	Translation services
Promotional materials	User manuals

ing various constituencies, inside and outside the company, to ensure that management formulates responsible policies. Inside the company, writers also often assume a central position in creating a corporation's identity and in clarifying its mission by drafting position statements, policy guides, and strategic plans of positions.

Because writing is a central function in business and manufacturing, jobs appear in all types of organizations across the country. *O'Dwyer's Directory of Corporate Communications 1997*, for example, "lists 10,000 PR and communications people at 6,500+ companies and associations. . . . Approximately 80% of the companies have formal PR/communication titles or departments." These corporate communicators write many varied types of documents to fulfill their wide-ranging responsibilities "for press relations, employee communications, local community relations, government affairs at the local and federal levels, environmental and safety affairs, financial relations including stockholder and Wall Street communications, corporate identity programs, contributions, corporate training programs . . . and exhibits, conventions and trade shows."

Marketing Communication (Marcom)

Marketing writers have to display the same versatility as corporate writers. However, whereas the corporate writer tends to concentrate upon the organization's need to connect with its internal and external publics, the marketing writer, in creating advertising and promotional copy, attempts to sell the company's products or services. A marketing communicator, for example, might publicize the company's new product at a press conference or write a press release about its features for trade publications. The corporate communicator would be a spokesperson for the organization at press conferences that address the larger relationship of the corporation with its publics, aside from any product or sales considerations.

Corporate-Based Documentation

The purpose of corporate-based documentation, which includes reports, instructions, and other documents, is to provide readers with information they need to do their jobs. Such documents might include policies, procedures, and instructions for operating products used in the organization. They might also include proposals to obtain business and reports to keep clients informed about the work the company has performed. For many businesses, documentation *is* their product. Consulting firms, for example, may study some aspect of a client's management practice and issue an analytical report or a feasibility study. Marketing research and polling firms produce intelligence reports, public opinion polls, and market surveys for their clients. Some companies, providing product or service support and training for clients, produce evaluation reports, manuals, guides, curriculum plans, and workbooks. In creating these communications, writers and editors research relevant literature, conduct interviews and use other methods of gathering information, perform analyses, interpret data, compile background information, create tables and charts, plan illustrations, and write the final text for their clients.

Often these communications must be written in multiple languages for an international readership. Whatever the language, information may reside in printed form in an electronic database, or in CD-ROM, readily accessible through computer search and retrieval. Working on screens in online, World Wide Web, or CD-ROM information systems, writers might also choose colors, typefaces, formats, and the information that goes on these screens.

By considering the intersection of the documents produced for different audiences—internal and external—and for different purposes, we can see that a corporate communicator might produce an astonishing variety of documents. Typical internal communications can be classified conveniently into three types, as shown in Table 1.1. *Employee communications* are used to pass on the latest news and policy decisions from management. *Operational communications* set out instructions or describe standard procedures or policies that help employees perform particular job-related tasks. *Planning communications* help in the process of creating products and services.

Employment Outlook

As we move into the next century, the American economy will continue to shift away from manufacturing and toward providing services, from fast-food and automobile repair to financial advice, insurance, health-care, and the like. The Bureau of Labor Statistics, U.S. Department of Labor, predicts that from 1994–2005, "business, health, and education services will account for 70 percent of the growth—9.2 million out of 13.6 million jobs—within services." Furthermore, "occupations which require a bachelor's degree or above will average 23 percent growth, almost double the 12 percent growth projected for occupations that require less education and training" (p. 4). These projections suggest that the professional and managerial ranks of our service economy are expected to grow at very healthy rates through the year 2005. Specialists in corporate communication, public relations, marketing communication, and corporate-based documentation can expect to see greater demand for their skills.

You must remember, however, that employment predictions are subject to the vicissitudes of local, regional, national, and international economies. Rates of employment are also highly industry specific. Thus, depending upon locale and general economic outlook, all these industries (such as health care, tourism, banking, and financial services) have differing employment projections that you should investigate before embarking on your career.

At the managerial level across a number of these industries, however, the employment outlook is consistently positive. The Bureau predicts that, because of "increasingly intense domestic and global competition in products and services," management opportunities through the year 2005 in advertising, marketing, and public relations will "increase faster than the average." In addition, "employment of marketing, advertising, and public relations managers is expected to grow much faster than average in most business services industries, such as computer and data processing, and management and public relations firms, while average growth is projected in manufacturing industries overall" (*Occupational Outlook Handbook* p. 62). Many openings will occur because of replacements, as middle managers move into top management positions. Competition for these positions will remain keen, but opportunities will vary by industry, the greatest number being available in data processing services, radio and television, motor vehicle, and business services, as well as "management and public relations firms" (*Occupational Outlook Handbook* p. 62).

The Bureau also tracks opportunities for writers and editors employed in the communication industry: newspapers, magazines, government agencies, radio, television, book publishers, journals, corporations, and public relations/advertising firms. Across all these occupational categories, the Bureau predicts that "through the year 2005," employment will "increase faster than the average," noting that the continuing expansion of scientific and technical information" will increase the demand for technical writers (*Occupational Outlook Handbook* p. 186). As one of these writers or editors, what salary might you reasonably expect to earn, at entry level and throughout your career?

Salaries

Because salaries for writers in business and manufacturing vary according to rank, years of employment, type and size of business, location, and industry, only general and somewhat tentative salary information is available. However, entry-level writers/editors in business and manufacturing can expect their salaries to average anywhere from $22,000 to $33,000. People with five to fifteen years' experience can anticipate that their salaries will span the mid-thirties to high forties, and senior employees can expect to earn salaries that range from the low fifties into six figures.

Two professional communication societies, the Society for Technical Communication (STC) and the Public Relations Society of America (PRSA), have conducted salary surveys of their membership and various practitioners. These surveys, although illuminating, represent limited data sources; thus, you should view their results with caution.

Generally speaking, the STC and PRSA surveys suggest the following about earnings for communication professionals in business and manufacturing:

- Practitioners in industrial/manufacturing concerns and utilities (such as heavy equipment and electronics manufacturers or gas and electric companies) enjoy the highest salaries.
- The larger businesses and manufacturers in high-risk industries or threatening, unstable environments (such as pharmaceutical, nuclear engineering, and chemical companies) tend to pay higher salaries.
- Communication employees on the east and west coasts command more money.
- Practitioners with expertise in investor relations, international or environmental affairs, issues management, or technology are in more volatile, higher risk businesses and therefore receive larger salaries.
- People with advanced degrees, course work beyond the bachelor's degree, or professional accreditation usually report higher salaries than those without.
- Managerial positions, because they involve greater responsibility, nearly always pay more than the relatively low-risk technician positions.

Let's look at each of the two surveys in more detail.

STC salary survey

As Table 1.3 shows, the STC survey reports the mean salary in 1997 for a technical writer/editor in the United States was $46,750 (Table 1.3). As the figures in Table 1.3 also suggest, an editor/writer in business and manufacturing with 2 years' experience or less could expect to make $39,180.

Because companies typically have various grades or levels of writers and editors, technical knowledge, time in grade, and demonstrated value to the company all boost salaries from this figure. As Table 1.4 shows, the highest salaries are earned by mid-level and senior managers, who have mean salaries of $53,980 to $70,930.

PRSA salary survey

In corporate communication, the salary picture looks brighter. The median salary in 1995/96 for all respondents was $49,070 (Table 1.5). Remember, however, that these salary figures will vary by geographic region, gender, and size of the practitioner's market (large metropolitan versus small city, for example).

As Table 1.6 shows, the highest paid respondents are practitioners in investor relations, issues management, environmental affairs, and government relations—all high-stakes or high-risk areas of business. The

TABLE 1.3.
STC Mean Salary 1997

Years of Experience	Mean Salary
2 years or less	$39,180
2–5 years	$30,030
6–10 years	$47,290
11 years or more	$53,660
All respondents	$46,750

Source: *1997 Technical Communicator Salary Survey.* Arlington, VA: Society for Technical Communication, 1997, pp. 4–5.

TABLE 1.4.
STC Salaries by Employment Level 1997

Employment Level	Mean Salary
Entry	$32,910
Mid-level, non-supervisory	$43,190
Mid-level management	$51,920
Senior management, non-supervisory	$53,980
Senior management	$70,930

Source: *1997 Technical Communicator Salary Survey.* Arlington, VA: Society for Technical Communication, 1997, pp. 4-5.

TABLE 1.5.
1995/96 PRSA Salary Survey

Position Title	Median Salary
Account Executives (junior, senior account executives, associates, assistants)	$32,580
Supervisors (account supervisors, supervisors, managers, coordinators, group managers, directors, vice presidents)	$52,860
Senior Management (senior/executive vice presidents, senior counselors, chairmen, presidents, partners, owners)	$76,790
All Respondents	**$49,070**

Source: Simmons Market Research Bureau, *Salary Survey of Public Relations Professionals,* New York: Public Relations Society of America, 1996, p. 13.

lowest paying careers are in marketing and advertising, relatively competitive positions, very popular with new college graduates. Generally speaking, throughout the occupation, salaries are directly related to supervisory scope: The greater the managerial responsibility, the higher the salary. In fact, "the highest corporate salaries are found at management consulting firms (median salary is $141,424)" (*Salary Survey*, p. 26). Thus, as you begin your career in communication, you should be aware of the distinctions between the non-managerial and managerial functions.

Entry-level salaries, as you might suspect, are significantly lower than the salaries reflected in Table 1.6. The median entry-level salary across the occupation is $23,030, with entry-level corporate, government, and nonprofit salaries nearly $2,500 above those for public relations firms (*Salary Survey*, p. 23). Further, if you begin your career on the west coast, you will make significantly more at entry-level ($25,790 median) than in the Midwest ($22,160 median) (*Salary Survey*, p. 24).

CAREER PATH

Early in your career, you will need to decide how to shape it beyond the entry level. Your decision will depend upon who you are and how you see yourself. You should take stock of your strengths and weaknesses. Assess your educational preparation and intelligence. Reflect

TABLE 1.6.
1995/96 PRSA Salaries by Area

Position Title	Median Salary
Investor Relations	$72,484
Issues Management	$66,300
Environmental Affairs	$65,881
Government Relations	$65,367
International	$63,964
Crisis Management	$59,523
Generalist	$54,600
Corporate Communications	$53,508
Technology	$52,114
Employee Relations	$51,032
Media Relations	$50,797
Special Events	$49,450
Community Relations	$49,157
Publicity	$48,886
Marketing	$48,869
Advertising	$45,577

Source: Simmons Market Research Bureau, *Salary Survey of Public Relations Professionals*, New York: Public Relations Society of America, 1996, p. 31.

upon your personality and drive. Find out specifically what will be expected of you in the workplace as you advance in your career. How you develop as a professional will depend upon whether you acquire increasing expertise as a technician or become a manager.

Technician

You may find a career as a communication technician very fulfilling. As a technician, you would actually produce the internal and external written materials discussed earlier. Or you might simply assist in larger promotional or documentation projects that your supervisor assigns. You will have relatively little, if any, say in establishing corporate goals. Instead, you will write the communication end-products that serve these goals (newsletters, brochures, instructions, policy statements, and manuals). Depending upon your skills, educational background, and desires, you might acquire wide-ranging experience in writing, editing, interviewing, presenting to various publics, designing publications, planning events, and the like. Many communication practitioners find this production aspect of their work to be amply rewarding as a creative outlet. The "deliverable" (finished piece) that results after hours of dedicated labor can rarely be equaled as a source of satisfaction, pride, and fulfillment.

In addition to preparing documents in print, online, or other media, recent dramatic changes in technology mean that you might, in addition to writing, maintain and produce the mailing and distribution lists, schedules, budget spreadsheets, project time lines, and office inventory. In short, writers and editors in business and manufacturing will find that, as technology becomes ever more sophisticated, so too will their careers. Success in technician-oriented communication occupations will require high levels of intelligence, flexibility, and creativity.

These sophisticated developments in technology, however, also dramatically underscore the need for managers who can supervise the increasingly complex communication tasks that result from the alliance of people and technology.

Manager

If you aspire to communication management, you must demonstrate ability that goes beyond proficiency in writing, editing, and production. Communication management demands special personal attributes and temperament. Initiating and managing projects call for skills in handling time, tasks, money, material, and people.

Time and task management, for example, are crucial in any undertaking, but especially in complicated projects where many people are producing components at various stages. The project manager must track the team's progress along a strict time line (with due dates that must be adhered to), as production moves toward the final deadline. The manager also initiates and oversees the project budget, making sure that costs are controlled, and guaranteeing that everyone has enough money to complete necessary tasks. Materials management consists of making sure that needed equipment is in the right place at the right time, that everyone has whatever is necessary to do the job (from computers to paper clips). And because so many projects depend upon a number of people working together, a manager needs to put together the most skilled team possible to help the members work well together.

Thus, as a manager, you will deal with budgets, vendors, and client, and therefore, you will have to possess strategic, tactical, and logistical abilities. You will be expected to define problems, recognize opportunities, and set goals for entire groups and projects. As a project begins, you will supervise primary and secondary research, implement activities, and oversee communication plans. One of your chief responsibilities will be to evaluate the results of your corporation's communication endeavors. In time, you will no doubt plan and implement larger, more complicated projects (such as overseeing production of an annual report or orchestrating a new plant opening).

Probably, the most critical aspect of communication project management is effectively dealing with people, those with whom and for whom you work. You must be adept at dealing with your superiors, subordinates, fellow managers, vendors, clients, customers, the general public, salespeople, editors, photographers, writers, graphic artists, freelancers, marketers, and engineers. You will have to know how to motivate and guide your project teams, committees, and task forces, and to understand why particular people work well together so that you can form effective groups. You will be called upon to negotiate vendor contracts, judge product quality, and establish deadlines. Quarterly or annually, you will evaluate employee performance. You will hire and fire. You will have to quell rumors, mediate disagreements, and resolve misunderstandings. Yet, even with these challenges, managing people can be its own reward.

As you have probably guessed, communication management expertise comes only with time and experience. Usually, a minimum of three to five years on the job with one company is necessary before you can break into even the lower level supervisory or managerial ranks. You must also realize that the number of management opportunities in a given industry or business can be severely limited. For example, technical documentation specialists in some companies have relatively few managerial or supervisory positions to which they can advance. To move into the management ranks, these technical writers and editors may have to become project leaders, quality assurance specialists, researchers, or trainers; they may even have to move into other corporate positions, such as marketing, promotions, production, public relations, sales, customer support, or human resources.

Because of the limited number of positions available in management within a given company, and because of the inevitable bureaucratic layering that results when too many people hold management positions, some companies are collapsing their managerial hierarchies into task groups. In these groups, each member assumes greater managerial and production responsibility for some aspect of an assigned project. This "flattening" of the managerial hierarchy, which spreads out management tasks, tends to increase productivity, decrease red tape, eliminate bureaucratic buck-passing, and boost morale—resulting generally in a more efficient use of a company's time, space, material, money, and personnel. As a manager, you may have to learn to lead such groups. However, even as a member of a project team, you may find that you are a manager—if not of people, certainly of tasks, material, money, and time.

Although much of what it takes to become a successful communication manager or technician results from experience, you can start acquiring this experience by carefully selecting undergraduate courses in your major and minor or by pursuing the appropriate post-baccalaureate certificate or graduate degree. The education of a business communicator, both as a technician and as a manager, must be built upon a solid foundation of college courses. Beyond these, you should consider specialized courses. The remainder of this chapter examines both kinds of preparation.

PREPARATION

Foundation Courses

The successful communicator in business can major in any undergraduate discipline that encourages creative approaches to problem solving, sharpens analytical skills, enhances verbal acuity, and provides insight into individual and collective human behaviors. Most majors that provide this background are located in the arts and sciences. They include business communication, communication, education, English, history, journalism, modern languages, philosophy, psychology, public relations, and sociology. No matter what the major, education in the liberal arts and sciences is always a good foundation for effective communication in business, simply because such disciplines tend to foster creative, inquiring, integrative, and analytical attitudes. You should thus combine a number of opposing attributes: be creative yet analytical, flexible yet focused; be detail-oriented yet a generalist, independent yet a team player. In sum, the effective communicator should enjoy learning across a wide variety of subjects, have knowledge of current events, and be reasonably comfortable with ambiguity and uncertainty. (A sample business communication curriculum is shown in Appendix A.)

In addition to knowledge, skills, and a flexible yet focused mindset, the best communication practitioners possess a strong sense of ethics that translates into principled behavior. The practitioner must abide by a code of ethics that guarantees responsibility to the truth, the client, the customer, the corporation, and the general public. Practitioners also take care never to violate communication law, especially as it relates to First Amendment rights, libel, and slander. Some communicators, in fact, have to know the law intimately. Investor relations practitioners, for example, must be schooled in the law on securities, financial disclosure, and insider trading. Marketing communicators must fully understand the law relative to copyrights, trademarks, logotypes, and trade names. Although you may be able to take courses that focus on these topics, you will more likely find them discussed in courses that touch on various aspects of corporate communication history, theory, and application.

Given this general profile, what particular abilities might the successful communicator in business and manufacturing be expected to have? And what course work helps to develop these?

Written Communication

The two most important skills you can possess in communication are good writing and editing. You should be creative within the confines of virtually any writing situation. To command such versatility, you will call upon many voices, adopt many styles. Courses that best prepare entry-level writers to be versatile and adaptable are those that introduce a variety of writing tasks, with teachers who, as good editors and writers themselves, will help you to master fundamental principles. Here are some courses that will give you a good foundation:

- technical writing
- technical editing
- business writing
- public relations writing
- marketing communication (brochures, ad copy, direct mail)

- feature writing
- news writing
- script writing
- report writing
- rhetoric
- managerial communication (case analyses)
- communication research methods

Often, these courses have more specialized, advanced sequels. Public relations writing, for example, may be followed by a case-oriented course in public relations campaign management. Other advanced courses may focus on writing for a specific industry such as finance, high-tech, health, sports, or tourism. With or without advanced courses, however, mastery of the fundamental principles of good writing and editing, combined with curiosity, native intelligence, creativity, ethical sensitivity, and plenty of practice on the job (under the careful tutelage of a mentor or supervisor), can ultimately lead to success in writing for business and manufacturing.

Oral Skills

Interpersonal, small group, and public speaking abilities are indispensable for anyone in communication. At some time, you will likely be called upon to brief or persuade fellow writers, editors, managers, staff personnel, members of other departments, clients, the media, and the public. Daily, your competence in interpersonal and small group communication will be tested (especially listening, interviewing, meeting, nonverbal, and negotiating skills). To help you attain proficiency in these areas, many colleges and universities offer the following specialized courses:

- public speaking (introductory and advanced)
- interpersonal communication
- small group communication
- interviewing
- intercultural communication
- organizational communication
- argumentation
- negotiation
- persuasion
- forensics
- debate

Because in business, promotions and raises are often tied directly to speaking abilities, you should master the requisite principles and application of public speaking, interpersonal, and small group communication.

Visual Communication

Writers in business and manufacturing will increasingly be expected to integrate text and graphic elements; they will also manage production in other media, such as film and video. Production courses in the visual arts are therefore necessary to introduce business writers to the potential problems and solutions inherent in design decisions. Courses that explore some of these include the following:

- Desktop publishing
- Computer-mediated design
- Graphic design and production
- Typography and design
- Publication design
- Presentation graphics
- Visual communication theory
- Photography
- Film making
- Television production
- Video production
- Visual communication management

You should remember that, although writers in business need not be gifted visual artists, the more you understand the strengths and limitations of desktop publishing, the World Wide Web, and other visual technologies, the principles governing effective integration of text and graphics, and the burgeoning new computer-mediated film and video technologies, the more communication options you will have to choose from.

Computers

As I suggest above, you will probably need to be familiar with text and graphics processing software in Windows, UNIX, or the Macintosh operating environments. Larger companies may have employees linked to a mainframe computer or to networked PCs, Macs, or workstations. Whatever the computer environment, you will be expected to learn the various file management, document formatting, printing, and text manipulation functions of at least one full-featured word processing program (such as WordPerfect or Microsoft Word). You will have an edge if you can tastefully use the program's typography and graphics features, especially proportional fonts, page layout, files importation, and construction of graphs, charts, and tables.

Many employers today assume that you will have some experience with a full-featured desktop publishing package such as FrameMaker, Ventura Publisher, PageMaker, or Quark XPress. Knowledge of a spreadsheet program (including Lotus 1-2-3, Quattro Pro, or Excel) and graphics or presentation software (such as Arts & Letters, PowerPoint, Aldus FreeHand, Corel Draw, or Freelance Plus), and internet software (such as FrontPage, Internet Explorer, Netscape Navigator, and various HTML coding utilities) will give you other important functional competencies. Although your prospective employer may not use software with which you are familiar, the fact that you are comfortable using full-featured programs and can produce tastefully designed documents argues persuasively for your communication effectiveness in any office. Courses that introduce you to computers in these areas of communication include the following:

- fundamentals of computing (word processing, spreadsheets, graphics, networks, and databases)
- desktop publishing
- publishing on the World Wide Web
- computer-aided design and illustration
- computer graphics
- software-specific short courses (in Access, HTML, PowerPoint, Lotus 1-2-3, Excel, MS Word, WordPerfect, FrontPage, PageMaker, etc.)
- corporate electronic publishing
- computer-based project management

As a communicator, your value to the corporation may be directly measured by your knowledge of these new computer-mediated technologies.

With a firm grasp of written, oral, visual, and computer competencies, you have a solid foundation upon which to build a communication career. You should, however, also devote some time to acquiring expertise in specialized areas.

SPECIALIZED PREPARATION

Although most opportunities to learn a business may come chiefly through experience, you can augment this experience formally through education. This specialized knowledge can be acquired in a number of ways: by taking courses in business and technology, by participating in an internship, and by pursuing an advanced degree or earning professional accreditation.

Business Courses

Many successful communication managers have had no formal course work in business; they simply have learned what they needed to know on the job. As competition for these positions increases, however, you would be well advised to give yourself the edge by taking business courses that lay a good foundation to serve you both as a technician and as a manager. What curriculum you choose depends, of course, on how you wish to shape your business career. Listed below are some courses that offer a comprehensive introduction to business:

- Accounting
- Business ethics
- Business law
- Business policy
- Business statistics
- Economics (micro and macro)
- Management (of organizations and behavior, and of human resources; sales management, retail management, operations management)
- Managerial finance
- Marketing (marketing, advertising, promotional strategy, consumer behavior, direct marketing, marketing of services, international marketing).

You would do well to minor in one of these areas. For example, if you wish to become an investor relations specialist, major in technical communication, business communication, or public relations and minor in finance. Marketing communication specialists could minor in marketing; business or economic reporters, in economics; communication managers, in management.

Technical Courses

Should you desire to concentrate less on business and more on the technical side of an industry, you would do well to take courses, as electives or as a minor, in the specialty of your choice. For example, if automotive writing appeals to you, courses in chemistry, physics, automotive design, metallurgy, and materials stress would be appropriate. Should you wish to become a writer in the furniture industry, courses in botany, chemistry, wood working, textiles, interior design, and furniture construction might be necessary. Writers in food science and nutrition need courses in food chemistry, botany, nutrition, and physiology. The list of technical specialties and their required courses could provide you with many opportunities to focus your future. What you must remember is this: Selected carefully, scientific and technical courses provide you with the operational and theoretical language of your industry. Mastery of this fundamental language, combined with proficiency in writing and speaking, is necessary for you to function well as a communicator.

Moreover, though writing and editing, speaking, visual communication, computer, business, and technical courses provide invaluable insights, you should view such courses simply as introductions, not as conclusions, to the communication opportunities and challenges you will face in the work place. No course or series of courses can prepare you for all the communication opportunities you will encounter in your business writing career. And in the work place, so much of what you must know will be industry-specific. Over time, your writing will become increasingly effective as you learn your industry and your field. This kind of knowledge is acquired chiefly through experience—by engaging in discussions with fellow employees, doing your daily work, reading trade publications, and conducting interviews inside and outside the company. Likewise, in attending conferences, trade shows, company meetings, professional networking sessions, and corporate training courses, you will expand your horizons. If you stay with a single organization, you will, in time, become very familiar with your company's product or service and its particular market as you learn more about its corporate mission, image, philosophy, and reputation. The more you know about your company, its technology, and its market niche, the more effective you will be as a communicator.

Though this kind of knowledge is acquired through experience over time, you can get a head start even while still an undergraduate. How? As an intern.

Internships

Internships introduce you to an actual work environment, where you will experience the daily activities of communication professionals. As an intern, you may have the opportunity to attend staff meetings, write copy, work with photographers, help plan conferences and special events, design small publications, attend video/photographic shoots, meet internal and external clients and employees from other departments in the organization (especially marketing, sales, graphic production, and the like), make media contacts, and generally acquire a solid feel for the business.

The internship is an opportunity to combine your classroom learning with supervised, on-site work experience. The on-site supervisor will work closely with you and your academic adviser to ensure that the internship is a valuable learning experience. If you undertake your internship for academic credit, you could obtain this credit by conducting research for the company, actually designing and analyzing a questionnaire, performing a literature review, and submitting a report of your findings. You could analyze some of your employer's communication practices, thus performing a small communication audit for your department. You could apply selected communication theory to work situations—especially valuable for many employers would be an analysis of their meeting management or interviewing techniques. Your employer might have you design and produce various corporate pamphlets, brochures, or reports (with accompanying analyses). Whatever the project, you should design it to expand your practical and theoretical communication expertise.

After one semester's on-site experience and some completed projects, you will most likely have become acquainted with a number of communication professionals who, knowing your work well, will supply you with recommendations as you begin your job search. Occasionally, internships turn into part-time jobs that, upon graduation, become full-time positions.

Advanced Degrees

As a communicator in business, you have a number of options for study beyond the bachelor's degree. Many colleges offer master's degrees in communication, public relations, rhetoric, composition and rhetoric, journalism, communication management, technical and professional writing, technical communication, radio and television, creative writing, and the like. If you already have an undergraduate degree in communication, business communication, or an allied major, do you need one of these advanced degrees? Possibly—especially if your employer desires, for purposes of advancement, that you certify your communication abilities beyond the undergraduate degree. You will recall that both the STC and PRSA salary surveys found a correlation between advanced degrees and higher income.

But before you decide to pursue an advanced degree in communication, be very clear about what you are looking for and why you might seek this advanced degree. After about three to five years' experience beyond your bachelor's degree, carefully assess your long-term career goals. Examine your educational strengths and weaknesses; then match these against the post-baccalaureate degree programs that appeal to you. Talk with the program directors, some of the faculty, and current students in the various programs. Be sure to ask these questions: How many years will this program take? Do the courses reflect state-of-the-art technology and current research? Can course selection be tailored to my needs? Are the faculty well qualified as practitioners, researchers, and teachers? Is this degree chiefly academic or practical? Does this degree justify its cost in time, money, and energy? Will my employer be able to pay for some or all of the courses? And the ultimate question to which the rest tend: What new personal and professional opportunities will this advanced degree provide?

If you wish to enhance your business mobility, an advanced degree in communication may not be right for you. Perhaps you should pursue an MBA instead, with a concentration in communication, computer systems, marketing, management, accountancy, or finance—especially if your communication expertise is strong, and what you really need to ascend into management is a deeper understanding of business functions. Maybe all you need is a course or two in some communication or business specialty, a six-week seminar that will shore up a weak spot in your education. If, on the other hand, you hope eventually to teach or conduct communication research in a four-year college or university, you will need to consider the Ph.D.

Remember, only you can answer the question of whether an advanced degree is important. As you examine your options, carefully balance the costs against the benefits. Above all, be an enlightened and discriminating academic consumer.

Professional Accreditation

In addition to, or instead of, an advanced degree, you may some day seek professional accreditation through the Public Relations Society of America (PRSA) or the International Association of Business Communicators (IABC). Accreditation is evidence that your peers in one of these associations are confident of your status as a professional practitioner. To achieve accreditation, you must be an association member in good standing, have practiced for a certain number of years (five for the PRSA), and demonstrate (through oral and written examinations) historical, theoretical, ethical, legal, and practical knowledge of the profession. In addition, the IABC requires a portfolio evaluation. The PRSA awards successful candidates the Certificate of Accreditation and the designation of "PRSA Accredited" or "APR" (Accredited in Public Relations). The IABC designates successful completion with "ABC" (Accredited Business Communicator).

Seminars, courses, and workshops are also made available through these professional associations so that practitioners can keep abreast of advances in communication knowledge, theory, and practice. With communication technology changing so rapidly, with research continually reshaping the theoretical body of knowledge, and with ongoing, sometimes profound, developments in international law, politics, and economics, communication practitioners are continually challenged to develop professionally. The associations thus employ accreditation and continuing education to monitor the quality of their members' contributions to themselves, their companies, their clients, their customers, and to society at large.

CONCLUSION

A career as a writer in business and manufacturing can be very rewarding. Whether you work for a manufacturer, wholesaler, or retailer, in goods or in services, your skills as a communicator will present many opportunities for advancement. The Bureau of Labor Statistics is optimistic about employment for the next decade: Communicators in corporate, marketing, and corporate-based documentation should find increasing and diverse opportunities in an expanding service economy. Whereas entry-level salaries for writers and editors may remain relatively low, salaries for people at the supervisory/managerial levels, especially in the high-risk areas of business, will most likely remain robust. The secret to your career success will be judicious planning. Make your early choices wisely (in selecting courses, a major, a minor, and the first job), and you will build your career upon a solid foundation.

In planning your career, examine the corporate annual reports, brochures, and pamphlets in your library or career planning center at school. Talk to your professors in a number of different subjects, not just communication courses. Conduct information interviews with communicators in businesses that interest you. Read articles and books like this one, for these give you a clear sense of available careers and advancement opportunities. (See the references and "Appendix C: Suggested Reading," at the end of this chapter.) Take courses that buttress your skills in written, oral, and visual communication, as well as courses in computers, business, and a technical specialty. Consider an internship. And when you are finally near graduation, begin your search for entry-level positions in industries you consider interesting. Remember that as a communicator, you must feel good about the industry, about your employer, and about the product or service you represent. For upon graduation, you do not want simply to begin a job. You want to begin a lifelong career.

PROFESSIONAL PROFILES

The following two profiles will give you an idea of the varied work that technical communicators do in business and manufacturing firms. Christine Makis creates marketing communications for a firm that develops computer software for scientific applications, while Mat Tavares is a technical communication manager for a large, international corporation.

Christine Makis

Christine Makis is the marketing communication coordinator for Galactic Industries Corporation, publishers of high performance data processing software for scientists in the fields of spectroscopy and chromatography. Communication plays a vital role in the scientific software business because customers need information about products, newly released products, and updates. Christine says that "Galactic has hired professional communicators since 1987, their first year of organization. For the first two years they used an outside public relations firm and then, realizing the importance of this area, hired their first internal marketing communication coordinator in 1989."

Christine is very enthusiastic about the challenges of being a marketing communication coordinator. She has performed numerous communication tasks. Besides writing press releases, Christine has written and designed advertising copy, direct mail copy, fact sheets, and brochures. She says that "the audience for most of these pieces is potential users, but often we target our current users as well." Christine notes that she spends time "meeting with advertising sales representatives, preparing monthly sales and leads reports, and designing, preparing, and demonstrating products at trade shows." She especially likes attending trade shows because of the opportunity to travel and meet interesting people.

"Professional communicators are very important in the scientific software field," Christine notes. "Anywhere you have highly specialized people in two different areas trying to communicate to each other, you always risk the chance of misinterpretation. In Galactic's case, our potential customers are spectroscopists and chromatographers who are not necessarily computer literate—and then there are the Galactic engineers, who know enough about these fields to program software, but they are truly programmers." Because the programmers are so immersed in the technical aspects of the product, Christine emphasizes that they "need professional communicators who understand the product and the benefits it will bring to the scientists. From that understanding, the communicators relay a message to potential customers without getting too technical."

A business communication major as an undergraduate, Christine began working for Galactic immediately upon graduation from Bentley College. Although this is her first position with the company, and her first full-time professional communication position, Christine points out that she gained a great deal of on-the-job experience working part-time and in an internship at Cahners Publishing Company in Newton, Massachusetts. During her one-semester internship as a senior, Christine was a promotion art assistant. She was involved in various "production tasks, such as type specing, mechanical paste-ups, mounting art for displays, and making corrections on the Macintosh." The internship was useful too because Christine learned how to manage projects. She "organized and managed logo and magazine files, performed various clerical tasks, ordered art, and obtained price quotes." Christine feels the internship with a major communication company like Cahners gave her a valuable head start in seeking her first position after graduation: "People who had read my resume knew Cahners, of course, and they were impressed that I had worked there."

Besides the internship, Christine gained valuable professional experience over the past few years working part-time as an editor for the Institute of Internal Auditors, Greater Boston Chapter. As editor, Christine designed and produced the chapter's monthly newsletter. She scheduled and organized articles, wrote and edited copy, designed page layouts, and oversaw production of the newsletter. Christine gained much of her layout and design experience in a summer job as a desktop publisher with Desktop Design, Springfield, Massachusetts. In this job, she formatted newsletters, magazines, and manuals. She also assisted in designing brochures, flyers, and advertisements. Christine says that one of the things she enjoyed most in this job was "consulting with customers about their design preferences."

With her varied experience and education, Christine feels very confident about her professional future. She says, "Working for a small company like Galactic, I have gained—and am still gaining—a great amount of experience and knowledge in written and visual communication." She hopes "to remain part of Galactic for quite a while." Although it is a small company, Galactic "is rapidly growing in every aspect, including," she notes, "my responsibilities and challenges. I would like to stay with Galactic as long as I am challenged and am confident that both parties are benefiting."

In reflecting upon her career, Christine doesn't think it is feasible to pick out one specific career path for someone who does what she does. She believes "there are many different avenues a person could take. The most reasonable and, depending on the person and the company, the most desirable career path would be to work your way up through the various levels of the marketing communication department until you hit the top." Christine feels "it is reasonable to focus on a single area like technical writing or graphic design and either open your own business or work for a firm established in this area."

Christine is excited about her work as a marketing communication coordinator and about her future as a technical communicator. She credits her early success to choosing business communication as an undergraduate major, for she was able to learn about both business and communication. Christine says that in addition to the ten business courses she took, she "was able to put together interesting combinations of communication courses like public speaking, technical writing, communication theory, public relations, and graphic design." Besides carefully selecting courses that would prepare her well as a professional communicator in business, Christine emphasizes "the importance of gaining experience through part-time work and an internship." Once employed full-time, she devoted herself to the job, working long, often challenging hours in a field she loves.

Mat Tavares

As operations manager for the Technical Services Operation of Raytheon Service Company (RSC), Mat Tavares oversees technical communication products and services that account for approximately $120 million in annual sales. RSC, a wholly owned subsidiary of Raytheon, provides these services worldwide for Raytheon companies and for a wide variety of other companies needing help in project management, systems engineering, training services, technical information services, and the like. Responsible for the day-to-day operations of RSC, Mat is involved in planning, directing, and controlling technical communication activities in all the major programs of this 1,200-person organization.

RSC operations include all areas of technical communication: writing and editing, basic research, computer graphics, training, video and film production, interactive videodisc production, graphic design, photography, photocomposition, custom exhibits, reprographics, information management, word processing, and printing. Mat's responsibilities are now managerial; that is, he no longer writes or edits projects. As a manager, he makes sure that the right personnel are assigned to projects, oversees proposals and bids, manages the budget, and makes sure that bid contracts are fulfilled. His ultimate responsibility is to ensure that RSC operates annually at a profit. Thus, with well over three decades of experience as a technical communicator, supervisor, and manager at Raytheon, Mat is familiar with all phases of careers in technical communication for business and manufacturing.

In what Mat calls a "deep tech" company (like his own, an engineering-based technocracy), a successful writing career must be carefully prepared for and nurtured over time. The fundamental qualification, Mat feels, is an undergraduate degree in a science, especially physics, computer science, or one of the engineering sciences. This scientific/technical education must be linked with good writing skills, of course, but Mat firmly believes that the ability to understand complex concepts, data, and technical plans constitutes the foundation for writing at Raytheon. After a few years' experience, a writer will probably have defined a technical niche, having become very familiar with a product area and its market. In time, then, a good "deep tech" writer becomes conversant with the concepts, operating principles, and technical language of the engineers and designers who form the various product teams.

Mat sees the writing field today as tremendously challenging. In addition to possessing good writing skills, the successful writer has to be adept at problem solving, especially in analyzing products, markets, and target audiences within those markets. Writers are thus becoming communicators in the fullest sense, because they have to choose, from among a bewildering array of communication possibilities, the exactly right medium or mix of media to convey technical information. Mat points out that the major developments in technical communication are directly linked to technological developments in media. Communicators in business and manufacturing should therefore become familiar with all aspects of technology, from paper-based publishing to electronic publishing (knowing both its software and hardware), to CD-ROM and online venues. In addition, communicators should know when and how to use the appropriate video technologies as well as various combinations of interactive computer and video.

For those communicators wishing to rise into the supervisory and managerial ranks, Mat emphasizes that a background in business is absolutely essential. Experience plus an undergraduate business degree, advanced studies certificate, or an MBA degree will help to provide the business understanding that communicators, functioning as supervisors or managers, will need to maximize a company's investments in personnel, technology, product development, and quality control. But this sort of understanding does not come simply from education or degrees, nor does it come overnight. Years of experience in an industry or with a company and its products, plus initiative, organizational ability, people skills, and an entrepreneurial bent are, to Mat, what ultimately spell success. His own career, in fact, illustrates well the upward path of a technical communicator in a "deep tech" corporate environment.

Coming to the Raytheon Company in 1961 as a senior engineering writer/supervisor, Mat's early experiences with the company were indeed varied. He planned and coordinated the efforts of the draftsmen, illustrators, and other writers to ensure consistent quality and compliance with specifications. As a senior engineer and instructor for Raytheon Company, Electronic Services Division, Mat planned and developed training courses on various guidance and target-tracking radar systems. As a senior instructor, he presented these courses to military, civilian, and government personnel.

Mat's demonstrated planning acumen made it possible for him to advance to technical writing manager, responsible for preparing corporate-based documents, such as system-and equipment-level manuals for publication. Mat assigned writers and estimated, planned, and controlled the various writing tasks. He was the liaison between the publications task group and the design and project management groups. As a manager, Mat was always on the lookout for new managerial talent. He evaluated the personnel directly under his supervision and was careful to develop their writing and administrative abilities so that his company could effectively groom its next generation of managers.

Mat himself moved on to become the assistant department manager at Raytheon's Technical Information Operation, a position he held for 11 years. He was responsible for the activities of over 800 technical information specialists involved in a wide range of military and commercial technical information programs aimed at internal and external audiences. An important part of his duties was to develop new business in markets requiring technical information services. Mat identified, assessed, committed resources, and judged the profitability of these markets and opportunities. He also established departmental objectives, strategies, and action plans. In performing these high-level business activities, Mat feels that his MBA degree was essential. The MBA, in fact, helped open the doors to his current position as operations manager at the Raytheon Service Company.

Mat Tavares foresees that communicators will continue to function as key players in development teams, from product inception through manufacture, delivery, operation, maintenance, and training. With quality control becoming ever more the watchword in business and manufacturing, communicators will play increasingly important roles in selecting, controlling, and communicating information to ensure their company's success. For those technical communicators who carefully plan their education and careers, who are versatile, intelligent, and willing to put in long hours, Mat sees a bright future.

APPENDIX A

The Bentley College Bachelor of Science Degree in Business Communication: A Sample Curriculum

The Business Communication (BC) major at Bentley College consists of eight courses selected from among a number of theory and applied electives. Students may also take BC-related electives in other departments (computer information systems, foreign language, literature, marketing, advertising, management, psychology, sociology, and the like) to complement their selection of business communication courses.

Business Core (10)	Major (8)	Minor (4)
Financial Accounting	Effective Speaking	Elective
Managerial Accounting	Comm theory elective	Elective
Business Statistics	BC elective	Elective
Computer Information Systems	BC elective	Elective
Managerial Finance	BC elective	
Business Law	BC elective	
Management	BC/BC-related elective	
Marketing	BC/BC-related elective	
Operations Management		
Business Policy		

ARTS AND SCIENCES (18)

Humanities:	Social Sciences:	Math & Science:
English Composition I	History I	Math I
English Composition II	History II	Math II
Literature I	Government	Computer Science
Literature II	Psychology/Sociology	Science I
Philosophy	Microeconomics	Science II
Humanities elective	Macroeconomics	Science elective

APPENDIX B

FURTHER INFORMATION

Professional Communication Associations
The Association for Business Communication (ABC)
Robert J. Myers, Executive Director
Baruch College, CUNY
Department of Speech
17 Lexington Avenue
New York, NY 10010
(212) 387-1620
Fax: (212) 387-1655
www.courses.sha.cornell.edu/orgs/abc/

The ABC is the oldest international association of business communication professionals in the world. ABC members include communication consultants, corporate communicators, and academics. The Association publishes the scholarly *Journal of Business Communication* and the *Business Communication Quarterly*.

Institute of Electrical and Electronics Engineers (IEEE) Professional Communication Society (PCS)
345 East 47th Street
New York, NY 10017
(212) 705-7900
www.comsoc.org

The Professional Communication Society is an organization located within the framework of a larger professional association, the Institute for Electrical Engineering Education. Its primary objective is to improve the communication of technical information.

International Association of Business Communicators (IABC)
One Hallidie Plaza
Suite 600
San Francisco, CA 94102
(415) 433-3400
Fax: (415) 362-8762
www.iabc.com

IABC is dedicated to fostering communication excellence, contributing more effectively to organizational goals worldwide, and being a model of communication excellence. In pursuit of this mission, IABC provides a full range of member services, adheres to sound fiscal and association management policies, and promotes better public understanding and recognition of the value of professional communication.

National Investor Relations Institute (NIRI)
Louis M. Thompson, Jr., President & CEO
8045 Leesburg Pike
Suite 600
Vienna, VA 22182
(703) 506-3570
Fax: (703) 506-3571
www.niri.org

NIRI is an association of investor relations executives, whose goals are to identify the role of the investor relations practitioner, to protect a free and open market with equity and access to investors of all kinds, to improve communication between corporate management and shareholders, present and future.

Public Relations Society of America (PRSA)
33 Irving Place
New York, NY 10003-2376
(212) 995-2230
Fax: (212) 995-0757
www.prsa.org

The PRSA was chartered in 1947 and, with a national membership of more than 18,000 in 109 chapters throughout the United States, is the leading public relations association in the world. PRSA members come from business and industry, public relations counseling firms, government agencies, educational institutions, trade and professional groups, hospitals, and other not-for-profit organizations. PRSA has a Code of Professional Standards, backed by effective enforcement procedures, to which all members must adhere.

The Society for Technical Communication (STC)
901 North Stuart Street, Suite 904
Arlington, VA 22203-1854
(703) 522-4114
Fax: (703)522-2075
www.stc.org

STC has over 20,000 members worldwide in "8 regions each containing approximately 20 local chapters." It is "the largest professional society in the world dedicated to the advancement of the theory and practice of technical communication in all media."

APPENDIX C

Suggested Reading

(1997). *Peterson's 1998 job opportunities for business majors.* Princeton, NJ: Peterson's.

Driskill, L. P., Ferrill, J., & Steffy, M. N. (1992). *Business & managerial communication: New perspectives.* Fort Worth, TX: Dryden.

Farr, J. M. (1994). *America's 50 fastest growing jobs* (2nd ed.). Indianapolis, IN: JIST Works.

Field, S. (1996). *Career opportunities in advertising and public relations.* (Revised edition). New York: Facts on File.

Field, S. (1996). *100 best careers for the 21st century.* New York: MacMillan General Reference.

Gould, J. R., & Losano, W. A. (1994). Revised by W. E. Kramer and M. K. Kramer. *Technical writing and communication careers.* Lincolnwood, IL: VGM Career Horizons.

Green, M., & Nolan, T. (1984). A systematic analysis of the technical communicator's job: A guide for educators. *Technical Communication, 31* (4), 9–12.

Guiley, R. (1995). *Career opportunities for writers* (3rd ed.). New York: Facts on File.

Kruell, C. (1995). The internal agency approach to managing and developing marketing materials. *Technical Communication, 42* (2), 231–235.

Mogel, L. (1993). *Making it in public relations: An insider's guide to career opportunities.* New York: MacMillan.

Morgan, B. J. (Ed.). (1993). *Public relations career directory* (5th ed.). Detroit: Gale Research.

Moore, S. (1996). *An invitation to public relations.* London: Cassell.

Noronha, S. F. R. (1994). *Careers in communications.* Lincolnwood, IL: VGM Career Horizons.

Teague, J. H. (1995). Marketing on the World Wide Web. *Technical communication, 42* (2), 236–242.

NOTES

[1]One of the more comprehensive salary studies is Fisher, H. S. (Ed.) (1997). *American salaries and wages survey* (4th ed.). Detroit: Gale research. For a glimpse at some regional salary figures, see "Advertising copywriter," p. 34, "Marketing, advertising & public relations manager," pp. 422, 427–428; "Public Relations,"

pp. 571–572; and "Technical Writer," pp.702 and 763–64. However, even Fisher's survey is spotty and should not be considered definitive.

[2]STC's 1997 *Technical communicator salary survey* represents the responses of over 900 of 2,000 members of the Society for Technical Communication in the United States and Canada. The response rate for the entire survey was slightly greater than 45 percent. STC has over 20,000 members. The PRSA Salary Survey results, conducted by Simmons Market Research Bureau, Inc., surveyed "a total of 6,000 sample members on an 'nth' basis: 1,000 APR-accredited members, 2,500 non-accredited members and 2,500 non-members [of the PRSA]" (p. 3).

REFERENCES

1997 Technical communicator salary survey. (1996). Arlington, VA: Society for Technical Communication.

O'Dwyer's directory of corporate communications: 1997. (1997). New York: Jack O'Dwyer Co.

Fisher, H. S. (Ed.). (1997). *American salaries and wages survey* (4th ed.). Detroit: Gale Research.

Simmons Market Research Bureau. (1996). Salary survey of public relations professionals. New York: Public Relations Society of America.

United States Department of Labor, Bureau of Labor Statistics. (1996). *Occupational outlook handbook: 1996-97 edition.* Bulletin 2205. Washington, DC: GPO.

chapter 2

Writing for Engineering Fields

Marian G. Barchilon
Arizona State University (East)
Mesa, Arizona

Jobs

- *Writing/Editing:* documentation analyst, developer, engineer, or specialist; information analyst or engineer; information product developer; marketing writer; multimedia developer; online information developer; proposal specialist; technical communicator; technical editor; technical editor/writer; usability analyst or engineer.
- *Designing:* graphic artist or designer, illustrator, visual communicator.
- *Managing:* communications manager, publications manager, publications supervisor.
- *Training:* trainer.

Responsibilities

Developing, designing, and managing print, non-print, and multimedia-based technical materials in support of engineering and engineering-related industries.

Employment Outlook

Generally, the outlook is good because there is projected growth in many engineering fields and projections of increased employment after recent downsizing. However, following a national trend, more and more technical communicators are becoming employed as freelancers, consultants, and contract employees.

Salary Range

Depending on your level of education and experience, salaries can range from a mean of $33,000 for entry-level communicators to a mean of $54,000 for those with 11 or more years of experience. Those with engineering or technology backgrounds can command higher salaries based on their technical expertise.

INTRODUCTION

Technical communicators perform a variety of communication tasks, both alone and in teams, in many engineering fields. While some of the chapters in this book focus on technical communicators in the aerospace, computer, and manufacturing fields, technical communicators can participate in other engineering fields as well. These engineering fields include agricultural, architectural, automotive, bioengineering, ceramic, chemical, civil, construction, electronic, electrical, environmental, industrial, marine, materials, mechanical, metallurgical, mining and geological, naval, nuclear, oceanographic, optical, petroleum, reliability, software, structural, systems, and welding.

While each engineering field has its own unique characteristics, all involve the same basic engineering functions: research, development, design, production, construction, operations, sales, and management. Therefore, technical communicators who are employed in these fields perform internal and external communication tasks related to one or more of these functions. These communication tasks will be described in detail later in the chapter.

To better understand the role of technical communicators in engineering, you first must understand what an engineer does. An engineer identifies problems and then applies principles of science to create economically feasible designs that solve those problems. Thus, the engineer is a creative problem-solver, who creates functional devices, systems, and processes that help improve the world around us. For example, a biomedical engineer bridges the engineering, physical, and life sciences in order to identify and solve medical and health-related problems. Biomedical engineers may design medical instruments and devices, including artificial hearts and kidneys, lasers for surgery, and cardiac pacemakers. In contrast, electrical engineers apply mechanical and electrical engineering principles to design and construct computers and auxiliary equipment. Thus, electrical engineers may be involved in the automatic control of machines and devices, such as autopilots for spacecraft and missiles.

YOUR LIFE AS A WRITER IN ENGINEERING

Technical communicators in engineering work in many different organizations, from small to large engineering and engineering-related firms, national laboratories, U.S. military and government offices, and universities. For the past eight years, *Graduating Engineer* has published its *Directory of Engineering Employers*, which lists potential employers by name, discipline, and industry. If you are interested in a position in a particular engineering field or in a particular industry, you'll be able to find many options listed here. For example, if you're interested in working in chemical engineering, the *Directory* lists companies such as DuPont, Fluor Daniel, and Merck. Likewise, if you're interested in the defense industry, you'll find such organizations as Lockheed Martin, Lawrence Livermore National Laboratory, Los Alamos National Laboratory, and Rockwell.

As a technical communicator in engineering, you would design, develop, and manage a great variety of communications related to the research, development, design, production, construction, operations, sales, and management tasks that engineers perform. We can most easily describe these communications by dividing them into two broad categories: internal and external communications.

Internal Communications

Internal communications involve communication within an organization. For example, you might write and edit internal employee communications, including corporate memos, letters, reports, and newsletters, or internal guides to help engineers prepare technical reports. You might also write in-house proposals, which are documents written to convince colleagues to adopt an idea, product, or service. For example, you might write a proposal suggesting that management purchase a new piece of technical equipment. Likewise, you might write in-house feasibility studies, which are documents written to show whether a proposal is practical. Or you might write policies, procedures, operating instructions, and manuals for products used in the organization, such as special machinery, lab equipment, or software. Finally, you might edit engineering specifications for designing a new product, or develop instructional and training materials that explain some technical product or process to its users.

You also might give informative and persuasive presentations for a variety of purposes. For example, you might speak to employees about products or team projects, addressing members of a department, committee, or task force.

External Communications

External communications involve communication outside an organization, such as writing and editing for clients, customers, other engineering professionals, the government, or members of the general public. This type of communication is particularly important in engineering since engineers design functional devices, systems, and processes that impact society. Thus, engineers are sensitive both to the impact of their designs and their communication, which reflects those designs. For example, a civil engineering firm understands the importance of a well-designed bridge, for a poorly constructed one may lead to serious accidents, litigation, and, consequently, a poor public image.

As a technical communicator working in engineering, you might write external proposals that help your company win contracts for products or services. Since these contracts are important sources of funding, teams of experts often work together on developing the proposal. For example, an environmental engineering firm may want to respond to a request for proposal (RFP) to secure a large contract to clean up contaminated waste at a local site. A team of technical communicators, environmental engineers and other subject matter experts (SMEs) may work on the response. Once the contract is obtained, you might have additional important documentation tasks to accomplish. For example, you might write formal reports to inform the clients about the work your company has performed. These can include progress reports, which document the work accomplished to date, and final reports that show the results of the completed work. Other types of external proposals include sales proposals, written to persuade clients outside the organization to purchase a service or product, and grant proposals, which attempt to persuade organizations to fund engineering research and other activities.

Other types of external communication include annual reports, which document the company's business and financial activities over the past year. You also might help engineers edit manuscripts for publication in journals or summarize the engineers' research in various external publications read by funding sources (see Tamara Locke's Professional Profile later in this chapter).

For external customers, you might write product documentation detailing how a product works or how a new, upcoming product will perform. You might also prepare user manuals to help customers use the product.

On the promotional side of an engineering or engineering-related firm, you might create advertising copy to sell your company's product or service in magazines, newspapers, or trade publications. Additionally, you might write technical newsletters, technical bulletins, flyers, brochures, datasheets (which provide data about a product) or catalogs, which also serve as promotional material for products or services.

You also might be asked to write a press release about a product's features for trade publications or persuasive copy for the general public, especially if the public has a negative attitude about potential hazards or products produced by your company. For example, if your employer is involved in chemical, petroleum, or nuclear engineering, your task might be to help establish a positive reputation for the company.

Using the latest technology, you might serve as a "Webmaster," designing World Wide Web pages to inform customers and clients about your company's products or services. Additionally, you might develop various multimedia products, online (electronic) documents, or interactive electronic technical manuals (IETMs) for instructional, training, and other purposes.

On the presentation side, you might be asked to create and even deliver presentations to external audiences for a variety of purposes. For example, if you had a biomedical engineering background, you might give a presentation informing hospital staff how a new medical device works. If you had an environmental engineering background, you might give a presentation informing a client of the project phases completed for a hazardous materials cleanup, or you might present hazardous waste research findings to concerned citizens. As a public relations representative, you might serve as company spokesperson in the event of an accident or crisis. In contrast, if you were employed in the marketing area of an engineering firm, you might give a persuasive presentation to convince prospective customers to purchase a new engineering product because it is safe, reliable, and economically feasible.

EMPLOYMENT OUTLOOK

Employment opportunities for technical communicators are often tied to job growth in specific engineering fields. Current research indicates projected growth in the following industries: computer hardware and software, telecommunications, photonics, biotechnology, manufacturing, pharmaceuticals, energy, environmental, factory automation, tests and measurements, subassemblies, medicine, defense, advanced materials, chemicals, and transportation. According to the National Association of Colleges and Employers, college graduate hiring in the engineering fields is up, with 78 percent of schools reporting an increase. This is because employers need new employees who can keep up with technological advancements and because employers see an increase in business and economic projections after recent downsizing trends. Also, according to the U.S. Department of Labor, the demand for technical communicators is expected to rise because of the continued increase in the volume and variety of technical communications and our society's growing need to communicate technical information.

In line with a national trend, more technical communicators are serving in temporary positions as freelancers, consultants, contingent workers, and contract employees. According to the Bureau of Labor Statistics, in 1995 there were 2.7 million temporary workers employed through agencies, nearly double the number five years ago. Factoring in contingent and contract workers, the figure jumps to 6 million. This figure compares with 117.2 million permanent and payroll workers.

Generally, greater employment opportunities exist for technical communicators in larger engineering and engineering-related companies. Larger firms offer more opportunities for employment, whereas for economic reasons, smaller firms often employ engineers as jacks-of-all-trades who also perform technical communication tasks.

Depending on your level of education and experience, your salary might range from a mean of approximately $33,000 if you are an entry-level technical communicator to a mean of about $54,000 if you have 11 or more years of experience. According to the *1997 Salary Survey* conducted by the Society for Technical Communication (STC), the mean salary for U.S. technical communicators is $46,750. However, based on anecdotal evidence, those technical communicators with engineering or technology backgrounds probably have higher salaries. STC's data does not distinguish between technical communicators with different educational backgrounds or in various engineering fields.

Career paths for technical communicators vary. Generally, however, communicators advance to positions as leads or seniors and then to positions as supervisors.

PREPARATION

Technical communicators employed in engineering come from a variety of educational backgrounds. However, you're likely to be most successful in the engineering fields if you have both a strong communication and technical background and an aptitude for technology. Technical communicators in engineering usually have degrees or course work in technical communication, English, and graphic design, in addition to engineering or the sciences, and some knowledge of the latest information technology tools.

However, regardless of your formal education, if you expect to adapt successfully in an engineering environment, you should understand how to (a) communicate technical information to a variety of technical and non-technical audiences; (b) work well with engineers; and (c) use new computer information technology, including software and hardware. Although technical communicators in engineering often rely on

SMEs to help them understand the technical content of communications they're working on, you'll be more employable if you have a multidisciplinary education because you'll already understand the subject matter. Also, because engineers rely on high technology, you'll be more in demand if you are adept at using the latest information technology, such as the Internet and World Wide Web. You should try to be multitalented, with the ability to develop, design, and manage a variety of print, non-print, and multimedia-based technical materials. Your computer experience should include knowledge of such basic tools as word processing, graphics, desktop publishing, presentation, database, spreadsheet, and multimedia software.

PROFESSIONAL PROFILES

The following three profiles will give you a more specific idea of the work done by technical communicators in the varied fields of engineering. Tamara Locke is a technical writer for a major U.S. government defense contractor, Marcia Bethel does similar work for a large manufacturer of computer components, and Roger Holt is a training and technical communications manager for a well known electronics firm.

Tamara Locke

Tamara Locke is a technical writer for Sandia National Laboratories. Sandia has research and development responsibilities for nuclear weapons, arms control, energy, the environment, economic competitiveness, and other areas of importance to the needs of the nation. Sandia's main mission is to ensure that the United States' nuclear weapon stockpile meets the highest standards of safety, reliability, security, and military performance.

Tamara edits technical reports, conference papers, and journal articles written by Sandia's scientists and engineers. She also publishes the *Guide to Preparing SAND Reports,* an internal guide distributed throughout the Labs to answer authors' questions about preparing technical reports and to provide current information on Sandia's writing and publishing standards. In addition, she is involved in the review and approval procedure for publications, verifying that authors have sent their publications to the appropriate departments for approval and that the documents meet basic formatting requirements.

Tamara also writes user guides to help engineers and designers build their own components, and she writes and edits articles for the magazine *Inside Sandia,* a corporate publication that showcases Sandia's technical achievements in order to generate interest in transferring Sandia-developed technology into private industry. To produce these articles, she researches previously published in-house reports and interviews scientists and engineers. Thus, Tamara not only prepares technical documents for scientists and engineers to use, but she explains Sandia's researchers' accomplishments to the public, which funds Sandia's research and benefits from it.

Before obtaining this position, Tamara edited military manuals for a year and worked in Sandia's Design Definition Department for eight years, designing printed circuit boards using Computer-Aided Drafting (CAD) software. This job was particularly appropriate because Tamara has an associate degree in drafting and design as well as a BA in English. She then became the Department's Component Database Manager, creating schematic and physical electrical component packages on computers for other designers and electrical engineers. Additionally, for one year she wrote administrative and technical articles for Sandia's newspaper.

Tamara sees that, recently, writers in her company have had to adapt to many changes, caused partly by staff reductions that have required them to take on additional responsibilities (such as contract administration) not necessarily related to writing. However, because of these staff reductions, she also sees potential for more outsourcing support in technical communication at Sandia.

Marcia Bethel

Marcia Bethel is a staff technical writer for Intel Corporation, a semiconductor company that supplies the computing industry with chips, boards, operating systems, and software. Intel's products are used by industry members as building blocks to create advanced computing systems.

Marcia has held her position at Intel for three years. Before that, she was a consultant to Intel for over six years. Her educational background consists of a certificate in data processing and undergraduate course work in business administration.

While Marcia's title is the same as Tamara's, her communication tasks are different. Moreover, she distinguishes herself from other technical communicators at Intel who hold such titles as information engineer or usability engineer. She says that the information engineers generally write for other engineers, and the usability engineers write for end users.

As a staff technical writer, Marcia writes for both Intel engineers (internal customers) and customer engineers (external customers). While preparing her engineering communications, Marcia always follows the Institute of Electrical and Electronics Engineers, Inc. (IEEE) and Joint Electronic Device Engineering Council (JEDEC) standards.

For her internal customers, Marcia edits engineering specifications written by marketing, design, and engineering staff to design a new product. For her external customers, she edits application notes that explain how a product works in a particular application. Additionally, she writes technical papers that tell how a new, upcoming product will perform. Marcia also writes user manuals and develops tables containing technical data for her engineering audiences.

Marcia plans and schedules projects for two writing teams that support four engineering groups. She interviews marketing staff, applications engineers (customer-oriented engineers who work inside the company), and design engineers (design-oriented engineers who work inside the company).

What does Marcia like best about her job? She likes interviewing engineers, finding out how things work, and then documenting the process. She believes that since engineers are highly technical people, technical communicators will gain their respect by being technically proficient.

Roger Holt

Roger Holt recently accepted a position as a training/logistics/publications supervisor at Motorola, which is in the electronics/aerospace field and conducts business for both government and commercial purposes. The company researches, develops, and manufactures communications equipment for earth and space uses. Roger currently oversees the preparation, production, scheduling, and time-phasing of publications and training for the ground-based portion of the IRIDIUM® System. The IRIDIUM® System is a new, satellite-based, wireless, personal communication network designed to allow common types of telephone transmissions (voice, data, and fax) to reach their destinations on Earth at any time. In using this system, it is unnecessary to know the location of the person you are calling; rather, you only need to know that person's system telephone number. The system consists of a handheld telephone (like a cellular phone), a series of 66 satellites in orbit, and a series of ground stations. The handheld telephone is used to originate and receive calls. Before taking this exciting position, Roger was a technical writer, a lead writer, and then a publications supervisor. He has a BS in physics and many years of on-the-job communication experience.

Because Roger is now in management, he attends frequent meetings with staff, managers, and internal/government customers; delegates tasks; and sets department goals and objectives. He is often involved in preparing project status reports, budgets, and schedules. To do these tasks, he often must use government military specifications, guidelines, and handbooks; Motorola internal policies and procedures; customer-supplied statements of work; and departmental guidelines for writing and production functions.

He says the future for technical communicators is bright as long as they can use all the modern tools (e-mail, computer, publications software, the Internet, and multimedia) and can adjust to customer requirements. Roger implies that flexibility is the key to success in the engineering environment. He says that technical communicators need to research and write information that communicates what clients need, but with more speed, accuracy, and timeliness than ever before.

Tamara, Marcia, and Roger have similar visions for the future of technical communicators in engineering. They testify to the importance of having good technical communication skills and knowing the technical field you're working in, but they also stress the impact of business and technological tools on their work. All agree that communicators must engage in continuous, lifelong learning in a variety of disciplines and always be ready to face new challenges in a fast-paced, competitive, and rapidly changing environment. Most importantly, they understand that despite the constant changes they see around them, their key roles remain remarkably the same: to provide fast and accurate internal and external information to a variety of technical and nontechnical audiences.

APPENDIX A

FURTHER INFORMATION

Associations

Institute of Electrical and Electronics Engineers (IEEE)

Professional Communication Society (PCS) [comsoc]

345 East 47th Street

New York, NY 10017

(212) 705-7900

http://www.comsoc.org

IEEE's PCS is a leading professional society in technical communication that is devoted to communicators in the engineering fields.

Society for Technical Communication (STC)

901 North Stuart Street, Suite 904

Arlington, VA 22203-1854

(703) 522-4114

http://www.stc-va.org

STC is the world's largest professional society dedicated to the advancement of the theory and practice of technical communication.

APPENDIX B

Suggested Reading

Amparano, J. (1996). Temps tackle bigger load as experts worry. *The Arizona Republic, 22* (December), A1, A28–A29.

Beakley, G. & Evans, D., et al. (1987). *Careers in engineering and technology.* New York: Macmillan Publishing Company.

Livo, L. J. (1990). What we call ourselves. *Technical Communication 37,* 51–60.

Woolever, K. (in press). *Writing for the technical professions.* New York: Longman Publishing Company.

REFERENCES

Directory of engineering employers. (1996). *Graduating Engineer 18,* 12–27.

Society for Technical Communication. (1997). *1997 Technical communicator salary survey.* Arlington, VA: Society for Technical Communication.

U.S. Department of Labor, Bureau of Labor Statistics. (1994). *Occupational outlook handbook* (Bulletin 2450). Washington, DC: Government Printing Office.

chapter 3

Writing in the Aerospace Industry

Rebecca O. Barclay
Knowledge Management Associates, Inc.
Portsmouth, Virginia

Thomas E. Pinelli
NASA Langley Research Center
Hampton, Virginia

Jobs
Writer/editor, visual communicator, multimedia/online information developer, documentation developer/manager, trainer/facilitator, and others.

Job Responsibilities
Developing, producing, and managing a wide variety of print, non-print, and media-based materials in support of the aerospace industry and its related products and services.

Employment Outlook
Good but subject to cyclic fluctuation.

Salary Range
$33,000 to $54,000 yearly.

INTRODUCTION

The large and complex aerospace industry, which employed approximately 850,000 people in 1994 (*Aerospace Facts,* 1994–95, p. 11), plays a vital role in the nation's economy. Although only a small percentage of those employed in aerospace are technical communicators, they perform a wide variety of communication duties in government and the private sector.

Aerospace is a dynamic, cutting-edge industry that is prone to cyclic fluctuations in employment. It is also a knowledge-rich industry that depends heavily on producing, transferring, and using information in many formats for different audiences and purposes. Thus, technical communicators are an important part of this industry.

YOUR LIFE AS A WRITER
IN THE AEROSPACE INDUSTRY

If you work as a technical communicator in the aerospace industry, you will rarely be bored, given the broad range of opportunities and challenges to communicate information effectively. A technical communicator interested in aerospace could work for one of several major government agencies. For example, the National Aeronautics and Space Administration (NASA) and the Department of Defense (DOD) rely on skilled writers and editors to help researchers produce highly technical publications that document research findings and a variety of print and non-print materials designed to disseminate information and transfer technology. These publications include technical reports and memoranda, journal articles, and conference presentations. The Federal Aviation Administration (FAA) employs technical writers and editors to prepare safety regulations and related documentation to ensure that aircraft are properly operated and maintained. The major producers of civilian and military aircraft, Boeing-McDonnell Douglas, Lockheed Martin, and Northrup-Grumman, and their subcontractors, vendors, and suppliers, also depend on technical writers and editors and other communication professionals, such as information developers, multimedia designers, and document management specialists, to create and manage documentation and other information products that support the aircraft industry. For example, according to Dr. Steve Poltrock of Boeing Computer Services, more than 70 manuals and documents totaling over 92,000 pages were developed for the Boeing 747–400 aircraft.

Professional societies like the American Institute of Aeronautics and Astronautics (AIAA), which provide journals for their members, and publishers of aerospace-related newspapers and magazines like *Aerospace Daily* and *Aviation Week and Space Technology* rely on the skills of trained communication professionals to write and edit articles for a variety of audiences. Airlines also use the services of skilled writers and editors to prepare process documentation and information products for internal and external customers. For example, information developers, writers, trainers, and others are called on to develop written and online training materials for flight and maintenance crews who must update their professional skills and learn new ones as advanced aircraft are placed into service. In addition, information developers, writers, and graphic designers prepare the safety instructions found in most airline seatback pockets and the major carriers' in-flight magazines offered to airline passengers.

CAREER PATH

You might begin your career in writing in the aerospace industry by working as an editor. As in other industries, editing often involves more than just correcting the grammar and spelling of technical material. Therefore, being a good editor requires that you be trained in and understand the fields in which you're editing. These fields include aeronautics and aerodynamics, computer science, space technology, physics, computational fluid dynamics, engineering, and environmental science.

Lynn Heimerl, an editor at the NASA Langley Research Center, who is profiled later in this chapter, adds this information about the duties of an editor: "The substantive edit that we perform at Langley . . . is very thorough. We must have solid writing and editing skills and know math, science, engineering, and aeronautics."

Substantive editing, whether done at Langley or elsewhere, means that editors ensure that reports

- are accurate, understandable, and clearly written;
- use math, symbols, and units correctly;
- contain appropriate terminology (such as that used in aeronautics or space physics);
- include data that are consistent in text, tables, figures, and appendixes;
- are complete, use a logical order, and have conclusions that are based on included data;
- cite references that are correct and available to the reader; and
- do not violate copyright law or endorse products and tradenames.

Such work might eventually lead you in many directions. Some technical communicators in the aerospace industry prefer to remain writer/editors and to increase their communication capabilities over the years, while others move into managing publications. Some former editors now work in the online dissemination of aerospace-related materials, or in multimedia development, in scriptwriting, or in book publishing, depending on their talents, personal interests, and the available jobs and salaries in these fields.

EMPLOYMENT OUTLOOK

Like many industries, aerospace continues to experience the effects of downsizing. And technical communicators in this industry will not be immune to layoffs, particularly if their work is not perceived as valuable to the organizations for which they work. The *Occupational Outlook Handbook* (1994) predicts that employment opportunities for technical communicators will remain good, however, particularly if persons trained as technical communicators also have academic preparation in a technical field (U.S. Department of Labor, p. 188). Moreover, in addition to an ongoing demand for the traditional writing and editing skills, forecasters predict a growing need for developers of multimedia products, interactive electronic technical manuals (IETMs), and World Wide Web page developers. Trainers and independent consultants who can create specialized materials like proposals, computer documentation, and indexes will also be in demand.

A 1997 salary survey conducted by the Society for Technical Communication (STC) indicates that the average yearly salary for an entry-level technical communicator is approximately $32,910. Salaries for technical communicators working in aerospace generally follow the results of this survey. Moreover, as is true in most professions, salary levels rise with years of experience and increasing responsibility. The average yearly salary for a senior manager is $70,390. An individual who has a bachelor's degree can expect to earn an average yearly salary of approximately $45,090; someone with a master's degree can expect to earn approximately $49,940 (Society for Technical Communication, pp. 4–5).

PREPARATION

Before the advent of technical and professional communication programs at the college and university level, technical communicators working in aerospace were usually educated in engineering or science. They developed many of the necessary writing and editing skills on the job. Today there is general agreement that communication professionals working in aerospace do need enough technical background to be able to understand the subject matter and communicate it clearly, although they do not necessarily need undergraduate degrees in engineering or science (Roper, 1993, p. 215). A more typical approach today is to work toward a degree in technical communication, communication arts and design, English, or journalism and to take courses in mathematics, physics, chemistry, or biology to provide the technical background that writer/editors will need in order to communicate with engineers, scientists, and other professionals in the aerospace industry.

Whichever approach you take, having a good technical background can be as important as good communication skills. For example, Janice Costa, a technical communications team leader at McDonnell Douglas Aerospace, who also is profiled later in this chapter, says, "My technical background is an asset when talking to engineers, and [studying] technical writing really improved my writing skills. If I were beginning today, I would get as much experience writing in as many different areas as possible—scientific, technical, business—in addition to learning the specific requirements of the job."

As a technical communicator in the aerospace industry, you would need skills in writing, editing, and grammar as a foundation. Janice says, "I would highly recommend taking several intensive writing courses and other communication courses in addition to technical writing courses. Try to find classes in different areas that help balance your writing skills—for example, oral communication or presentation design. The communication courses are also necessary because so many employers specify good written and oral communication skills. Besides, there is a high probability that some day you will have to present your work to a group, or to your management. Learning effective skills now makes you more marketable later."

Of course, you could prepare for a career as a technical communicator in aerospace by pursuing a degree in aerospace engineering and supplementing that course work with statistics, mathematics, science, and communication studies. Courses in computer science also are a must for anyone who will work in a technical field.

In addition, courses in the basics of law for publishing and business, marketing, and public relations will be critical in the future as more communication jobs move from large publishing houses and government organizations, which traditionally have stressed a more layered and segmented approach to communication, to small companies and computer organizations, in which one person performs many jobs requiring diverse skills. These courses would also be helpful for someone planning to work in a setting that provides information products for the public.

Another area that is becoming increasingly important is multicultural communication. According to Janice, "A change that I cannot emphasize enough is the growing multicultural emphasis in industry. 'Diversity' is one of the latest buzz words, and having some knowledge of multicultural communication is a great help. Multicultural communication does not mean speaking many different languages. It is the awareness that not all cultures are like our own; our way is not the only 'right' way of doing things, and we can unintentionally send the wrong message by our behavior." Fortunately, there are many places to go to find information on different cultures. Knowing where to find the information as it is needed is more important than trying to memorize everything about all cultures before beginning a new job. "I am lucky," Janice tells us, "multicultural communication courses were required for my degree. I am still studying the field, however. I think anyone who wants to stay in aerospace, or any industry, needs at least a fundamental understanding of multicultural communication."

In addition, you need to be comfortable using basic word processing programs, graphics software, and standard desktop publishing packages. Lynn Heimerl points out that "the field of technical communication is changing at a tremendous rate, more so than at any other time I can remember." In the past, print predominated in most communication organizations and jobs. Today, however, technical communication involves a wide array of formats, media, and avenues for disseminating information. This flexibility will increase as new technology makes new formats easier to use and within the reach of the public. "The emphasis on online publishing and multimedia has far-reaching effects on training to be a technical communicator," explains Lynn. "Now, you must have solid basic skills, be comfortable with and keep up to date with changes in computer systems, and continue to learn to keep pace with the field and the technology."

Janice Costa also finds that good computer skills are vital to any type of communication at McDonnell Douglas. "All of the writing and presentation materials are on computer, much of the information needed is in company-wide computer files, and other information can be found by performing online searches outside of the company." Although McDonnell Douglas still produces hardcopy documentation, there is growing emphasis on having all information in a company-wide computer system. "Quite a lot of our documentation is already in the system, so anyone who needs the information can get it quickly," says Janice.

As the effects of the "information superhighway" change the publishing workplace, using new information technology now requires that editors know how to edit a document on a computer without ever seeing it on paper, use standard word processing packages (for example, Microsoft Word or Novell WordPerfect), handle graphics software (such as Adobe Illustrator or Photoshop), use desktop publishing programs (Adobe FrameMaker or Aldus PageMaker), and put information online on the Internet.

Putting information online requires keeping up to date about changes in the systems that employers use (UNIX, Macintosh, PCs), determining how to get graphics images online (for example, using GIF and JPEG files), and learning how to prepare the print material to be read online (using Hypertext Markup Language and conversion software packages that convert the written word to electronic documents). It also requires knowing the latest software programs so that you can perform your job more efficiently and accurately. Therefore, you should not limit yourself to knowing only one type of program. You'll need facility with many different types, including word processing, graphics, spreadsheets, databases, statistics, and mathematical processors. And skill in publishing online and the ability to work with and understand a variety of computer platforms will be essential.

Lynn adds, "There is one piece of advice I'd give someone who is beginning a career in technical communication [in the aerospace industry]. Take a number of projects that you know how to do well and do an outstanding job on them. But also take some projects that are high risk, that you are not sure you can handle, and learn as you go . . . sometimes these projects bring the biggest chance to learn and grow!"

To get the chance to take risks, learn, and grow, Lynn and Janice both stress the importance of on-the-job experience. According to Lynn, "If I were trying to start a career as a technical communicator today, my best advice would be to get as much work, internship, or volunteer experience in the field as possible before looking for a full-time job." Janice agrees, "If possible, take an internship or a volunteer position that uses the same skills. Even if you do not keep the job, you have started a network of other people in the field. This network can be very important later in your career." It can help you learn about possible job openings, because many jobs are never advertised. If you are trying to move from your educational institution into the workplace, you should find educational programs that have summer or school-term co-op programs. Internships and cooperative education programs typically can provide you with valuable work experience and opportunities to apply skills that make you highly competitive on the job market. Spending time with a placement counselor at your college or university to see who is hiring and what skills are being used is also smart. Then work to get those skills.

Technical communication in the aerospace industry can be a wonderful job, especially if you enjoy working with people, writing, and doing research. According to Janice, "If you enjoy writing research papers in school and interacting with others, you would probably enjoy a career in professional communication."

The best advice we can offer for preparing for lifelong employment in the aerospace industry is to look at communication in the broadest possible context. Realize that the roles of writers and editors are changing rapidly; you may find yourself working on projects that would not have been considered in the purview of technical communicators ten years ago. Remain flexible and open to learning, recognize that you may be called on to perform many different kinds of communication tasks in a team setting, and seek out opportunities for professional growth.

PROFESSIONAL PROFILES

This section profiles two professional communicators who work in different sectors of the aerospace industry. Lynn Heimerl is a technical publications editor and manager with more than ten years of experience, who works at the NASA Langley Research Center in Hampton, Virginia. Janice Costa is a communications team leader with seven years of experience, who works for McDonnell Douglas in Long Beach, California.

Lynn Heimerl

Lynn Heimerl has worked as a technical publications editor for the NASA Langley Research Center for four years. The Langley Research Center is one of NASA's premier, basic research centers that studies aeronautics, atmospheric sciences, and space research and technology.

NASA Langley was the original National Advisory Committee for Aeronautics (NACA) center that developed and tested almost every aircraft that flies today, worked with the original manned space program, and developed the thermal tiles that now keep the Space Shuttle from burning up upon re-entry into Earth's atmosphere. Today, Langley develops new, safer methods to fly and track airplanes as they leave and enter airports, designs the technology for future aircraft, studies space and how to live and work in it, and leads worldwide research in studying the atmosphere, such as the ozone hole and the burning of vegetation and its effects.

Technical communication has been an important part of the history of NASA. NASA's original charter, approved by Congress, was "to provide the widest practicable and appropriate dissemination concerning its activities and the results thereof." NASA's mission today is not only to perform research and transfer new technology to industry but also to communicate what has been learned in studying aeronautics, space, and the environment to the public, to colleges and universities, and to other researchers in the United States and abroad. NASA also plays an active role in communicating advances and skills in science and mathematics to public school students.

As a technical publications editor and manager, part of Lynn's job is to edit such NASA research documents (referred to as "formal reports") as technical papers and technical memoranda, which contain scientific and technical information aimed primarily at researchers, U.S. aerospace companies, and educational institutions. NASA Langley requires an extremely high level of edit for these documents, the substantive edit defined earlier in this chapter. "These reports are reviewed both for technical content and for readability and completeness; the NASA reports are considered high-quality technical documents that have a worldwide readership," says Lynn.

Lynn's responsibilities also have included writing and editing proposals and even re-engineering NASA editing and production policies. (Re-engineering is the total redesign of how NASA handles production and publishing.) Production work at Langley involves editing, typing and typesetting, correcting and inserting graphics, page setup, printing, and entering the report in the NASA database so that others can retrieve and use the document.

A typical day for Lynn might also include numerous other writing and editing projects that require multiple skills, such as working on a team that is reviewing how to streamline the procedures at Langley, writing and editing a proposal for new services, writing copy concerning new technology and how it affects the public, and putting information on a "home page" (a page on the Internet that tells about NASA Langley and what it does). Langley is actively putting reports and other information on the World Wide Web (WWW) on the Langley and Technical Report Servers. These reports can be accessed by anyone via the Internet, by using uniform resource locators (URLs): for example, http://techreports.larc.nasa.gov/cgi-bin/NTRS. "Putting documents online requires using a variety of computer skills," says Lynn. "These skills constantly change as the technology changes."

NASA editors handle a wide variety of types and lengths of documents. According to Lynn, "Assignments are extremely varied. This year I was project manager for a full-length (550 pages) history of Langley called *Spaceflight Revolution* by James Hansen, and then I also worked on projects that involved writing the copy for a magazine article and an ad for a technology transfer magazine."

Lynn's duties have required her to develop multiple skills and to learn new skills on a continuous basis. Her projects have required skills in copywriting, graphics, design and layout, desktop publishing, computer technology and online publishing, and printing techniques for both print media and documents that will be published on the Internet.

Lynn originally was trained in communication, with a minor in art and a concentration in science. Through her first series of jobs, she learned the standard communication policies and formats commonly used by technical communicators.

These first jobs included working as an editor for a NASA contractor for six years. While working for the contractor, Lynn had a chance to perform the high level of editing that the NASA Langley Research Center requires and to learn the Agency's publication standards. Before taking that job, she worked as a writer in a state government educational library, was a newspaper reporter for a weekly newspaper, wrote for a daily newspaper, was a copywriter for an advertising and public relations agency that handled both technical and educational accounts, and handled public relations and information for a large Head Start program. In addition, Lynn did freelance work for a number of technical companies in the Hampton Roads, Virginia, area prior to working with NASA. "I enjoyed both writing and science," says Lynn. "I can combine both interests in my current job, which makes it exciting."

After working for the NASA contractor, Lynn returned to college and took postgraduate work in science, math, computer science, aeronautics, and aerodynamics. "It is important to have a broad background in communication, but it is also necessary to get specific training in the field in which you are working," advises Lynn. She is continuing to concentrate on courses in aeronautics, computers, and environmental science.

"If I were training for my first job today, I'd be sure to get the specific skills that are necessary to begin," explains Lynn. "I would also concentrate on acquiring broad skills that would transfer from job to job and that would prepare me for living and working in a constantly changing world."

Lynn says that despite uncertain times in working for the government as it downsizes, she really enjoys her work at NASA, and "each day brings a new project with new challenges." An essential element to being successful in a job is to have solid skills and to like what you do. "What I really love about working for NASA," observes Lynn, "is that the job is always changing. It involves using every skill that I have learned in the past, and it also requires continuing to learn so that I can keep pace with what needs to be done."

Janice Costa

Janice Costa has worked for over seven years in several communication areas at McDonnell Douglas Aerospace, a firm that has an interest in space systems, defense systems, and commercial aircraft. The corporation is divided into many subdivisions; the West Coast is home to the commercial aircraft company (DAC) as well as the space systems company (MDA–W). DAC designs and manufactures the MD–90, MD–80, and MD–11 airplanes; it also has close ties with the C–17 project, which is co-located at the Long Beach facility.

McDonnell Douglas was Janice's first employer. "I was in college, majoring in electrical engineering," she explains, "when I interned at DAC. My first assignment required a lot of communication skills, including writing and interpersonal skills. While I was still working at DAC, I graduated from California State University, Long Beach, with a bachelor of arts in speech communication in 1992. Although I did not enjoy engineering, the technical experience has been invaluable to me at McDonnell Douglas. I am currently working on a graduate degree in communication, with an emphasis in organizational and multicultural communication. I also have taught interpersonal communication to undergraduate students at the university for the past year. My undergraduate and graduate programs both have strong emphases in writing, which have been very beneficial for my career."

Janice's initial responsibility as a technical communicator was to create users' manuals for computer programs, which her department generated, for airline customers. "I have also been involved with creating and presenting various classes related to process and product improvement and customer satisfaction," she notes. Most recently, she worked in the technical library, cataloging, performing data searches, and assisting customers.

When asked to explain her current duties, Janice first explains a little more about the company and the role of communication in it. The goal of McDonnell Douglas is to design and build superior airplanes and to be a world-class competitor in the commercial aircraft business. There are many different types of communication within the company—for example, writing technical manuals and procedures, and meeting with other McDonnell Douglas employees, regulatory agencies, customers, and suppliers. A particularly important kind of communication is the extensive documentation of aircraft design specifications so that the company's departments can meet or exceed industry standards for quality. This documentation is part of the communication that is vital to all processes because most of the employees traditionally have little contact with those people in other areas (engineering with manufacturing, for example). For this reason, McDonnell Douglas offers training in many aspects of communication (effective presentations, technical writing, proposal writing) to help employees improve their skills.

Currently, Janice is a team leader in the Integrated Product Development (IPD) group, a unit that is responsible for a number of different activities. IPD trains other groups in such new business practices as Process Based Management and Quality Function Deployment, is responsible for the Total Quality Management-Interactive Education (TQM–IE) activity in their area, directs the engineering training, and finds and researches new business practices to improve DAC's capabilities. IPD also provides user support and training for a number of different computer systems.

As the leader of the communications team in IPD, Janice spends much of her time writing and revising documentation on business processes and practices to be used by McDonnell Douglas employees. The documentation often requires different versions of the same process to be used at different levels of the corporation to improve the employees' performance and enhance the competitiveness of McDonnell Douglas.

Other components of Janice's day-to-day job responsibilities are compiling and editing the group's status report, creating the quarterly newsletter, organizing the monthly meeting with the vice president, and assisting in special projects as they arise. Janice says, "I write my department's status report, which goes to our vice presidents, general managers of other departments, and the other members of my department. It is produced every three weeks and is generally seven to ten pages long. Our newsletter, which is only about four pages, focuses on a few key issues, but it has more depth than the status report."

Special projects are often presentations to or from management on a variety of subjects. "I am currently helping to revise a report on our integrated product development process," Janice says, "which will be given to all of the D&T (development and training) managers, and assisting in the development of a step-by-step instructional series on integrated product development, which will also be given to the D&T managers." The report and instructional series about integrated product development will explain the importance of the process and the procedures necessary to comply with the process. All of the processes and procedures are guided by regulations from the FAA, ISO 9000 requirements, and the Malcolm Baldridge criteria. Conforming to ISO 9000 requirements for quality systems is becoming increasingly important for U.S. companies competing in world markets. This is because complying with established standards for quality during all stages of product development and avoiding potential international product liability are important for building and maintaining relationships with customers both at home and abroad.

Though Janice's job requires a great deal of attention to detail, she emphasizes, "that does not mean the job is boring. . . . Much of the information I need is obtained by working with the other people in my group. Every new assignment is a chance to learn about a new subject."

REFERENCES

Aerospace facts and figures 1994–95. (1994). Washington, DC: Aerospace Industries Association of America.
Roper, D. G. (1993). How much technical knowledge do editors need? The authors' perspective. In Proceedings of the 40th Annual Conference of the Society for Technical Communication (pp. 215–217). Arlington, VA: Society for Technical Communication.
Society for Technical Communication. (1997). 1997 technical communicator salary survey. Arlington, VA: Society for Technical Communication.
U.S. Department of Labor, Bureau of Labor Statistics. (1994). Occupational outlook handbook (Bulletin 2450). Washington, DC: Government Printing Office.

chapter 4

Writing for the Environmental Sciences

Melinda Thiessen Spencer
Independent Consultant
Olympia, Washington

Jobs

Technical editor and writer, community relations specialist (public participation specialist, risk communication specialist), environmental educator, environmental journalist, proposal writer, grant writer, public information officer, and regulatory compliance specialist.

Responsibilities

Identify information needed by the audiences to understand environmental protection or natural resources management issues and provide that information in an understandable, accurate, and interesting way.

Employment Outlook

Good, especially for those with science backgrounds, ability to work on varied projects, and initiative in identifying users' needs.

Salary Range

From the low to mid-$20,000s per year for entry level with bachelor's degree to the $50,000s per year for senior-level managers.

INTRODUCTION

Environmental science is the discipline concerned with understanding and solving the problems caused by the interaction of natural and cultural resources. The environmental field has grown out of our struggle to preserve clean air and water, protect wildlife and habitats, accommodate increased demands for outdoor recreation, and balance economic growth with the preservation of open space. Young and dynamic, the environmental field is constantly changing as the public demands a more central role in decisions that affect them and as new laws are passed to protect natural resources. Environmental professionals combine their skills and experience in the sciences with a love for the environment to understand and solve the problems that result when society's goals conflict with natural systems.

Environmental issues can be grouped into two broad categories: environmental protection and natural resources management. *Environmental protection* involves assessing environmental quality, evaluating environmental impacts, enforcing government regulations, and developing technologies to prevent and clean up pollution. Hazardous compounds in the environment present a major threat to the health of people, plants, and animals. As a result, much attention in recent years has focused on hazardous waste management, which involves controlling how hazardous materials are used and disposed of. Joan Strawson Dollarhide's chapter later in this book provides an in-depth look at the roles of environmental communicators in hazardous waste management efforts.

Natural resource management, the second major category of environmental service work, is concerned with managing the earth's resources for the benefit of humans. This field encompasses a wide range of activities, such as land-use planning, growth management, and land acquisition for recreation and habitat preservation.

As issues in both of these areas become more complicated and diverse, environmental communicators are needed to help scientific experts communicate with the public and with each other. From government agencies to popular media, consulting firms to wildlife sanctuaries, the product of every environmental study is information. Making this mountain of information accessible and useful to the public and to decision makers is what environmental communicators do.

In this chapter, I describe the legislative foundation upon which the environmental professions are built; what you can expect in your life as an environmental communicator, including settings and environments where environmental communicators work; typical jobs and responsibilities; employment outlook; how best to prepare yourself for work in this field; profiles of two environmental communicators; and resources for further information.

LEGISLATIVE FOUNDATION
OF THE ENVIRONMENTAL PROFESSION

The public's increasing concern about environmental protection and natural resources management has led to the passage of extensive environmental legislation at all levels of government. Many jobs in the environmental field are a direct result of legislation and the regulations passed to enforce this legislation. Environmental communicators must become familiar with the legislation that defines the field. The list below identifies major federal legislation; updates are available from professional associations (many of these associations are listed in Appendix B) and from state and local government agencies.

Major Federal Environmental Legislation

- Wilderness Preservation Act (1964): established the National Wilderness Preservation System, which designates certain lands as wilderness areas.
- National Environmental Policy Act (NEPA, 1969): landmark legislation that imposed environmental responsibilities on all agencies of the federal government, specifying that they prepare detailed environmental impact statements for all federal projects that may significantly affect the environment.
- Federal Clean Air Act (1970, amended in 1977 and 1991): established limits for emissions from stationary and mobile sources of air pollutants to protect air quality.
- Federal Water Pollution Control Act (1972), Clean Water Act (1987): defined pollution limits, required water quality monitoring, and studied waste water treatment options.
- Coastal Zone Management Act (1972): established a coastal zone management program that provided grants to states for coastal planning and management.
- Federal Safe Drinking Water Act (1974, 1977): limited the amount of pollution allowed in drinking water sources.
- Resource Conservation and Recovery Act (RCRA, 1976): established a hazardous waste management program to regulate organizations and individuals who generate, store, transport, and dispose of hazardous waste.
- Toxic Substances Control Act (1976): empowered the U.S. EPA to require chemical manufacturers to test toxic substances that enter the environment in substantial quantities or present the likelihood of substantial human exposure.
- Comprehensive Environmental Response, Compensation, and Liability Act (CERCLA, 1980): authorized the President to require cleanup of toxic material releases. Established Superfund, which is financed by a tax on the production of toxic chemicals, to pay for restoring natural resources that have been damaged by toxic chemicals.

- Superfund Amendments and Reauthorization Act (SARA, 1986), including Title III, the Emergency Planning and Community Right to Know Act: strengthened the U.S. EPA's mandate to involve the public in the decision-making process at Superfund sites.
- Environmental Education Act (1990): coordinated educational efforts at federal, state, and local levels.

YOUR LIFE AS AN ENVIRONMENTAL COMMUNICATOR

Whether you are concerned with environmental protection or natural resources management, as an environmental communicator, you will perform a wide range of tasks in fast-paced environments, where a missed deadline can send a company executive to jail or cost thousands of dollars per day in penalties. The duties and responsibilities of environmental communicators vary depending on whom they work for, their geographic location, and their technical knowledge.

Environmental communicators edit, write, and coordinate the production of technical reports that interpret data and recommend environmentally sound decisions; they prepare direct sampling at suspected pollution sites so that these areas can be cleaned up quickly and thoroughly. They also prepare educational materials for the public and elected officials. If they work in research and development, they edit technical reports written by scientists and ghostwrite journal articles and conference papers. If they work in public affairs, they write and edit news releases, brochures, videotapes, and public service announcements for radio and television. And if they work for an environmental service organization, they define in writing the scope of the organization's activities and win the resources needed for research.

One of the best things to happen to the field of environmental communication is the adoption of community right-to-know policies in the Superfund Amendments and Reauthorization Act. These policies give environmental communicators the mandate to build bridges between scientists, elected officials, and the public by providing unbiased information about environmental and public health risks caused by chemical use and disposal.

Environmental communicators often travel a lot, going where the action is. If they are working with the community near a hazardous waste site, they go to that community. If they are involved in environmental education, they go where they are needed to disseminate information. Depending on whom they work for, environmental communicators may handle projects from a number of groups, departments, and agencies. Or they may work with a team of communicators in one agency or department. Their days are a combination of working independently and in teams with scientists, graphic designers, printers, and editors.

The boundaries of environmental communicators' jobs change daily. Environmental communicators fulfill many roles, some of which they will not have anticipated and may not have been trained for. Because they must write and speak effectively and be able to translate technically complex information into terms that various audiences can understand, environmental communicators are often the best people to interact with the public and the news media at press conferences, public meetings, and facility tours.

WHERE YOU MAY WORK

The primary employers of environmental communicators are government, industry, consulting firms, environmental organizations, and news media.

Government

Government agencies that employ environmental consultants exist at the federal, state, and local levels. Federal government agencies involved with environmental research, regulations, and enforcement include several agencies connected with land-use management and the protection of the environment:

- Department of the Interior—Fish and Wildlife Service, National Park Service, and Bureau of Land Management;
- Department of Agriculture—Soil Conservation Service and Forest Service;
- Department of Energy; and
- Environmental Protection Agency.

As an environmental communicator in any of these organizations, you might find yourself

- drafting proposed legislation;
- preparing reports and studies for federal facilities to ensure that industries are complying with environmental regulations;
- preparing guidance manuals to help industries comply with environmental regulations, conducting training courses on a variety of envi-

ronmental issues, including how to handle hazardous wastes, and facilitating the flow of information between agencies;

- publishing materials for the public that describe national parks and forests, along with interesting aspects of their wildlife and geology; and

- preparing environmental impact statements for facilities within the federal government's jurisdiction to show the effects that projects, such as dams, power plants, or airports, will have on the environment.

You could also do similar work at the state level. State government agencies include air and water quality control boards, environmental health and safety departments, and departments of toxic substances control. State governments implement, enforce, and even design environmental protection policies, often taking the initiative in matters such as land-use planning and special habitat protection. In addition to completing the tasks mentioned above—drafting public policy and legislation and preparing environmental impact statements—you might also be involved in preparing reports of field investigations and inspections, and providing timely and accurate information about environmental issues to federal and local agencies, business and industry, environmental interest groups, trade associations, citizen organizations, and the news media.

Local government agencies mirror the efforts of state governments, ensuring that environmental policies adequately protect the local environment. You might be involved in the following tasks at the local level:

- preparing reports about facility compliance with applicable regulations;

- addressing citizen concerns about the environment in public meetings;

- preparing materials for the public on topics such as the proper use and disposal of household toxic compounds;

- helping local businesses reduce their use of toxic compounds; and

- writing grant proposals to fund local zoos, parks, museums, and nature centers.

Industry

Many industries use chemicals and processes that have an impact on the environment. Given the penalties for polluting, industries have realized that minimizing environmental impacts makes sound business sense. It helps them avoid bad publicity and lawsuits, and they can often save production costs if they recycle some of their materials or use less hazardous substitutes.

Companies communicate environmental information to consumers, regulatory agencies, and each other. For example, the Chemical Manufacturers' Association, composed of many chemical companies, founded the Community Awareness and Emergency Response (CAER) groups that bring industry leaders, elected officials, emergency responders, and public health professionals together in groups across the country to share ideas and resources for avoiding chemical-related environmental emergencies. CAER member organizations have found that it makes good business sense for companies to operate in an open, cooperative fashion in their communities.

Companies involved in oil exploration and development, chemical manufacturing, timber sales, and waste management employ environmental communicators with a broad range of skills, including public relations, media coordination, graphic arts, government relations, environmental journalism, and law. These environmental communicators produce materials such as

- requests for proposals to procure the research materials needed to run the industry;
- annual reports for shareholders;
- reports for government agencies and consumers about advances their companies have made in reducing pollution and waste;
- reports required by various environmental laws, including air and water monitoring reports, hazardous chemical inventory reports, and emergency response plans; and
- public relations materials, such as speeches, press releases, and videotapes, to enhance their employer's public image with regard to environmental matters.

An example of the public relations aspect of an environmental communicator's job in the timber industry recently appeared in my newspaper. The text at the bottom of an advertisement about fish spawning reads, "At Weyerhauser, we're working with university scientists, government agencies, environmental groups and Native American tribes to study watersheds, analyze problems and find solutions that will make life a little easier for fish in forest streams. For a copy of our Annual Environmental Performance Report, call 1-800-551-4803." Accountability to the public is an integral aspect of business today.

Consulting

Environmental consulting firms are composed primarily of scientists, engineers, and technicians, whose services are sold to businesses and government agencies that cannot afford, or do not need, to maintain a large environmental staff. In an effort to be competitive, government agencies and industrial companies are reducing their in-house environmental staffs and are relying on consultants to develop and implement programs to solve environmental problems and to keep them in compliance with regulations.

Consultants perform projects such as investigating soil contamination at industrial sites, determining human health impacts from exposure to airborne pollutants, and analyzing proposed housing tracts to determine if they will disturb sensitive plant and animal habitats. The product of these activities is information, which must be conveyed accurately and on time to the client, government officials, and the public.

In an environmental consulting firm you might perform one or more of the following tasks:

- research and write communications to clients, detailing research findings in the field;
- manage support staff—for example, word processors, graphic designers, and printers;
- coordinate proposal-writing efforts;
- prepare audiovisual materials for public meetings; and
- teach engineers, chemists, and geologists how to write clearly and effectively.

Environmental Organizations

Environmental organizations include interest groups, educational organizations, and research institutes that focus on public education, research, advocacy, and natural resource stewardship. They are often nonprofit organizations. The missions of these groups vary; they promote recycling, educate the public and legislators about endangered species and habitats, raise public awareness about water pollution, build trails and restore habitats, and manage natural areas through land trusts.

If you decide to work for an environmental organization, you could expect to perform some of the following tasks:

- write grant proposals, research reports, journal articles, and presentations for scientists;
- write press releases, brochures, and annual reports;

- prepare mass mailings on advocacy issues;
- conduct educational seminars and community surveys;
- present testimony at public hearings or legislative committee meetings;
- review and analyze proposed legislation;
- research and prepare position papers on specific environmental topics; and
- facilitate meetings among agencies, industry, and the people affected by environmental activities.

News Media

The public gets most of its information about the environment from the news media. If you live in a large metropolitan area, you have probably noticed that special reporters are assigned to each type of story covered in the daily newspaper and televised news programs. Abundant and complex information on the environment has made it necessary for reporters to specialize in order to readily understand the importance of new environmental findings and integrate this information with what the public already knows. Communicators who have this specialized training in environmental science provide a significant service to their audiences, who get a more complete and meaningful story, and to the organizations that make the news, because their stories are conveyed more accurately.

Environmental communicators are employed by newspapers, television networks, trade associations and other special-interest organizations, and magazines. Many perform freelance work, writing books and preparing documentary films and videos about their areas of expertise.

JOBS AND RESPONSIBILITIES

The term "environmental communicator" encompasses many jobs. Seven of the most common environmental communication jobs are described here:

- technical editor/writer,
- community relations specialist (this position is now frequently called "public participation specialist") and risk communication specialist,
- environmental educator,
- environmental journalist,
- proposal and grant writer,
- public information officer, and
- regulatory compliance specialist.

It is impossible to draw fine distinctions among these job descriptions, since some of these positions require fundamentally the same skills and entail similar responsibilities as others. In addition, as the environmental field continues to redefine itself, new careers are being created in response to demands from the changing marketplace. Nevertheless, I describe these positions below.

Technical Editor/Writer

Entry-level environmental communicators usually start their professional lives as technical editors. In this capacity, they usually do a lot of proofreading. However, because so much information passes through their hands, technical editors have a great opportunity to learn about the organizations they work for and the types of communications these organizations produce. Technical editors spend a lot of time at their desks or on the telephone, clarifying issues presented in the materials they are working on. They usually work with other environmental communicators in teams to ensure that complex information is presented effectively. Editors also regularly take on project management roles, such as coordinating the efforts of writers, artists, and production staff; accepting responsibility for meeting deadlines; and ensuring that finished communications contain no errors in logic or presentation.

Editors often grow into more specialized positions after a few years, especially if they continue to work for the same organization and thus become increasingly familiar with its issues, services, and language. As their knowledge about environmental issues increases, their ability to take on the role of the novice reader often decreases. When this happens, many technical editors become more involved in authoring and managing communications. For example, they design and prepare multimedia presentations, applying their writing skills in popular media such as video and internet productions. Often they become primary writers and project managers, designing reports, brochures, and articles; interacting with their own or a client's staff to negotiate project definitions and budgets; and making sure publications get to the right audience on time and within budget. They may also represent their organization in public meetings and to the media, and they may market their organization's skills through proposal and grant writing. Of course they continue to analyze and interpret technical information.

Technical editors and writers are employed by all of the organizations discussed earlier in this chapter. Moreover, as they become more expert in the technical aspects of their organizations' work, many forge ahead into the roles described below.

Community Relations Specialist and Risk Communication Specialist

Community relations and risk communication specialists are liaisons among the community, government, and industry at sites contaminated with hazardous materials and in areas where controversial development is proposed. The job of the community relations specialist is covered in depth in the next chapter. However, I describe it briefly here so that the relationship of this part of environmental communication to the whole is clear.

Community relations specialists are third parties who give each side in an environmental controversy equal time to express their views. Community relations activities are characterized by a two-way flow of information—from an agency or company to the public, and from the public back again. Community relations specialists must understand the technical aspects of environmental issues so they can explain them to the public. They listen to the public's concerns and reliably relay questions and answers between community members and scientists involved in the cleanup. Listening and responding in a meaningful way to citizens' environmental concerns is essential to building trust between citizens and government or industry.

Community relations activities are closely associated with risk communication. Risk communication specialists use their technical knowledge of environmental issues to help the public understand conclusions presented in health risk assessments (HRAs), perhaps the most crucial documents that result from environmental studies. HRAs provide scientific estimates about how humans, plants, and animals may be exposed to contamination and possible short- and long-term health effects of that exposure. In preparing an HRA, scientists must make many assumptions to evaluate possible exposure to contaminants. For example, scientists use "best guesses" to estimate how much contaminated soil a child may ingest through eating homegrown produce and playing outdoors. Because so many judgment calls are involved in the process of quantifying health risks, someone who understands the entire process is needed to explain what the results mean to an affected community.

Risk communicators are employed by government agencies and consulting firms. Like community relations specialists, people in this role must be perceived by the community as being neutral. Therefore, while many communicators in environmental organizations and industry may have job responsibilities that are similar to community relations specialists, they cannot be effective risk communicators if the public feels that they have a vested interest in the outcome of an environmental problem. To be of greatest help to community members, risk communication specialists must understand the public's perceptions of risks associated with a particular project, help them become more knowledgeable about complex data and terminology, and develop communication channels for citizens to provide constructive feedback to industry experts and government decision makers. To make sure information gets back to the public, risk communication specialists must find effective ways to simplify and yet accurately present complex technical concepts to public groups, coach agency or industry spokespersons in how to talk about health risks to the public, and prepare and implement strategies to release critical health risk information to the public and the news media as soon as it becomes available.

Environmental Educator

Environmental educators work in a wide range of settings but share a common objective: to foster public awareness of and concern for the environment. Many environmental educators develop curricula and support materials for public schools. By 1989, 45 states had adopted environmental education plans, which provide a curriculum structure for local schools (Environmental Careers Organization, 1993, p. 119). Environmental educators work in many other settings, too, including botanical gardens, museums, and zoos, interpreting scientific information for the public. Nature centers, such as those supported by the National Park Service or the U.S. Fish and Wildlife Service, hire environmental educators to help visitors understand and appreciate the significance of environmental assets, such as old-growth redwood trees, or environmental advances, such as the cleanup of an oil-soaked coastline.

As an environmental educator, you might work in any of the following settings and prepare any of these communications:

- School districts and state education departments: preparing daily curricula and special programs for events such as Earth Day.
- Municipal, county, regional, and state park systems, including zoos, aquariums, arboretums, youth camps, museums, and cleanup programs: preparing brochures, signs, videotapes, and multimedia educational programs.
- Local agencies whose programs require widespread changes in people's behavior, such as curbside recycling programs: writing brochures, press releases, and community awareness communications.
- Regulatory agencies, consulting firms, and industry: helping legislators, scientists, and managers stay up to date on environmental issues such as toxic spill control and emergency response procedures; preparing reports, regulations, and updates.

- Federal agencies, including the Bureau of Land Management, Army Corps of Engineers, U.S. EPA Office of Environmental Education, and U.S. Forest Service: preparing reports for public and technical audiences on current cleanup sites and land management issues.

- Environmental organizations, such as those that treat injured birds and reintroduce them into the wild: creating brochures, videotapes, public awareness documents, and multimedia presentations.

- Cruise lines and ecotourism groups: promoting low-impact visits to fragile areas like the Arctic Circle and recreational facilities like the Epcot Center at Disney World. This involves creating multimedia and print communications to foster public awareness of the ecology of these areas.

- Citizen-interest groups, such as the League of Women Voters, that rely on timely and unbiased information to make community-based, environmentally aware decisions: writing speeches, presentations, and print and multimedia materials.

- Civic groups, such as the Rotary Club, and youth organizations like the Girl Scouts or Big Brothers: helping members learn about protecting natural resources, which involves coordinating events, planning presentations, and organizing learning activities. For example, the Rotary Club might sponsor a Creek Clean Up Day and would need to know how to avoid disturbing bird habitats.

Environmental educators must be effective and engaging speakers, with a strong technical background in their specialty areas, such as wildlife habitat preservation or chemical emergency response. Their challenge is to effectively relate complex technical information to audiences with varying degrees of knowledge about the topic, providing enough basic information so the novice can understand, and the sophisticated professional can remain interested.

Environmental Journalist

Most of what we know about environmental issues comes from newspapers, magazines, newsletters, and television. The environmental journalists who prepare this information are in influential positions and have a responsibility to make sure their materials are interesting, timely, and accurate.

Environmental journalists get their stories from press releases and interviews, and from being observant members of their communities. They cultivate relationships with contact people to learn the background information that gives depth and credibility to their stories. Environmental journalists have a responsibility to present all perspectives. Moreover, the people and organizations that make environmental news, such as government agencies, military installations, environmental organizations, and universities, want to avoid inaccuracies and exaggerations. Therefore, to help journalists gather information for these environmental stories, these organizations hold conferences, conduct facilities tours, and design press kits.

For example, when I was an intern for a university department that researched groundwater contamination, we sponsored a Groundwater Conference for Journalists, which was attended by journalists from across the country. Technical experts clarified issues about how pesticides and solvents move through soil layers into underlying water reservoirs, how these contaminants affect the plants and animals that come into contact with the contaminated water, and how scientific methods for measuring such effects are limited. By taking the time to educate journalists about background issues, the people who make the news, such as university researchers, can feel more confident that their stories will be presented accurately and fairly by the media. And since the journalists' hallmark is accuracy and timeliness, they, too, benefit by educating themselves about current environmental issues.

Environmental journalists are employed by newspapers, magazines, professional associations, and television and radio stations. Newspaper reporters focus on issues of interest today, such as proposed revisions to the Endangered Species Act. Magazine writers, on the other hand, focus on issues with more longevity, such as the ethics of breeding nearly extinct species in captivity. Industrial trade associations employ environmental journalists to prepare materials such as newsletter articles on regulatory changes that will affect a particular industry, or success stories such as the implementation of a community recycling program. Professional associations hire environmental journalists to edit journal articles and ghostwrite conference proceedings.

Proposal and Grant Writer

Grant and proposal writers are the unsung heroes in many environmental organizations. Grant writers are responsible for winning grant money to conduct environmental research; they may also persuade clients to give their organizations the resources needed to conduct environmental business. With a knack for highlighting an organization's strengths and minimizing its weaknesses, grant and proposal writers sell their organizations to prospective clients.

Grant writers are employed by environmental organizations, universities, and facilities such as zoos and parks, to bring in operating and research funds. Grant proposals for operating funds describe the inherent value of a facility and why it should receive funding, while proposals for research grants describe why certain research should be conducted, who will conduct the research, how they will do it and with what resources, and how much money is needed to complete the proposed project.

Proposal writers persuade clients to hire their organization to conduct environmental investigations and prepare reports. They respond to requests for proposals (RFPs) issued by industry or government agencies. RFPs describe work that needs to be done. The proposal that is written in response to an RFP emphasizes an organization's innovative and cost-effective approach for accomplishing the work on time and within (or below) budget and describes the organization's experience on similar projects. Consulting firms live and die by the success of proposal writers in winning work for the company.

Grant and proposal writers must take the initiative in finding out about available grants, sponsoring organizations, and clients, and they must be well-versed in the art of reading between the lines and anticipating and addressing the needs of a potential client or grant-giving organization. For example, picture yourself as the proposal writer for a consulting firm. You have learned through your professional contacts that the potential client awarded its last project to your competitor, who very effectively used color graphics to convey information about air pollutant dispersion. Even though the RFP does not specify that the consultant have color graphics capabilities, you should anticipate that the client will expect you to highlight your company's experience and success by also using color graphics. Grant writers, too, must anticipate what a sponsoring organization wants to know and provide that information in a creative and memorable way.

Public Information Officer

Public information officers are the link between any organization and everybody that the organization comes into contact with. As such, they perform any combination of the activities described throughout this chapter. Their job is to anticipate public and media reactions to their organization's environmental actions and to help other organizations, the public, and the media understand those actions.

Public information officers are employed by every organization mentioned in this chapter. In government agencies, they interpret federal environmental laws so the public understands and supports those laws. In environmental organizations, consulting firms, and industry, they prepare press releases, respond to media inquiries, and prepare many other types of informative materials to help other organizations and the public understand their employer's goals and activities. Public information officers must be skilled in oral and written communication and experienced with audio and visual media, such as the World Wide Web and CD-Rom presentations. They present their organization to the public, and they must be comfortable in that role.

Regulatory Compliance Specialist

Regulatory compliance specialists interpret a myriad of federal, state, and local environmental regulations as they apply to specific businesses and industries. These specialists are employed by government agencies to make sure the businesses and industries within their jurisdiction meet all environmental requirements. They are also employed by industry, consulting firms, and environmental organizations to identify compliance issues and to establish a plan to comply with applicable regulations.

Responsibilities of regulatory compliance specialists include

- researching and interpreting environmental regulations to determine their applicability to an industry or organization;
- documenting whether or not a facility is complying with the regulations;
- providing guidance to industry and agencies to help them comply with environmental regulations;
- tracking the status of proposed environmental legislation; and
- preparing and presenting training sessions to update the regulated community on changes in the environmental laws.

EMPLOYMENT OUTLOOK

Current and Future Availability of Jobs

Environmental communicators can look forward to the growing availability of jobs. As the economy gains momentum, environmental employers are scrambling to find qualified staff. Practically any career with the adjective "environmental" in front of it will offer excellent job opportunities for environmental professionals in all disciplines into the next century, according to *Washington CEO* magazine ("An Industry on the Move," 1994, p. 79). Worldwide, revenues generated by the environmental industry are expected to double between 1993 and 2000 (p. 81). As borders open up all over the world, a substantial amount of environmental work will need to be done, from cleaning up industrial sites in the former Eastern Bloc to protecting unique habitats that are just coming to the public's attention.

Some of the top jobs in the environmental field include environmental educators and communicators. The job of writer/editor is included among the *100 Best Jobs for the 1990s and Beyond* (Kleinman, 1992, pp. 238–240). The Department of Labor (1994, pp. 187, 188) suggests the demand for technical writers is expected to increase because of the continuing expansion of scientific and technical information and the increasing need to communicate it. Although the communications field is keenly competitive, opportunities will be good for technical writers (including environmental communicators) because not many writers can write effectively about technical material. Some job listings from the *Seattle Times* newspaper, provided in Appendix A, give you an idea of the range of current job opportunities in the environmental communications field.

Salaries

Most people entering the environmental field do so for reasons other than to make the highest salary possible. But even though communicators in the environmental profession are often motivated more by their commitment to environmental issues than by financial reasons, they can, and do, make a good living. Salaries for environmental communicators vary widely, depending on one's employer, location, position, education, and experience. However, based on my experience, median annual salaries for environmental communicators are within the following ranges:

* entry-level with bachelor's degree: $20,000–$25,000
* mid-level (master's degree or 5 to 7 years of experience)
  -non-management: $25,000–$35,000
  -management: $35,000–$40,000
* senior management: $40,000–$50,000

Government employees are paid less than their counterparts in industry or consulting. However, federal employees are generally paid more than state employees, who are, in turn, paid more than local government employees.

Employees of nonprofit environmental organizations can also expect to be paid less than their counterparts in government, industry, or consulting. Because nonprofit environmental organizations often depend on donations and grants for their operating budgets, the money must be stretched so that the greatest good is done for the fewest dollars. To make up for lower salaries, however, many employees in these nonprofit organizations often derive a greater sense of job satisfaction because they work directly with the public to increase awareness of and activism about environmental issues.

Salaries for environmental communicators in the news media vary so widely that median salaries have not been cited. For example, writers of popular books, journalists on assignment for *National Geographic,* and the environment reporter for *Good Morning America* earn very high salaries that are not typical in this profession. However, the majority of environmental communicators employed by the media earn salaries comparable to other specialty reporters.

PREPARATION

Formal education and hands-on experience are equally important in preparing for a career as an environmental communicator. As you learned earlier in this chapter, environmental communicators can apply their skills in many new careers being created in response to new laws and public demands for better information. No formal training program exists for every job, so employers look at an applicant's skills and experience as much as at education.

An increasing number of environmental professionals have very specialized backgrounds in subjects like environmental toxicology, geophysics, and atmospheric modeling. This trend will continue as more sophisticated information is needed to study environmental issues.

However, environmental communicators complement specialists by providing a broad-based, integrated understanding of environmental issues. One of my environmental communicator colleagues, Mary Kay Coker, has noted that, because it is an interdisciplinary field, environmental science is harder to prepare for than some of the more traditional sciences. For instance, you may be asked to write something on the health effects (biology) of nitrate compounds (chemistry) found in drinking water (hydrology) in certain areas (geography and geology). Just as all aspects of the environment are interrelated, environmental communicators must be able to draw connections among specialty areas to form a comprehensive understanding of environmental issues.

Education

A four-year college degree is crucial if you plan a career in environmental communication. The type of degree can vary, but environmental communicators must have a combination of skills in science and communications. As an undergraduate, you will want to take a variety of courses in biology, chemistry, geology, physics, and especially courses that emphasize environmental issues. You may choose to get your degree in a science with a minor in English, journalism, or technical communication, or vice versa. In either case, courses in technical or scientific writing and editing will be a must. If your degree is in a completely different field, be prepared to demonstrate your interest and understanding of environmental issues through post-graduate courses or volunteer work. Regardless of educational background, the common thread weaving environmental communicators together is their commitment, demonstrated through educational choices, previous paid or volunteer work, and extracurricular activities.

To enhance your opportunities for advancement, continue to educate yourself even after you finish school:

- Read voraciously to keep up to date on what's happening in the environmental field.
- Enroll in training seminars at university extensions, community colleges, or professional associations.
- Volunteer or intern in an environmental agency or organization. (See the Placement section later in this chapter.)
- Join and participate in professional associations to develop a network of practicing professionals. (See the "Further Information" section in this chapter.)
- Check the *Encyclopedia of Associations* at your library for a more extensive list of associations.
- Talk to people who work in the field. Your first contacts could come from professional associations. Be sure to ask them to recommend other contacts.

Special Skills and Personal Attributes

Potential employers look for employees with a wide range of skills that often are not taught in the classroom. In addition to strong communication and research skills and sound scientific knowledge, you should exhibit the following characteristics:

- Ability to concentrate amid confusion, produce under pressure, and prioritize conflicting demands.
- Tact in giving and receiving criticism.
- Awareness of an audience's information needs.
- Ability to interpret highly technical information for different audiences.

- Ability to work with people from a wide variety of backgrounds, who hold divergent points of view.
- Ability to deal tactfully with controversial topics.
- Ability to question what experts say. Often, your job will be to play devil's advocate, representing the most challenging contingent of an audience.
- Willingness to accept new responsibilities, such as representing your employer at public meetings. You will need to be confident in your ability to talk about what you know, and know when to defer to other experts when you are out of your depth.
- Familiarity with software programs for desktop publishing (word processing, graphic layout, spreadsheets) and multimedia and video production.
- Personal belief in your work.

Benefits of Experience

One thing that distinguishes the environmental field is the amount and variety of work done by interns and volunteers. It is now almost a prerequisite for environmental professionals to have internship or volunteer experience before they search for their first professional position. In these part-time and often non-paid positions, volunteers and interns gain valuable work experience, get to learn about their chosen profession, and have the opportunity to demonstrate their abilities and commitment to potential employers. Two organizations that can help you organize internships and volunteer work are the Environmental Careers Organization (formerly known as the Center for Environmental Intern Programs, or CEIP) and the Student Conservation Association. Addresses for both are provided in Appendix B.

Think carefully about what you want to learn before deciding where you want to work. Most interns and volunteers want positions in which they can develop specific skills, such as writing press releases or preparing video storyboards. Know what you want so you can focus your efforts on those organizations that will give you the experience you seek.

Once you have decided where you want to work, contact the person who is in a position to hire you. Be prepared to assess the organization's needs and propose your own position. You may need to persuade people that they would profit from employing an environmental communications intern or volunteer. Many people do not know what environmental communicators do, so be able to describe your work in terms that your prospective employer is familiar with. Otherwise, you may get an answer like, "Well, we don't really need a technical writer. Our scientists do their own writing." Focus on specific projects with tangible results. Ask the manager of the organization you wish to work for, "What projects have been sitting in your in-basket for a while that I could take a lead on?" An offer like that would be difficult for any busy manager to refuse.

Here's another example of how to get your foot in the door. Imagine that you've just read a newspaper article about how your county's recycling agency must increase the percentage of household waste that it recycles by 25 percent in two years. The agency manager is a member of the National Association of Environmental Professionals, which you recently joined. Approach her at the next NAEP meeting and say something like, "I read in the newspaper that your agency is increasing the percentage of household waste that is recycled. I wonder if you've considered a public information campaign as an initial step in meeting that goal. You could tell people how to do a better job of separating their recyclable materials from their garbage and remind them about why recycling is so important. I have writing and research experience in issues related to waste management from my technical communications program at the state university. Perhaps you could use an intern to brainstorm your agency's public information campaign." Despite your efforts, you still may not get the position, but the people you talk with will appreciate your initiative and will likely give you new leads to follow.

Internships are more competitive and structured than volunteer positions. Contact your local, state, and regional offices of federal agencies in the fall if you are interested in working for them the following summer. Local government agencies like to hire local citizens, so begin your search close to home. Nonprofit organizations also look in their own backyards first when hiring new interns or volunteers. Many corporations have environmental and health and safety departments; these are good places to start if you are looking for an internship with them.

If you are looking for an internship in a consulting firm, you may be able to capitalize on the peak-and-valley nature of consultants' workloads. Often consulting firms have more work than their staff can handle. Letting an intern who is paid $5 per hour proofread a 2,000-page report makes better business sense than having a staff writer who is paid $15 per hour do that job. The down side is that some consulting firms may take advantage of an intern's economic value by working him or her too hard. In addition, because the work pace is usually very fast, consulting firms rarely provide much training or management for their interns.

When the organization you want to work for expresses interest in you, write a proposal that describes how the services you are offering will meet the organization's needs. Define the types of work you might do for the organization, the skills you have that enable you to do this work, and a time frame for completing the work. The most successful internships focus on one or two specific projects, are well-supervised, run on schedule, and have an end product. However, because you are there to explore your chosen field, be wary of internships in which your manager travels a lot or is otherwise unable to give you guidance on a daily basis.

PROFESSIONAL PROFILES

This section profiles two environmental communicators working in different areas of the profession. Lora Moerwald is the water quality project coordinator for a county environmental agency, and Cecilia Franz is a freelance writer who has co-authored an environmental textbook and writes grant proposals and other materials for various clients, including the Center for Reproduction of Endangered Wildlife, the research arm of the Cincinnati Zoo and Botanical Garden.

Lora Moerwald

Lora Moerwald is employed by King County, Department of Metro, in Seattle, Washington. Her department has developed an interagency program called the Local Hazardous Waste Management Program in King County. This program operates in conjunction with the county's public health and solid waste management departments, the Association of Suburban Cities, and the City of Seattle. The program was developed in response to a state law that mandated that local areas had to implement programs to deal with hazardous waste from small industries and private households (called "small quantity generators").

Lora's primary function is environmental education. She visits businesses to see if they are in compliance with applicable regulations, explains regulations, and provides information to help them get into compliance. She often follows up her visit to a business with a letter that provides recommendations to help the business identify and manage its hazardous waste, including suggestions for process changes. "The goal is to keep small quantity generators of hazardous waste in compliance with environmental laws," she explains. "We do this by providing technical assistance, giving them on-site help, answering questions, and doing research to help reduce the amount of waste that is generated." These goals are met through a combination of direct contact and written materials. Members of Lora's department prepare brochures, fact sheets, and booklets on topics including

- how to determine if waste is hazardous or nonhazardous,
- how to label waste containers so they are handled and disposed of properly,
- how small businesses and specific industries can comply with environmental regulations, and
- how to replace hazardous materials with nonhazardous substitutes.

In addition, department members staff a hot line to answer questions from the business community and produce public service announcements for the local media.

Lora prepared for her career by earning a B.S. in environmental policy analysis and planning. She has worked in various aspects of environmental communication for eight years, starting out as a technical editor for an environmental consulting firm and moving into positions of increasing responsibility in city and county agencies. She likes the role she plays in helping businesses reduce the volume of hazardous waste they produce, although she says walking "cold" into all types of industries is difficult. She never knows what she'll find, and some business people resent what they see as the government's intrusion in their operation. While she would like to develop expertise about one or two of the industries her department works with, she recognizes the importance of her role as a generalist, pulling together regulatory information for the myriad industries she encounters in the field.

Despite the difficulties of the job, Lora says, "We feel good about the approach we take—educating businesses to achieve compliance instead of following the enforcement approach." This educational approach— seeking cooperation from businesses by helping them do what is right instead of punishing them when they do something wrong—is being monitored by the U.S. EPA, which may eventually emulate it. Lora says government agencies are realizing that, "businesses respond better when someone comes in to inform them and work with them to avoid a problem, and not just to slap them with a ticket."

Cecilia Franz

Cecilia Franz enjoys a busy career as a science writer and environmental educator. She is director of the Biosphere 2000 Project at Miami University and copartner in Two Herons Consulting, which specializes in providing educational communications about environmental issues.

Directing the Biosphere 2000 Project includes ongoing work on an already published textbook entitled *Biosphere 2000: Protecting Our Global Environment* and for the nonprofit, grant-giving Global Heritage Endowment (GHE). Cecilia and textbook co-author, Donald Kaufman, have already completed work on the second edition of *Biosphere 2000*. Cecilia researches, writes, and reviews text; incorporates other reviewers' comments; and pulls all the pieces of the book together into a cohesive whole. "The first edition of our book was recently awarded second place in Anheuser Busch's A Pledge and a Promise program, a national competition for environmental projects," Cecilia says. "And I'm even more pleased with our second edition," which was published in the summer of 1995.

Profits from the sale of *Biosphere 2000* are fed directly into GHE to fund undergraduate environmental research, activist, and educational projects. As director of the foundation, Cecilia is responsible for making environmental science professors and students aware of the book and the GHE grant monies that are available. She accomplishes this by preparing promotional materials and conference presentations, and giving presentations about the foundation on university campuses. She organizes the grant proposal process and ensures that members of the selection committee have all the information they need to select grant recipients.

If this is not enough to keep Cecilia busy, she is also very involved in the work of Two Herons Consulting, which she and Don Kaufman founded in 1990. Two Herons Consulting provides environmental and educational information to clients. One recent project involved performing an environmental impact assessment of a wetland area along the Ohio River where riverboat gambling was proposed. The wetland is an important flyway for migratory birds. Cecilia says of her work on this project, "We found that many species would be vulnerable if riverboat gambling were allowed on this part of the river. Aside from the wetland habitats that would be affected, this area has archaeological significance, too. It was an important crossroads for native American tribes. To preserve these resources, we needed to make sure people understood the potential impacts of riverboat gambling development in this area."

Until Two Herons prepared their environmental impact assessment, landowners along the river did not realize that they could prevent the proposed development. Cecilia has found that "people don't always know the options that are available for protecting their resources. Our job is to provide accurate information so people can use it to make informed decisions." The information provided in the report helped the landowners understand their options with respect to the proposed development. Although the State of Indiana approved a license for casino development in the area, the developer still had to apply for a permit from the Army Corps of Engineers. Once the permit was approved, the developer had to comply with strict regulations designed to protect the floodplain, wetland, and surrounding area.

"What I like best about my career is the independence and creativity," Cecilia says. "While it's important to present a balanced view of any issue, in my job I get to take a stand. I get to present my point of view, which, of course, is based on extensive research. In many technical communication jobs, I wouldn't have this freedom." Cecilia intends to continue her work in environmental education, and she plans to write additional articles and books about environmental issues for general audiences.

Cecilia prepared for her career by earning a B.A. degree in English literature and a master's degree in technical and scientific communication. Her first job in the field of environmental communications was the internship required as part of her master's degree. She interned with a communications firm that produces training manuals, computer documentation, and environmental communications, including some related to the first edition of *Biosphere 2000*.

APPENDIX A

Sample of Current Job Advertisements

Public Information Officer/State of Washington Part-time salary: $33,600–$46,000 + benefits. The Puget Sound Water Quality Authority seeks candidates for a part-time Public Information Officer to manage its media relations program 4 days a week. The preferred candidate will have 3 years' experience managing a public information program and extensive experience in journalism, marketing, environmental, legislative, and local government relations.

Environmental Educator/Community Organizer. Thurston County Public Health salary: $2,692/mo. Develops, plans, carries out, and evaluates education and awareness programs for groundwater protection and household hazardous waste pollution prevention. Develops action-oriented activities, workshops and programs, and promotes groundwater protection and household hazardous waste awareness and prevention. Bachelor's degree in science, public health, or related field required, plus 3 years' experience in water quality/hazardous waste issues and community involvement.

Environmental Technical Advisor for environmental section of a large law firm. Qualifications: Minimum 1-3 years' experience in environmental consulting or with regulatory agency. Applicants must be familiar with environmental regulations, have strong research and writing skills.

Proposal Manager. ENSR Consulting, Engineering and Remediation, a leader in providing environmental management services, seeks an individual to manage a national government proposal support center. Position requires hands-on leadership, coordination and development of government consulting, engineering, and remediation proposals and presentations. Outstanding written and verbal communication skills, ability to interact with senior technical, sales, and management staff, ability to meet critical deadlines and superior strategic planning/organization skills are essential. BS/MS in related field and 5+ years' experience in government and/or environmental proposal writing required.

Regulatory Specialist/Project Manager. Consulting/remediation firm seeks regulatory specialist/project manager familiar with RCRA, NEPA, MTCA, HAZWOPER, & WA state Danger Waste Regulations. Prefer MS + 5 years' experience. Successful candidate will prove report-writing ability.

Technical Editor/Publications Coordinator. Nation's leading consulting firm seeks a technical editor/publications coordinator. Bachelor's degree in English, journalism, or a related discipline and a minimum of 3 years' editorial or technical writing experience required. The position encompasses strategizing, organizing, writing and editing scientific reports, tables, maps, and diagrams for consistency, clarity, grammar, and style; supervising publications staff; and coordinating workloads with other regional offices. Consideration will be given to detail-oriented, well organized individuals with excellent writing/communication skills. Applicants must have the ability to interact/coordinate with executive, marketing, technical, and publications personnel; meet in-house production schedules and client deadlines, often under short time constraints; and demonstrate a willingness to work hard to produce high-quality documents.

Public Involvement Specialist—Editor/Writer. Foster Wheeler Environmental Corporation is seeking an individual for a combined role as technical public involvement specialist/editor with 2–4 years' experience editing scientific/engineering documents. Must make public presentations, facilitate meetings, write newsletters, and edit and coordinate production of reports using graphics and word processing software. BA in communications or related discipline, knowledge of NEPA, SEPA, CERCLA, EISs and hazardous waste studies preferred. Requires flexible working hours in interactive environment.

Public Educator. Salary: $3,037–$3,348/mo. A local air pollution control agency seeks professional to organize, coordinate, and implement public education strategies to support air quality programs. Will have lead responsibility for information, education, and outreach activities related to transportation and planning issues. Must have in-depth knowledge of integrated communications strategies, techniques, environmental issues; will demonstrate ability to research, design, develop communications programs; translate technical information; communicate effectively orally and in writing; develop variety of written/presentation materials for various audiences; use desktop publishing software. Minimum qualifications include BA in journalism, communications, public relations, etc. plus 3 to 5 years' progressively responsible experience in communications or related field, including media relations, publications, and community outreach.

APPENDIX B

FUTHER INFORMATION
Organizations

Americans for the Environment
1400 16th Street, NW
Washington, DC 20036
(202) 797-6665
Fax: (202) 797-6563
http://www.ewg.org/pub/home/afe/homepage.htm

Canadian Science Writers' Association
40 Alexander Street, Suite 1111
Toronto ON M4Y 1B5
(416) 928-9624
Fax: (416) 924-6715
http://www.interlog.com/~cswa/

Environmental Career Opportunities (bi-weekly newsletter)
The Brubach Corporation
P.O. Box 560
Stanardsville, VA
(804) 985-8627
Fax: (804) 985-2331
http://www.ecojobs.com/

The Environmental Careers Organization
http://www.eco.org/site/welcome2.htm
The Environmental Careers Organization has regional offices throughout the United States:

* Northeast
  179 South Street
  Boston, MA 02111
  (617) 426-4783
  Fax: (617) 426-8159

* Central
  50 Public Square, Suite 1515
  Cleveland, OH 44113
  (216) 861-4545
  Fax: (216) 861-6727

* Northwest
  1218 Third Avenue, Suite 1515
  Seattle, WA 98101-3021
  (206) 625-1750
  Fax: (206) 625-924

* Southwest Region
  381 Bush Street, Suite 700
  San Francisco, CA 94104-2812
  (415) 362-5552
  Fax: (415) 362-5559

* Satellite Office
  50 Pine Street, #312
  Montclair, NJ 07042
  (201) 744-6256
  Fax: (201) 744-6257

* National Office
  179 South Street
  Boston, MA 02111
  (617) 426-4375
  Fax: (617) 423-0998

Environmental Law Institute
1616 P St., NW, No. 200
(publishes the *Directory of State Environmental Agencies*)

Washington, D.C. 20036
(202) 939-3800
http://www.eli.org/

National Association of Environmental Professionals
6524 Ramoth Dr.
Jacksonville, FL 32226-3202
(904) 251-9900
Fax: (904) 251-9901
http://www.enfo.com/NAEP/

National Association of Science Writers
P.O. Box 294, Greenlawn
NY 11740
Phone: (516) 757-5664
http://test.nasw.org/
National Environmental Training Association
http://www.envirotraining.org/about_ne.htm
E-mail: neta@envirotraining.org

North American Association for Environmental Education
P.O. Box 400
Troy, OH 45373
Phone/fax: (937) 676-2514
E-mail: jthoreen@igc.apc.org
http://www.nceet.snre.umich.edu/naaee.html

Society of Environmental Journalists
P.O. Box 27280
Philadelphia, PA. 19118
(215) 836-9970
Fax: (215) 836-9972
http://www.sej.org/

Society for Technical Communication
901 N Stuart St., Ste. 904
Arlington, VA 22203-1854
(703) 522-4114
Fax: (703) 522-2075
http://www.stc-va.org/

Student Conservation Association
http://www.sca-inc.org/

SCA office locations:

- Headquarters
  P.O. Box 550
  689 River Road
  Charlestown, NH 03603
  (603) 543-1700
  Fax: (603) 543-1828

- Southeast
  1800 North Kent Street, Suite 1260
  Arlington, VA 22209
  (703) 524-2441

- Northwest
  605 13th Avenue
  Seattle, WA 98122
  (206) 324-4649

- Midwest
  1370 Pennsylvania Avenue, Suite 330
  Denver, CO 80203
  (303) 831-7172

- Southwest
  655 13th Street, Suite 304
  Oakland, CA 94612
  (510) 832-1966

- Northeast
  P.O. Box 32369
  Newark, NJ 07102
  (201) 733-4450

Printed Materials

Allen K., Keller, S., & Vizza, C. (1996). *A new competitive edge: Volunteers for the workplace*. Arlington, VA: Volunteer—The National Center.

Encyclopedia of environmental information sources. (1993). Detroit, MI: Gale Research. ISBN/ISSN: 0-8103-8568-6

Environment encyclopedia & directory 97, 97th edition. (1997). Detroit, MI: Gale Research. ISBN/ISSN: 1-85743-028-X

Ethics/Science/tech writing —

Z286. S4 L33

PE 1404 P665

T 11 P73

Vidal → PS 3543 I26 T46

PS 3543.I26 w5

Environmental career directory. (1993). Detroit, MI: Gale Research. ISBN/ISSN: 0-8103-9153-8

Environment encyclopeida. (1993). Detroit, MI: Gale Research. ISBN/ISSN: 0-8103-8856-1

Environmental industries marketplace. (1992). Detroit, MI: Gale Research. ISBN/ISSN: 0-8103-8569-4

European enviromental information sourcebook. (1994). Detroit, MI: Gale Research. ISBN/ISSN: 0-873477-20-1

Gale environmental sourcebook, 2nd edition. (1993). Detroit, MI: Gale Research. ISBN/ISSN: 0-8103-8510-4

Rittner, D. (1992). *Ecolinking: Everyone's guide to online environmental information.* Berkeley, CA: Peachpit Press.

Science and technical organizations and agencies directory, 3rd edition. (1993). Detroit, MI: Gale Research. ISBN/ISSN: 0-8103-5464-0

The student contact book. (1992). Detroit, MI: Gale Research. ISBN/ISSN: 0-8103-8876-6

Volunteer! The comprehensive guide to voluntary service in the U.S. and abroad. New York: Council on International Exchange Services.

World environmental business handbook. (1993). Detroit, MI: Gale Research. ISBN/ISSN: 0-86338-458-7

World environmental research directory. (1993). Detroit, MI: Gale Research. ISBN/ISSN: 0-902799-95-9

REFERENCES

Coker, M. K. *Environmental communication.* Unpublished internship report prepared for the master's degree in technical and scientific communication, Miami University, Oxford, OH.

Environmental Careers Organization. (1993). *The new complete guide to environmental careers.* Washington, DC: Island Press.

Kleinman, C. (1992). *100 best jobs for the 1990s and beyond.* New York: The Berkeley Publishing Group.

U.S. Department of Labor, Bureau of Labor Statistics. (1994). *Occupational outlook handbook* (Bulletin 2450). Washington, DC: Government Printing Office.

An industry on the move. (1994, October). *Washington CEO,* 79–85.

chapter 5

Writing in Hazardous Waste Management

Joan Strawson Dollarhide
Toxicology Excellence for Risk Assessment
Cincinnati, Ohio

Jobs

Technical writer or editor, community relations specialist, technical adviser, environmental health scientist, trainer.

Responsibilities

Gathering and interpreting data, such as data about the concentrations of chemicals in soil. Writing and editing documents such as technical reports, proposals, or environmental impact statements. Conducting public meetings, such as meetings that inform people about environmental problems in their community. Explaining technical concepts, such as the risk posed by environmental contaminants, to a lay audience.

Employment Outlook

Variable. Opportunities exist for people with good communication skills, but most employers prefer employees with a strong technical background.

Salary Range

$18,000 to $25,000 per year for an entry-level position and up to $50,000 or more per year for a senior position.

INTRODUCTION

As Melinda Spencer's chapter on "Writing for the Environmental Sciences" points out, environmental science is the study of how we can better understand and solve problems caused by the interaction of natural and cultural systems. As you're now aware, this interaction has given rise to a significant aspect of environmental communication—that concerning waste management. One part of the field—hazardous waste management, has received much attention in recent years. This part of environmental science aims to prevent hazardous chemicals from reaching the environment and to remove them as quickly and safely as possible when they have been released. Because hazardous waste management directly affects peoples' health and the quality of their lives, considerable financial resources have been invested in it, and there are many jobs for environmental scientists and communicators in this area. The rest of this chapter focuses on writing opportunities in hazardous waste management, detailing more specifically the legislation that has given rise to these opportunities, the contexts in which documents are written, the specific documents you would write, and the more specific preparation you would need to be involved in this specialized field.

ENVIRONMENTAL LAWS

As Spencer points out in her broader survey of environmental laws, jobs communicating in hazardous waste management have been created largely by legislation developed over the last two decades. For example, the National Environmental Policy Act (NEPA), passed in 1969, required the development of environmental impact statements for all projects using federal funding.

Passed in 1976, the Resource Conservation and Recovery Act (RCRA) established a hazardous waste management program to regulate organizations and individuals who generate, store, transport, and dispose of hazardous waste. All phases of the waste management program require extensive technical documentation, including record keeping, reporting, and labeling requirements for people who generate hazardous waste and who store hazardous chemicals on their property. For example, people who transport hazardous waste from their factory to a landfill must implement a system to track the waste from the place it was generated and follow it along transportation routes to its final place of disposal. Personnel at treatment, storage, and disposal facilities are required to apply for and obtain operating permits. In addition, RCRA has public participation and community relations provisions, which necessitate documents such as community relations plans and fact sheets or newsletters. These documents, which are described later in this chapter, inform the people living near a treatment, storage, or disposal facility about how the facility is being managed and what steps are being taken to prevent chemicals in the facility from contaminating the environment.

In 1980, Congress enacted the Comprehensive Environmental Response, Compensation, and Liability Act (CERCLA), which authorizes the U.S. Environmental Protection Agency (EPA) to respond to releases of hazardous chemicals and to clean up abandoned hazardous waste dumps.

This program, which has become known as "Superfund," was enlarged by the Superfund Amendments Reauthorization Act (SARA) of 1986. SARA strengthens the U.S. EPA's mandate to involve the public in decision making at Superfund sites. For this provision of the Superfund program to work effectively, however, there must be extensive, effective communication between site officials and the public so that the public can make informed decisions. Thus, SARA requires that site officials conduct community relations activities such as public meetings, which keep the public abreast of site activities. SARA also provides the public with the opportunity to comment on site documents, and it requires organizations that use or store hazardous chemicals to inform the public about the amounts and health effects of chemicals in their possession. Finally, the Superfund program allows citizen groups near a Superfund site to receive up to $50,000 to obtain technical assistance in interpreting information related to a site.

In 1986, the Worker Right-to-Know laws were enacted to ensure that workers were informed of the potential hazards present in their work environment. Under these laws, employers must establish training and information programs for workers exposed to hazardous chemicals. These programs are designed to enable employers to communicate to workers about the hazards present in their work environment.

As a communicator interested in hazardous waste management, you could work for a private company affected by these laws or for a government agency or consulting firm that helps companies comply with the laws. Or you could establish your own environmental science communication business. In any of these situations, you might conduct public participation activities, provide technical assistance to local citizens' groups, prepare technical documentation, or train workers. These different positions are described below.

YOUR LIFE AS A COMMUNITY RELATIONS SPECIALIST

If you are interested in acting as a liaison between the community members living near a Superfund site and the scientists cleaning up the site, consider taking a job as a community relations specialist. You could work as a community relations specialist for either the government, a consulting firm, or with your own environmental science communication business. In this position, you would be part of the community relations program required by laws such as RCRA and CERCLA. This community relations program would serve to aid the peoples' understanding of the events taking place at the Superfund site and to increase public participation in decisions regarding the site.

Since the "community" is composed of many types of people, with different knowledge and experiences, one of the first activities you will undertake as a community relations specialist at a Superfund site will be finding out exactly who your audience is. You will start by interviewing local people to understand the structure of the community and to find out what type of information the community knows and needs to know. You may also interview the scientists involved in the cleanup to learn about the Superfund site itself (the size of the site and types of chemicals present, for example) and the schedule of research and cleanup activities that will take place. Based on the information you gather, you will decide what types and frequencies of communications will best serve the needs of the community. You will undoubtedly include in your communications a community relations plan (CRP), which will describe for both the EPA and the local community how the community relations program will be conducted during the Superfund investigation. You will generally prepare a CRP at the start of a Superfund investigation, although you may revise it periodically as the community's needs and scientists' strategies change. A community relations plan is generally about 80 pages.

Another kind of document you might prepare is a two-to-six-page fact sheet that explains technical concepts or processes to the community. At a Superfund site, fact sheets may describe how a well is installed to sample groundwater, or how contaminated soil will be cleaned up. Newsletters are also a good way to keep the community informed about the general status of any environmental project. These 10-to-15-page documents are usually published on a regular schedule, such as every other month. At a Superfund site, newsletters are used to describe new activities, such as the collection of some new soil samples, to answer frequently asked questions, or to introduce site personnel. Newsletters often include pictures of the site and of the investigation activities so that the community members can see what progress has been made.

Your role as a community relations specialist preparing these communications will vary. You will gather the information to be included by interviewing the scientists doing the work. Using this information, you will write the fact sheets or articles for the newsletter. You may also travel to the site to photograph the cleanup activities, or you may use computer graphics to draw maps of the site. Finally, you may put your graphic design skills to use by pasting up the documents and overseeing their production.

One of the most important aspects of your job as a community relations specialist will be to organize and conduct public meetings that offer people the opportunity to ask questions and express concerns about the cleanup. For example, citizens may want to know how the chemicals at the site may affect their children's health, or they may be concerned that the method chosen to clean up the site may not permanently remove the contamination. At these meetings you, scientists, project officials, and citizens will provide information which contributes to the decisions made about the project.

Again, your role in preparing for meetings will vary. You may be asked to develop the agenda for the meeting and to write the speeches that the project officials will make. You may create exhibits which will be displayed at the meeting to visually communicate complex issues to a community. These displays are composed of photographs, drawings, maps, and text that illustrate some aspect of an environmental project to the public. An exhibit can be created on a poster board or on an entire wall, depending on the amount of information to be communicated. On the evenings of the public meetings, you will work hard carrying audio-visual equipment and your exhibits to the meeting place, setting up the room, and greeting citizens as they arrive. You may work until midnight or later on meeting nights.

The job of a community relations specialist can be stressful when emergencies arise and deadlines change. However, your work will be fast-paced, and you will not be bored.

YOUR LIFE AS A TECHNICAL ADVISER

As Spencer points out, concerned citizens' groups are increasingly hiring technical advisers who can help them understand technical, site-related documents and act as an advocate for them in the decision-making process. Since citizens are usually looking for someone who can be impartial, you will not work for either the government agency regulating the site or the company cleaning up the site. More likely, you will be self-employed or work for a consulting firm whose mission includes advising citizen groups.

If you choose to work as a technical adviser, you will find that your daily activities will combine features of both the community relations specialist and the technical writer. You will most certainly review and interpret all site-related documents, such as the investigation report or the risk assessment. (These documents are explained in the next section.) And you will explain the contents of these documents to the group that hires you. You may participate in informal meetings with your group to explain what is known about the nature of the contamination at the site, and you may assist your group with the production of fact sheets or newsletters, which it will distribute to the rest of the community. You may assist in preparing the group's public comments and travel to meetings and hearings to represent the group before EPA officials, ensuring that your group's concerns are addressed. Finally, you may visit the site periodically during the remedial action to observe the progress of construction activities and provide technical updates to your group's members. Realize that the people who have hired you are working people themselves; thus, you can expect to conduct much of your business with your group in the evenings.

YOUR LIFE DEVELOPING TECHNICAL DOCUMENTS

If your interest lies in developing the technical documents produced during a hazardous waste management project, you could be employed by the government or a consulting firm either as a technical writer, technical editor, or environmental health scientist, depending on the strength of your technical expertise. However, regardless of your job title, working as a communicator developing technical documents requires that you have a greater knowledge of engineering, geology, chemistry, or ecology than is usually necessary to work in community relations.

The development process is generally the same for all these technical documents, including work plans, site investigation reports, feasibility studies, risk assessments, or environmental impact statements. To prepare these documents, you will often work as part of a team that includes engineers, geologists, and other scientists; and you will spend much time meeting with your team to plan, review, and revise your document. The exact role of each team member, including yourself, will vary according to your employer's wishes and your level of technical expertise. If you have little technical experience, your role may be that of editor and coordinator. If you have a high degree of technical expertise, your role may be that of primary author, gathering information from the engineers and scientists and freeing them for further field work. In this role, you may be required to interpret data, such as analyses of the chemicals present in soil and water, and draw conclusions regarding the locations and extent of the contamination at the site. Technical documents contain many maps and tables illustrating the contamination at the site, and you may be asked to draw these displays using computer-aided graphics. And of course you will spend much time writing, rewriting, and rewriting again.

Although you will prepare many different kinds of documents, each document is written for the same audience: the Environmental Protection Agency or some other regulatory agency, such as a state health department. In a regulatory agency, the individual readers are most often scientists and engineers with a detailed knowledge of the issues involved in cleaning up a hazardous waste site. These people use the documents you prepare to make decisions about how to clean up the site. The company that contaminated the site is ultimately responsible for cleaning it up. As a technical writer, you might work for that company, for a consulting firm hired by that company, or for the government agency overseeing the cleanup. However, since documents are also usually made available for public comment, the community members living near the site are a secondary audience. Thus, as the technical writer, you must balance the scientists' need for detailed technical information with the community's need to have complex information explained simply.

The rest of this section describes the types of documents named above. Each of these documents is prepared just once by the organization overseeing the hazardous waste management project, although it is then revised in response to comments received from the EPA and the public. Each document is at least several hundred pages long and can be several volumes.

Work Plan

At the start of a hazardous waste management project, a work plan is prepared by the organization overseeing the project to describe how the project will be conducted. At a hazardous waste cleanup, the work plan tells how and where soil and water samples will be collected, how samples will be chemically analyzed, and what safety procedures will be used to protect worker health. The community relations plan described in an earlier section is actually a part of the overall site work plan. However, the CRP describes communication activities rather than scientific activities.

Investigation Report

This report describes the results of an investigation undertaken to understand the nature of contamination at a hazardous waste site. Again, it is prepared by the organization conducting the cleanup. The following sections are usually included in this type of report:

- site history (e.g., the site is an abandoned waste dump that contains wastes from a pesticide manufacturing plant);
- physical characteristics of the site (e.g., the site is five acres and holds 30,000 barrels of waste);
- descriptions of the soil types at the surface and underground, which provide information that helps engineers decide which cleanup method is going to be most effective;
- description of the groundwater, including how far below the surface it is, in which direction it is moving, and how fast it is moving;
- the location and concentration of chemicals in the soil, groundwater, and streams; and
- suggested approaches for cleaning up the site (known as "remedial actions").

Feasibility Study

A feasibility study evaluates the feasibility of using various engineering techniques or strategies for cleaning up a hazardous waste site. Each remedy is assessed for its ability to protect public health, its effectiveness in permanently reducing the volume and toxicity of contaminants, its cost, and its compliance with all regulations. The feasibility study also describes any laboratory experiments conducted to evaluate the proposed remedies.

Human Health Risk Assessment

This report describes the health effects caused by the contaminants at the site and estimates the degree of risk posed by the contaminants (for example, if the contaminants are not cleaned up, they will cause 1 out of every 1000 people to get cancer). It also evaluates the pathways by which contaminants can reach people living near the site (such as eating food grown in contaminated soil or drinking contaminated water).

Environmental Impact Statements

The National Environmental Policy Act specifies that agencies proposing new construction and other environmental projects, such as dams, power plants, or chemical storage facilities, must prepare an environmental impact statement (EIS), which assesses the effects the project will have on the surrounding environment. The following topics are usually included in an environmental impact statement:

- air and water quality analysis (e.g., the presence and concentration of contaminants);
- demographic characterization (e.g., the age, education, and other characteristics of the people who live in the area, which help investigators understand the needs of the people living near the project);
- cultural, historical, and archaeological resource assessment (e.g., the presence of sites with cultural or historical significance that may be affected by the project);
- noise survey (e.g., to determine if the project will create a level of noise unacceptable to the community);
- traffic analysis (e.g., to determine how the project will affect traffic flow in the area);
- economic assessment and cost analysis (e.g., to determine how the project will affect the local economy, such as lowering property values or increasing the number of jobs); and
- land-use and zoning analyses.

Your life producing technical documents may be less varied than that of the community relations specialist, but it is often less stressful. Schedules for the major phases of an environmental project are developed at the start of the project, so work on the documents generally proceeds at a predictable pace. Even so, you may have to work long hours as a document deadline approaches.

YOUR LIFE AS A TRAINER

A subset of working as an environmental educator (discussed in the previous chapter), a career as a trainer in a work-site communication program would enable you to teach about environmental issues that affect workers. The Occupational Safety and Health Act requires that employers inform employees of workplace hazards. Therefore, most employers provide training courses to their workers that teach about health and safety procedures and the health effects of chemicals used in the workplace. In addition, many employers offer training courses that help employees learn new job skills, such as operating environmental monitoring equipment.

As a trainer, you could play a part in designing, teaching, and evaluating courses that inform workers about the presence of dangerous chemicals and other hazards in their environment. You might work directly for an employer, or you might work for a consulting firm that develops courses and offers them to a variety of employers. To design a training course, you might read work-site publications to understand which chemicals are present in the workplace. You might tour the workplace observing jobs for potential hazards, or you might analyze reports of workplace accidents to understand the accidents' causes. All these activities may serve as sources of information about hazards at the work site and as topics to address in your training course. You must also understand your audience, so you may interview workers to understand their knowledge and skills and to find out the kinds of questions they have. You will then prepare the training manuals, including the lesson plans, instructional materials, fact sheets, and visual aids that will be used when the course is taught or when it is presented on the World Wide Web. If the course is taught in a classroom, and you are comfortable speaking to groups, you may actually teach the course.

WHERE YOU MAY WORK

Recall that each of the jobs described in the previous sections is available either with the government or with a private employer.

Local, state, and federal governments all employ people in the environmental sciences, although more jobs are available at the state and federal levels. The U.S. Environmental Protection Agency, as Spencer has noted, is the federal government's leading agency for environmental science; it employs more people in the environmental sciences than any other federal agency. However, the following agencies all do work that is related to hazardous waste management:

- The U.S. Department of Agriculture
- The Food and Drug Administration
- The U.S. Department of the Interior
- The National Institute for Environmental Health Sciences
- The Centers for Disease Control
- The National Institute for Occupational Safety and Health
- The U.S. Fish and Wildlife Service

Most states have agencies that parallel the U.S. EPA and are designed to protect the environment and public health. For example, most states have an environmental protection agency and a health department. Moreover, most states handle issues relating to worker health and safety through a state occupational safety and health administration.

As a communicator at any of these agencies, you would have the opportunity to prepare technical documents or work in public information. For example, with the U.S. Department of Agriculture, you could write an investigation report that describes the effects of pesticides on the water supply, or a fact sheet telling farmers how they can prevent soil erosion. At the National Institute of Occupational Safety and Health, you could write a risk assessment that evaluates the effects of chemicals found in the workplace on workers' health, or you could prepare a training course that helps workers avoid accidents in the workplace.

As described in the previous chapter, you could work in the private sector. You can find a job with an environmental consulting company, a corporation, or a nonprofit organization. Consulting companies offer environmental services to corporations or governments on a short-term basis. These services might include: advice to a chemical manufacturer about how to modify their smokestacks to lessen the amount of air pollutants in a particular area; information about how to solve a hazardous waste problem, such as chemical contamination of an aquifer; or assistance with sample collection for soil and water data analyses. As a communicator with a consulting company, you might also be asked to prepare any of the documents described earlier.

On the other hand, large corporations, such as Dow Chemical or Procter and Gamble, may have environmental departments that ensure that the corporation is meeting all environmental regulations. As a communicator in one of these departments, you could either work in community relations or prepare the documents that the corporation submits to the government. These documents might include reports on the kinds and amounts of chemicals used by the corporation or a work plan detailing how the corporation will safely store and transport chemicals.

If you are interested in self-employment, opportunities for freelancing and consulting are becoming more common as corporations and technical consulting firms turn to writers and editors who specialize in environmental communication. As a communication consultant, you might be asked to coordinate an entire community relations program for a cleanup site or to prepare just one element of the program, such as a newsletter. You might be asked to design a training course, or write fact sheets describing the hazards of chemicals found in a particular workplace. All of the documents mentioned above are described in detail in the sections titled "Your Life as a Community Relations Specialist" and "Your Life as a Trainer." One area ripe for the small business person is technical advising, described in the section on "Your Life as a Technical Adviser." Advising citizens' groups would be a conflict of interest for most government agencies and private consultant firms involved with cleanup activities at a hazardous waste site. Thus, a market exists for freelancers and consultants who provide this advisory service.

EMPLOYMENT OUTLOOK

The environmental industry is one of the few that is continuing to expand and hire new people, and people all over the country are doing the kinds of communication jobs described in the earlier sections of this chapter. However, employers do not always hire professional communicators to do these jobs. Often, employers hire engineers or scientists with good communication skills to write reports or do community relations. In a recent edition of *The Washington Post*, all advertisements for environmental scientists, environmental research assistants, environmentalists, or environmental specialists listed "excellent writing and communication skills" or "public relations skills" as a requirement for employment. Employers seem to feel that hiring an engineer with good communication skills will give them an employee who can do two jobs, that of engineer and that of writer. Therefore, your best chance of getting a communication job in the environmental industry is to develop strong technical skills. If you don't major in a scientific or technical field, you will certainly need to develop strong technical skills to complement your communication degree.

Typical private sector salaries for communicators in hazardous waste management start at about $18,000 per year and may go as high as

$25,000. After three to five years of experience, you can expect to earn about $30,000 to $35,000 per year; and after many years' experience, you can earn $50,000+ per year. However, in many private companies, communicators are considered less "professional" than scientists or engineers. Thus, you may receive the low end of the salary range if you are hired as a technical writer, but the high end of the salary range if you are hired as an environmental scientist. Furthermore, salaries for environmental communicators really depend most on the organization and the field. For example, nonprofit conservation groups will usually pay a technical communicator less than will a consulting firm that works on hazardous waste cleanup.

The federal government pays employees by the General Schedule (GS) system. Thus, each employee meeting the education and experience requirements for a particular job will receive the same pay, regardless of whether the job is as a communicator or as a scientist. In general, a bachelor's degree will qualify you for a GS-5 ($17,000) to GS-7 ($21,000) job, depending on your work experience. However, a master's degree will generally qualify you for a GS-9 ($26,000) to GS-11 ($31,000) job, depending on your work experience.

Career advancement opportunities are uncertain for communicators in hazardous waste management. Often, as a writer, editor, or community relations specialist, you will be the only professional communicator in an organization, regardless of whether you work for the government or in private industry. If there is a communications group, you may advance to manager of that group. However, in order to advance to a position of more responsibility and authority, you will most likely have to leave communications. Positions into which communicators often move include marketing, administration, and, if their technical background is strong enough, technical project management.

Despite the prevailing bias of employers, the career outlook for environmental communicators in hazardous waste management is improving. Professionals in the environmental science industry anticipate a growing need for communicators in the field. Larger firms are expected to hire more communication specialists to help develop the community trust and confidence that must be a part of every environmental field project.

PREPARATION

You can prepare for a career in hazardous waste management the same as you might in other areas of scientific and technical communication: You'll need to plan your education carefully and try to obtain on-the-job experience.

Education

The education required for a communications job in hazardous waste management will vary from employer to employer. One employer will seek a candidate with a strong English education, feeling that the candidate can learn the necessary science on the job. Another employer will only hire a candidate with an advanced degree in engineering or science and the ability to write, feeling that the candidate should be able to fill either a technical or a communications position. Thus, you could prepare by majoring in some type of communication and minoring in a science, or vice versa. Journalism, public relations, or technical communication are useful communication majors. In particular, courses that would help you prepare for a career writing about hazardous waste management include writing and editing, graphic design, and desktop publishing. If you are interested in a career in training, you might also take some courses in education. However, be sure to take enough science courses to enable you to understand the topics you will be communicating about. Such science courses would include environmental science, ecology, chemistry, geology, and environmental engineering.

Some of these disciplines—engineering, geology, environmental science, or chemistry—are also useful technical majors. Particularly helpful are laboratory classes in which you learn to evaluate data and discuss experimental results in written reports. But as above, be sure to supplement your science classes with technical writing and editing classes.

An advanced degree can be either desirable or essential for finding a job, depending on the employer. However, consider earning an advanced degree that complements your undergraduate education. For example, you could earn a master's degree in environmental science if you have a journalism bachelor's degree, or earn a master's degree in technical communication if you have an engineering undergraduate degree.

Work Experience

As Melinda Spencer notes, experience is the key to finding a job as an environmental communicator. This experience is especially crucial when you are trying to locate a job in hazardous waste management. Entry-level jobs are almost nonexistent in this area; employers want people with one to three years' experience. To gain experience, you can do an internship or participate in a co-op program, in which you spend some time in school and some time working each year. Or you can try getting a summer job in which you prepare environmental communications. Volunteer to work for a nonprofit organization that does the kind of conservation work you are interested in. These organizations, especially, need people to write grant proposals, informational brochures, and educational materials. The point is that any type of environmental work will provide you with invaluable experience.

Even if you cannot find a job, you can take several actions to gain experience before you begin your search for a permanent job. Start by writing environmental articles for your school newspaper. Join clubs at your school that have an environmental mission and become active in their programs. Or simply become interested in the environment and issues surrounding its conservation—potential employers like job candidates who are aware. If your community is debating an environmental issue, such as siting a land-fill, become involved in the citizens' group leading the discussion. Attend public hearings and lobby for your point of view; the experience will be invaluable when you apply for a position in community relations.

FINDING A JOB

You will find that there are many effective strategies to finding a environmental job communicating about hazardous waste management, but probably the best is to go out and meet people. Attend the meetings of the local chapters of professional societies such as the Society for Technical Communication or the Society for Risk Analysis, go to training courses and seminars on environmental communication, attend job fairs sponsored by the environmental industry. Whenever you are in the company of other environmental professionals, introduce yourself to strangers and ask questions. Discuss your interests, career goals, and experience. You will find that you receive more offers to interview on the recommendation of someone who remembers you as a knowledgeable, articulate person than from all of the letters you could write.

Join professional societies, both in communications and environmental science, and participate in their job placement service. (See the Appendix on Further Information in this chapter and the previous one for a list of societies dedicated to environmental communication.) Look at the classifieds in your local paper or the papers of cities in which you would like to work. To learn about job openings in the federal government, look in your local phone book for any federal agencies in your area. The personnel office at any federal agency should post a list of job openings at all federal agencies in the area and may even have notices of nationwide job openings. Also, the personnel office should be able to give you the address and phone number of the Federal Job Information Center that serves your area. There are many of these centers around the country, and most of them offer a job information telephone service. Finally, be patient: It could take you several months to a year to find the job you want.

PROFESSIONAL PROFILES

This section focuses on two writers who communicate information about hazardous waste management. Robert Johnson has worked for the U.S. Environmental Protection Agency for 10 years and is currently a senior community relations coordinator in the Office of Public Affairs. Laura Loiseau works as an editor for a small environmental consulting firm. She has been an editor with the firm for two years.

Robert Johnson

Robert Johnson (his name has been changed) works in Chicago as a senior community relations coordinator in the Office of Public Affairs at a regional office of the U.S. Environmental Protection Agency. He has been with the U.S. EPA for 10 years, since earning a master's degree in urban and regional planning. His bachelor's degree is in chemistry, and before becoming a community relations coordinator, Robert spent three years with the EPA's Air Management Division reviewing air quality reports.

Robert is assigned specific Superfund sites within his region, for which he manages all community relations activities. "Primarily, I am a liaison between the public and EPA at EPA's Superfund sites," says Robert. "In that role, I respond to citizen, industry, and media requests for information and assist them in making sense of the details of the site. Also, through information sharing, I empower citizens in making decisions that affect site activities."

In order to carry out these responsibilities, Robert must conduct a variety of communication activities. He spends much time on the telephone explaining the Superfund program and other environmental laws to citizens who call with questions. He writes letters to residents living near Superfund sites explaining site actions, and he writes general information fact sheets about Superfund activities, which will be read by the people living near Superfund sites in his region. He may conduct community interviews with residents near Superfund sites to learn their information needs, or he may work with EPA's project managers to plan the community relations strategy at a site.

Robert is currently evaluating his future with the EPA. He feels that after seven years, the work he does in community relations has become limiting, and he is considering whether his career path lies within the EPA or with a private consulting company. "There is no clear career path for government employees in this field," he says. "If I stay with the EPA, I would like to shift away from site work and get more involved in EPA's research programs on effective communication strategies. If I leave EPA, I would like to market environmental communication services to the private sector."

However, Robert notes that it is difficult to move from the government to the private sector and that most communicators in the government just shift from one agency to another.

Overall, how does Robert feel about the importance of communication to environmental science? "We are getting our place at the table. As public involvement continues, our role [as professional communicators] will become more and more crucial. We are finally recognized as an integral part of the process."

Laura Loiseau

Laura Loiseau (her name has been changed) works as the lead technical editor at Advanced Sciences, Inc., a small private engineering company that conducts environmental investigations at Superfund sites. She has been with the company for two years and started as a community relations specialist before she became an editor. Laura earned master's degrees in environmental science (concentrating in policy making and administration) and international relations. Laura has no formal education in writing and editing (her bachelor's degree is in history), but her work as an associate editor for a scientific journal, before her current position, gave her the experience she needed to become a technical editor.

As technical editor, Laura oversees all aspects of document preparation. The documents she edits are used to report the results of environmental investigations to the U.S. EPA and to provide information to the community near the site. She works on every document that the company prepares, from work plans and investigation reports to newsletters and fact sheets. Her primary responsibility is to edit and rewrite until the organization, style, content, tone, and grammar meet the company's standards. Through her work, Laura strives to keep a uniformity among the documents. To accomplish this goal, she has developed a style guide, which the engineers and scientists must use as they prepare drafts. Among other things, the style guide tells scientists the appropriate format for various documents. Laura also writes "boilerplate" sections of the documents. Boilerplate means standard paragraphs, such as a description of the Superfund site, which usually appear in every document developed. Finally, Laura develops strategies for reducing the size of the documents (each report can be thousands of pages) without compromising quality.

Surprisingly, Laura's daily routine can be quite varied. She participates in technical meetings with the scientists to ensure that she has all the information she needs to review and prepare documents. She also oversees the production of documents (e.g., photocopying and compiling multiple copies), and she frequently travels to different sites to work with the technical staff to help them meet publication deadlines.

Like Robert, Laura is also evaluating her future. "Hazardous waste management tends to be temporary work," she points out. "The cleanup of a Superfund site is finite; once the work is done, the people move on. The project may change, but the work stays the same." Because Laura's company is small, she has just about reached the limit of her career advancement, even though she has a great deal of responsibility and authority. However, in a larger company, Laura may be able to move into management, overseeing other editors.

Overall, how does Laura feel about the role of communication in environmental science? "In this field, the documents are the products. As companies realize how much of their image is portrayed through their documents, people like me will be increasingly needed."

APPENDIX

FURTHER INFORMATION
Books

The Center for Environmental Interns Program (CEIP) Fund. (1989). *The complete guide to environmental careers*. Washington, DC: Island Press.

Hance, B. J., Chess, C., & Sandman, P. (1988). *Improving dialogue with communities: A risk communication manual for government*. Trenton, NJ: New Jersey Department of Environmental Protection.

Krimsky, S. & Plough, A. (1988). *Environmental hazards: Communicating risks as a social process*. Dover, MA: Auburn House.

National Research Council. (1989). *Improving risk communication*. Washington, DC: National Academy Press.

Newsletters

Exposure
National Center for Hazard Communication
University of Maryland
Center for Professional Development
University Boulevard at Adelphi Road
College Park, MD 20742-1668

Federal Career Opportunities
Federal Research Service, Inc.
P. O. Box 1059
Vienna, VA 22183-1059

Professional Societies

Society for Risk Analysis
Risk Communication Section
800 Westpark Drive, Suite 130
McClean, VA 22101
(703) 790-1745

National Association for Government Communicators
80 South Early Street
Alexandria, VA 22304
(703) 823-4821

Women in Communications
1244 Richie Highway, Suite 6
Arnold, MD 21012-1887
(410) 544-7442
http: //www.womcom.org

chapter 6

Writing for the Computer Industry

R. John Brockmann
University of Delaware

Christopher Velotta
NCR Corporation
Dayton, Ohio

Jobs & Responsibilities

- *Technical communicator* (or information analyst, information product developer, information engineer): creates manuals, online documentation, and other print and multimedia communications for technical and nontechnical audiences. These audiences may be both within and outside the organization that creates the information products.
- *Technical editor:* edits the communications described above to ensure that they are accurate and useful for their intended audiences. Editors also ensure consistency within a communication and across information products.
- *Usability analyst:* designs and administers various usability tests to monitor information product usability and provide direction for improvements.
- *Graphic designer/artist/illustrator:* develops the graphic components of information products, including page and computer screen design.
- *Senior technical communicator* (editor, usability analyst, graphic designer): In organizations with a number of writers, editors, testers, and designers, these senior-level people typically focus on the high-level analysis and design work required for information products. They may also serve as leaders on large projects, coordinating a team of contributors.

Employment Outlook

In the 1990s, the computer industry has assumed a more stable and typical growth pattern of 10 percent per year rather than the skyrocketing unstable growth of the 1970s and 80s, when growth reached 200 percent to 300 percent per year. Also, much of the growth of the 1970s and 80s was tied to growth in defense-related industries, which are now shrinking. Thus, the percentage of new jobs in the industry each year will decrease. In addition, fewer technical communicators will be directly hired by companies, and more will be hired indirectly as freelancers or through contract employment bureaus.

Additionally, as the industry stabilizes and information products proliferate into increasingly more sophisticated media such as CD-ROM and hypermedia, the required prerequisite level of knowledge and training will increase. Companies will require that new technical communicators in the computer industry be knowledgeable in special computer languages, hypermedia authoring tools, telecommunications, multimedia design, and usability testing.

Salary Range

Depending on the individual's level of education and experience, salaries can range from around $30,000 for a new writer, editor, analyst, or graphic designer to over $59,000 for consultant senior technical communicators and designers with over 10 years' experience. The 1997 Salary Survey conducted by the Society for Technical Communication lists the mean salary for U.S. technical communicators as $46,750.

INTRODUCTION

Writing for the computer industry encompasses the design of hardcopy documentation; online documentation; multimedia products, such as performance support systems, World Wide Web pages, and computer-based tutorials (CBTs); and teleconference, videoconference, and videotape instruction for computer hardware, software, and services. It also includes developing advertising and sales literature about everything from personal computers and mainframes to the software they use. These materials are developed for every type of user, from computer experts to elementary school students. Moreover, these communications can appear in many types of media from print to oral briefings to multimedia formats that integrate video, audio, animation, text, and graphics into one presentation that can be run on a computer. These communications serve users in every part of the world and in companies that create, sell, maintain, or simply use computer hardware and software. In short, the universe of writing for the computer industry is so large and is expanding so fast that it is only unified by its subject matter, computers.

In addition to the developing the types of products described above, more and more technical communicators are assuming new responsibilities for usability testing. Typically, these experts get their start designing and conducting usability tests for the information products they create. By observing participants in usability tests, technical communicators obtain valuable information about how to improve the accessibility, clarity, and effectiveness of their information products. They also gain unique insights into how to improve the usability of the computer products they are supporting. These insights can prepare technical communicators to make important contributions to product design efforts. As a result, some technical communicators have been asked to manage usability testing, not just for information products but also for their employer's entire range of computer products.

YOUR LIFE WRITING FOR THE COMPUTER INDUSTRY

Briefly, in writing for the computer industry, you could fill many different roles, develop many different types of communications, and have many different things to communicate about. Let's get a little taste of this variety by imagining what your job as a technical communicator in the computer industry might be like.

Let's assume you work for Financial Software, Inc., a California company that produces software used by banks to process information (e.g., reading and canceling the checks that customers send to the bank and preparing their monthly statements). At the most basic level, you develop information products for the bank personnel who use or maintain your company's software. From your information products, they learn how to install, update, customize, and use the software. In many cases, the people who install and maintain the software are not the same as those who use it, so you have to tailor each information product to the tasks that a specific audience will be performing.

In addition to creating hardcopy and online documentation, you develop short sales support brochures and computer-based demonstrations that describe your company's software to prospective purchasers. Thus, the types of writing projects that you and your colleagues work on are varied—from marketing communications to tutorials, reference manuals, and online help. Most important, the communications you create are essential.

Without them, the banks would have a much more difficult—if not impossible—time figuring out how to process checks with your software.

Your present task is to create a user's guide, "How to Use Check Processing Software," for purchasers of this software package. Because this is a software product, your users will also need online help available at the touch of a function key or from a menu. The procedures that users must follow are the same regardless of whether you explain them on paper or on-screen, so you will design your user's guide so that you can either print it on paper or compile it for access through the Check Processing Software program itself. By having just one source for both the hardcopy and online versions, you will be able to maintain and update the user's guide much more efficiently, and the online help will always stay current with the hardcopy. In addition, you will require only one development effort for both versions of the user's guide, which will save your company money and allow you to keep up with a short development schedule.

To create the user's guide, you will work with a team, including a programmer, a graphic artist, an editor, and a usability expert, and you will use a standard development process. A typical information product development process contains eight phases:

- *Analysis.* Analyze your audiences and the tasks they will perform. Plan information product sets, and determine which media (e.g., paper, diskette, compact disc, Web, videotape, audio tape, etc.) you will use to deliver each information product. Test for oversights in planning, such as missing audiences or tasks, incorrect task definition, or inappropriate media selections.
- *Design.* Set objectives for the communication and for users' tasks. Then create successively finer models of the information product (e.g., outlines and storyboards). Test the models for structural errors, such as illogical organization or missing sections.
- *Development.* Develop the information product prototype (e.g., the first draft of a document). Then test the prototype for accessibility problems, inaccurate information, or unclear writing.
- *Validation.* Conduct usability testing with a representative sample of the intended audience and a near-final draft of the communication. If the information product is an online help system that is integrated with the software product, conduct integration testing to make sure all of the links between the software and the help are functioning properly.
- *Production.* Make revisions based on the results of your validation and create reproducible masters of the information product. These masters may include camera-ready copy for hardcopy documents, disks which contain the text of online help systems, master video-

tapes for video presentations, and master computer tapes for CD-ROM.

- *Manufacturing.* Generate the required number of copies of the information product. Some information products must be reproduced and stocked in large numbers to meet the audience's demand, while others may be reproduced on demand as orders come in. The decision about which approach to use should be made in the analysis phase.

- *Delivery.* Deliver the information products to the intended audience in a timely and cost-efficient manner. Some information products may be mailed separately, while others may be shipped with the product itself. As with manufacturing decisions, the decision about which approach you use should be made back in the analysis phase.

- *Customer Satisfaction Assurance.* Actively collect and act upon audience feedback about the information product. Typically, you would use this data in four ways:

1. to assess your audience's satisfaction with the timeliness, accessibility, clarity, accuracy, and general usefulness of the information product;
2. to determine if employees actually learned what they were supposed to learn from the information product;
3. to determine if employees were able to use what they learned in order to do their jobs more effectively; and
4. to determine if the information product has been a cost-effective means of delivering information.

You will use this feedback to improve existing documentation. However, you may also use this audience feedback to ensure that future information products better satisfy your audience's needs and to improve the development process itself.

While you are developing information products, you will often collaborate with an artist, who creates graphics to help users visualize the steps you explain in your text. Or you may develop your own graphics and integrate them with your text, creating finished pages or screens with desktop publishing software, such as PageMaker or Quark Xpress.

As you develop your instructions, they are reviewed by programmers and analysts for technical accuracy, as well as by an editor for various quality checks, such as grammar, style, and clarity. And because you work for an enlightened company, your information product will be reviewed as described previously in the validation phase. Your company will bring in typical users, who will test your instructions to see if their ease-of-use could be improved. The people who supervise the tests are another kind of technical communicator in the computer industry, called usability analysts.

When your user's guide and online help is completed, you turn it in to your manager, who will supervise the final printing and distribution of the hardcopy document as well as compiling and testing the online help version; you continue working on other assignments. You generally work on more than one project at a time. For example, while you were writing the first draft of "How to Use Check Processing Software," you would probably have been given another assignment, such as creating updates for an existing information product. These other assignments are often worked into openings in your schedule (e.g., while you are waiting for reviews to be completed and returned to you). Or you might work mornings on one project and afternoons on another. You may also schedule time to assist peers in your department by reviewing their work and providing feedback.

After some time with the company, you will come to understand that your manager does not write, edit, or develop graphics, even though she's an expert in these matters, especially after more than 10 years in the field. What she does do is ensure that your department has the environment required to do consistently high-quality work. She accomplishes this by justifying expenditures for the equipment, money, people, and time needed to complete projects properly. She also quantifies the value added by her department to the company's information products by compiling information about the lower costs of supporting these products, increased customer satisfaction with the products, and increased usability of these products. She is responsible for coordinating the efforts of information product teams, developing budgets and timelines for producing materials, and encouraging everyone on teams to do their best.

Even though work is performed by teams at Financial Software, Inc., in many companies, you may operate alone as your own technical communicator, editor, usability analyst, and manager. For example, you could be working in the branch office of the First National Bank of Milton, Virginia, that purchased Financial Software's Check Processing Software. The primary product that your bank manages or produces is not software, but financial services; however, it's so important that the bank staff know how to use the Check Processing Software that you have been hired as a technical communicator. Your job at the bank is to take the user instructions provided by Financial Software, Inc.—which were designed to be used by all banks—and rework the material to fit the specific needs of your tellers in Milton. Again, you are gathering information from one source, interpreting it, and making it better suit the information needs of the user.

As we indicated earlier, your work includes more than developing hardcopy documents. Your job also entails using computers as tools for creating products that users see and hear at the computer terminal. If you have programming knowledge, you might end up developing the help messages that come up on the computer screen to give users explanations when they ask for specifics about features of programs they are using. You would make up the wording of menus that appear on the screen and the error messages that tell users that an error has occurred and how to fix the error. Even though the material you are writing appears on the computer screen, you would still be called a technical communicator because your primary objective is to communicate to the user how to perform certain tasks and how to become more productive with your company's products.

This focus for technical communicators is known as "performance support" because its objective is to allow end users to become productive as quickly as possible by providing guidance within the product itself. A benefit of this approach is that users can get the guidance they need without having to interrupt the task at hand to search out the information. The product walks the user through a task or even performs the task for the user.

There are many authoring tools on the market to help you create sophisticated online and performance support documentation systems, which can either be self-standing or embedded in a software program. An example of a self-standing system would be a demonstration program that you would create to show the look and functionality of a software program your company is developing. You might use this demonstration as a marketing tool to help sell the program. An example of an embedded online documentation system would be a context-sensitive help system that is accessible from the software program through a function key or menu. If the user presses the Help function key, the help system opens to a section that contains information about whatever it is that the user is trying to accomplish (i.e., the help system tracks what the user is trying to do and offers information specific to that task). For example, if a user has the "File Save" window open and is not sure how to name a file, he or she can press the Help function key to go directly to a section of the help system that explains how to save files. In other circumstances, the user might want to browse the help system by opening the "Help" menu and selecting the "Help Contents," "Index," or " Keyword Search" headings.

Other kinds of information products may be video-oriented. For example, a technical communicator who works at a company that produces instruction manuals for the car mechanics in one of the Big Three automotive companies in Detroit not only writes in print, but also designs multimedia information products that are presented on computer screens to mechanics. Thus, she gets the opportunity to collaborate closely with experts in animation, audio, and video techniques. When she got her degree in journalism 10 years ago, she never dreamed that she would end up using a computer to "cut-and-paste" video sequences for mechanics on how to perform certain car repairs and then integrate them into a multimedia document that would help them do their jobs more effectively. Her video teaches a process, but she uses the computer screen as the medium of communication. The focus of her responsibilities is performance support, and she provides her audience with an integrated combination of tools to help them operate as independently as possible.

She uses essentially the same development process as the one used for other types of information products. One difference, however, is that she works with a broader team of specialists, including media specialists, to develop the various components. For example, she would create an overall design for the multimedia information product, and the media specialists would create the video, animation, and audio segments, which she would then integrate with the overall package.

In summary, you can see that your life writing for the computer industry might include writing for a wide variety of audiences and purposes and developing many types of communications in different media. Such variety would keep you on your toes, and you would be constantly stretching to learn new methods for producing communications. The exciting part of being a technical communicator in this field is that you get to think of creative ways to use technology to meet the needs of users who have varied learning styles and increasing demands on their time.

WHERE YOU MAY WORK

The impact of growth in the computer industry and its effect on the profession of technical communication has been nothing short of phenomenal. Most businesses use computers, and their employees all need to know how to operate them. In addition, computer companies need a way to support the performance of their own field engineers (who install, repair, and maintain the computers) and sales staff. That's where you come in. The types of companies that might employ you are widespread, and potential employers of technical communicators exist in every part of the world.

Some of these are large, international corporations, while others are smaller companies. In addition, an increasing number of technical communicators work for technical communication consulting firms or contractors, or as freelancers. When choosing where you want to work, you should consider the different characteristics of each option and decide which one offers the best overall work environment for you. Some things to consider include availability of training, amount of control over the development of your information products, opportunities for promotion, and compensation.

Availability of Training

Large corporations typically offer access to training opportunities from internal and external sources. Many have in-house training departments to help their employees keep their skills up to date. If you need training in an area not supported by in-house sources, you will likely be able to get approval to attend an external training workshop. In addition, many large corporations provide tuition reimbursement for employees who want to pursue college degrees. Typically, the employee pays the tuition for a college course and is then reimbursed if he or she earns a grade of "B" or higher in the course.

Smaller companies may also offer training opportunities, although it is less likely that they will have their own in-house training for employees because it is often not cost-effective for them to offer programs for the small number of employees they have. You may find that fewer small companies offer tuition reimbursement because they do not have the same volume of cash flow as larger corporations to support this expense. What you probably will find is generous support for seminars and courses on topics that are directly and immediately applicable to your current work assignments.

Independent contractors and freelancers generally find that they have to pay for any training they need out of their own pockets. It is one of the expenses of running their own business. Independents may choose to recoup the cost of their training over time by adding a percentage to their hourly rate to cover their estimated training costs for the year. Or depending on their individual tax situation, they may choose to simply use their training expenses as a tax deduction.

In any of these three cases, training budgets are often the first to be cut when revenue or profits are down. Therefore, the availability of training will very likely not be a constant wherever you work. It will be up to you to carefully plan your career and actively seek out the training you need for your own professional development. If you put off this important activity, you may find that the training you need is not available for your next career step.

Amount of Control

If you choose to work for a large corporation, you should be prepared to work on pieces of projects and to rely on colleagues to complete other parts of the total development effort. Large corporations often divide work into specialized functions. For example, on an information development team, one employee may conduct the analysis and then design the material, another may develop drafts and conduct reviews, another may implement usability tests, and still another may create the illustrations and produce the final copy. All of this collaboration may also take place within the context of cross-functional teams that include developers and even customers. This form of collaboration is typical and can be very rewarding when you see what the team has accomplished.

Smaller companies commonly offer a wider degree of control over the development of their information products. You may be the only technical communicator in a company, which means that an entire project will be in your hands. This opportunity to be a generalist is often very satisfying for those who are just beginning their professional careers and are eager to practice the many skills they've developed in school. You also may feel strong pride of ownership in the finished product because you will have been responsible for every stage of its development.

Independent contractors may work on some projects from beginning to end and only on pieces of other projects. For example, some companies hire independents to complete just one stage of the process, such as the organization and design of the material, and others hire independents to complete the entire process. As an independent, you must be ready to offer whatever level of service your clients require.

Opportunities for Promotion

Because large corporations often have many offices around the world performing the same functions, you generally will have a fair number of opportunities for promotions or transfers. Promotions take you into higher levels of responsibility. To prepare for these responsibilities, some employees pursue a consulting track, in which they develop highly specialized technical skills, allowing them to take on more and more complex projects. Others pursue a management track, in which they develop their coaching and financial management skills. Lateral transfers allow you to broaden your skills and experience, preparing you for other roles in the corporation. Although they do not necessarily mean an increase in pay or a promotion to the next job level, transfers can be extremely important because they increase your value to the company and let others in the company see your capabilities.

Smaller companies may not have the same number of opportunities for promotions, but they frequently do offer higher levels of responsibility earlier in your career because fewer management layers exist between you and the head of the company. In addition, transfers are sometimes easier to accomplish in smaller companies because boundaries between departments are often not as formal or rigid as in larger organizations. In addition, you may quickly get to know everyone in the company and may be more aware of new opportunities within the company than you would be in a larger corporation.

Promotions and transfers are not applicable to a career as a contractor or freelancer. Independents are not part of a company family and do not move up from one level to the next. However, as they develop their skills and experience, independents can demand higher consulting fees. The more well-known and experienced consultants are, the more they can charge for their services. You would broaden your experience as an independent contractor, not through transfers within a company, but through many and varied assignments in a range of companies and departments.

Compensation

One final suggestion is to look at the total compensation package for each of your options. Areas to consider include the following:

- Salary
- Pension programs
- Employee savings and company-match programs
- Health benefits
- Bonuses
- Stock purchase programs
- Merit increases
- Cost-of-living adjustments
- Profit sharing

Compensation packages vary from company to company, regardless of whether you are targeting large corporations or small companies. One company may be higher in one area of compensation but lower in another, so you must compare the total value of the various packages. As a freelancer, you should be sure to set your fees so that they provide a total compensation package because you will have to fund each of the areas out of your own consulting fees.

Depending on your level of education and experience, salaries can range from around $30,000 for a new writer, editor, analyst, or graphic designer to over $59,000 for consultant senior technical communicators with over 10 years' experience. The Society for Technical Communication's *1997 Technical Communicator Salary Survey* lists the mean salary for technical communicators in the computer industry as $46,750. The Society for Technical Communication (STC) also reports the following average salaries for members with different levels of education; however, these figures are for all STC members, not just those who work in the computer industry.

TABLE 6.1.
STC Average Salaries by Education Level 1997

Education Level	Average Salary
Bachelor's degree	$45,090
Master's degree	$49,940
Doctorate	$55,810

Source: Society for Technical Communication, *1997 Technical communicator salary survey*, pp. 4-5.

EMPLOYMENT OUTLOOK

Most entry-level positions for technical communicators in the computer industry are for information product developers and editors. The career path then may include moving laterally to designer and tester on up to senior-level information product analyst or manager of a writing group or department. This path is clear, but at the department manager level, the path in writing and communication usually stops. Most often, the next steps are into such areas as quality assurance, marketing, or human factors.

Until the 1990s, most communicators in the American computer industry were directly employed full-time by software and hardware development companies. However, in other countries—Australia, for example—the hiring arrangements were quite different. Most Australian technical communicators in the computer industry were freelancers, and few worked full-time for a single company. This meant that they worked either out of their homes or in small offices of their own.

In the 1990s, American technical communicators have become more and more like those in Australia. This shift to independent contracting and freelance work has occurred because of the national downsizing of American white-collar workers. With the rise in the number of consultants and freelancers, a glut in the marketplace has occurred, and competition is increasingly fierce. In some cases, technical communicators leave their company after some 15 years and begin work as freelancers, directing their career paths toward starting their own businesses.

The future is unclear. The market has recently been inundated by both large and small computer companies. However, until emerging technologies such as parallel processing, hypermedia, virtual reality, and neural networks offer customers a new "must-have" product, such as the spreadsheets or word processors of the past, growth for technical communicators in the computer industry will be sluggish compared to the explosive growth in the 1970s, 80s, and the early 90s.

PREPARATION

When Joseph Chapline began writing about computers in 1947 as the first writer in UNIVAC, he had no training or background in writing or editing, but he did have some experience running the mechanical precursor to the computer, the differential analyzer. Today, however, companies require a broad range of communication knowledge and experience from new employees, and many are looking for candidates with undergraduate or graduate degrees in technical communication. For example, companies hiring information product developers, editors, designers, and testers expect knowledge in written and visual communication, as well as expertise in computer hardware and software.

To meet this need, academic programs in technical and scientific communication are becoming more rigorous and are growing rapidly. For example, the latest survey of programs conducted jointly by the Council for Programs in Technical and Scientific Communication and the STC identified over 180 academic programs in this area.

Because computer hardware and software are changing continually, it's difficult to describe the ideal preparation for an information product developer in the computer industry. However, in-depth knowledge of a particular generation of hardware, software, or computer languages is less important than the ability to learn new information quickly and to communicate easily in a variety of media, on a variety of subjects, to a variety of audiences.

Historically, the best preparation for dealing effectively with a changing environment is a bachelor's or master's degree, with a major or a significant amount of course work (up to 18 semester hours) in technical writing, editing, and graphic design.

In addition, if you are thinking about writing for the computer industry, you would benefit from a minor or a cognate area in computer science, which will provide you with a technical foundation that will help you cope with the rapidly occurring change in this field. At a minimum, you should develop a cognate area in a specific technical discipline (even if it's not computer science) to build confidence in your ability to understand and appreciate technical material and to demonstrate that you have technical aptitude.

You might also take courses in photography, art, and computerized illustration. And because you will need to know the latest techniques in desktop publishing, you will need to be conversant with digital typography and methods of working with laser printers and scanners. Much of this kind of knowledge can be effectively developed through internship experiences and preparing assignments for your course work.

To become an information product manager, you should not only be familiar with all of the areas of knowledge mentioned above, but you should know how to develop budgets and realistic deadlines for documentation projects, coach people to help them do their jobs more effectively, and negotiate with outside vendors such as printers, binders, and CD-ROM manufacturers.

Many academic programs in technical communication address these areas, but if such a program is not available to you, you should take additional course work, even if it means going outside your major. Useful topics if you wish to develop information products or become a manager or project leader include the following:

- project management
- management styles
- performance evaluation
- process management
- quality assurance
- cognitive psychology
- usability testing

Although you are not likely to find courses that deal exclusively with some of these topics, you may find courses that treat the topics.

PROFESSIONAL PROFILES

The three profiles in this section were chosen to give you a taste of the range of jobs available if you choose to write for the computer industry. The first describes the experiences of an entry-level technical writer; the second discusses the duties of an experienced documentation writer, who now works as a freelancer; and the third provides a portrait of a multimedia developer in a multinational corporation.

Jim Jeffers

During the summer vacation before his senior year in college, Jim Jeffers worked as a new information producer with a computer consultant company, Technical Communication, Inc, in Wilmington, Delaware. Jim was a double major at the University of Delaware in computer science and technical communication, and it was his expertise in programming that gave him the ability to work successfully in a position that most technical communication students apply for only after graduation.

It was hard for Jim to get the hang of professional corporate communication culture after leading the life of a student, beginning to study at midnight and going everywhere on a mountain bike. It was hard to get up every morning and appear bright and chipper at 8:00 a.m., to weather the suspicious looks of coworkers in jackets and ties, and to get used to the IBM PC desktop publishing software—especially after years in a world of Macintosh computers.

Besides adjusting to corporate life, Jim's major task was to take the very rough draft of a user guide developed by programmers in a client company and edit it, test it, and produce it using desktop publishing so that it could be sent back to the company and used by nonprogrammers. With his knowledge of computers, Jim was not afraid to use the program on his terminal to see if it performed in the ways described by the programmers' design documents. But after finding numerous omissions and incorrect statements, Jim found himself on the phone pretty regularly with the programmers who had created the original document.

Typical conversations went as follows:

"Did you know that if a user presses the PF1 key on menu 5 that all the information previously entered by the user is erased?"

"Well, no ..."

"What's the meaning of the error message, 'Queue Overload,' that appears when a user presses the 'Print' button a number of times, and what should the user do about it?"

"Oh, well ..."

Jim found that he had to be a good interrogator to ferret out how the software really worked—he had mistakenly assumed that the programmers would have written this all down in their design document. But it was fun to help in the development process, and his expertise in the eyes of his manager certainly soared when the company called to compliment him by saying they were surprised to see writing and programming skills so well-matched in one person.

Despite his success with the programmer, Jim found it hard to deal with all the edited drafts of his work that were returned to him by his editor and manager. It seemed that just when he felt he had unburdened himself of that manual, it reappeared on his desk demanding further care and attention. And it was disappointing that after all those weeks of working and reworking the draft, his manual was still "out for review" at the client site when it came time for him to leave.

He did enjoy working with the other technical communicators; they were all young, most had been on the job only a few years, and they all had an easy way of getting along with each other and editing each other's drafts before they were submitted to the boss. It was ironic to return to school to learn about writing in the computer industry when he had already been doing it successfully for three months.

Sandra Whittle

Unlike Jim, who is new to writing in the computer industry, Sandra Whittle has been designing computer documentation for six years. During that time, she has worked for a variety of organizations, from government departments to insurance companies to automobile companies, including Elders IXL, AT&T Bell Laboratories, the Electricity Trust of South Australia, Employers Mutual Indemnity Insurance, the Roads and Traffic Authority of South Australia, the State Attorney General Department, and Toyota Motor Corporation of Australia. Sandra is currently a technical communication consultant with IBM Australia.

In 1987, Sandra completed her thesis for an honors degree (the equivalent of a U.S. master's degree) in psychology by studying the "differences between user performance of those using online documentation and those using paper manuals." Thus, Sandra began her career as one of the few people with an academic background that could be used directly in her technical communication career. Sandra was so enthusiastic about technical communication in the computer industry that in the following year, 1988, she founded the South Australian Society for Technical Communication in Adelaide, South Australia.

Her move from company to company during her career reveals much about this field of communication. Sandra began as a technical communicator in a company that produced software, but she found her pay poor because her work was categorized as clerical. Because of this attitude on the part of her managers, her career was blocked, and she left the company. But while at this company, she gained valuable experience by

- researching the functionality of new computer systems;
- constructing concise, clear user manuals;
- reviewing and testing her manuals in accordance with stringent guidelines; and
- working closely with software project teams that included programmers, analysts, and users.

Because of this self-directed experience, Sandra got the opportunity to work with the User Interface Laboratory in the Human Factors group at the AT&T Bell Laboratories in Holmdel, New Jersey. This laboratory is one of the premier places of research and development for finding out how to put together a computer system that enhances user performance. She worked on a project team with software and hardware engineers, psychologists like herself, and interface and design specialists. While at Bell

Labs, Sandra functioned as a scientist, evaluating the availability of online user help and computer based training (CBT) systems. In this capacity, she wrote a paper entitled "A Literature Review of Online Assistance" and participated in weekly work review meetings. She also gave oral presentations on her team's work to various management groups.

Upon her return to Australia, Sandra had her first experience as an independent consultant, working as a technical communicator for the Electricity Trust of South Australia, a government agency. As a consultant, she was asked to evaluate their use of automated desktop publishing equipment and to produce paper manuals on topics ranging from basic computer concepts to advanced procedural handbooks. Her texts included the following:

- *Using the IBM Computer*
- *Cataloguing and Tooling—Materials Management System*
- *Debt Administration User Manual*
- *How to LogOn to the VAX Computer and Use Some Common Control Keys*
- *VAX Computer Training Manual for Inexperienced Users*

Over 400 people were trained using her manuals.

In her latest position, as an independent writing consultant with IBM Australia, she is both a trainer and a writer. As a trainer, Sandra teaches the IBM staff how to use their own automated desktop publishing product, called BookMaster, which runs on a mainframe. She also has been asked to write instruction manuals for two different software products created by IBM as well as to help IBM information product developers produce their own documentation. Her current project has an international flavor because she is helping technical communicators create manuals for Persian, Indian, and Turkish audiences.

Michael Burke

Michael Burke is an information engineer on a multimedia development team for NCR Corporation in Dayton, Ohio. The Information Engineering Department creates documentation and customer training for the installation, configuration, and use of hardware and software. This department also creates marketing and collateral materials, and software demonstrations.

Michael started his career at NCR about 11 years ago as an entry-level technical communicator and was primarily responsible for writing technical user manuals for mainframe computer customers and field engineers. He quickly became interested in online documentation and initiated development of the first NXE ITX Help Facility. His division then created a graphical, icon-driven way of accessing NCR's mainframe operating system; Michael also developed the first help system for this graphical user interface. He also initiated and directed a research project in partnership with the University of Washington to analyze customer needs and preferences for online information content and delivery methods.

In continuing to explore new ways of delivering information, he developed a procedure for packaging print documentation as electronic files. These files are shipped with the other software products created by the division, and they enable customers to simply send the appropriate document files to an electronic printer, providing them with the information they want—in hardcopy—when they want it.

Michael has spent about four years in multimedia research and development, and his current role is to serve as the "multimedia evangelist" for Information Engineering's multimedia endeavors. He looks for situations in which information can be delivered more effectively (in terms of cost, timeliness, and usability) in a multimedia format. He then designs and develops appropriate multimedia information products to meet the needs of users both inside and outside his company.

His first substantial multimedia project was a presentation describing the various functions and products developed by the Information Engineering group. It incorporated interactive audio, video, animation, and graphics in a computer-based presentation illustrating what the team could provide to customers. Its audience included internal organizations that might benefit from using multimedia in their products. He has also developed a multimedia computer-based training program, both for internal use and for use by external customers. In addition, he has developed a demonstration of the behind-the-scenes operations of a software product; this demonstration illustrates with graphics and animation what is otherwise invisible to users of the software.

When multimedia started becoming practical, Michael helped design a "suite" (or group) of multimedia training products that included an online tutorial, audiotape, videotape, and satellite broadcast for one of the division's messaging products. He also helped realize the company's first multimedia lab on the West Coast, where they demonstrated and promoted the capabilities of multimedia and encouraged its use as a delivery method for documentation, training, demonstrations, and marketing materials.

Before joining NCR, Michael worked as an electronics technician, as a member of an artillery battery crew, as a science and math teacher, and as a freelance writer and photographer. Now, his daily tasks include designing multimedia projects, attending meetings, and communicating through electronic mail. He also searches the World Wide Web and professional journals, attends professional conferences, and evaluates other information products to keep up with the latest developments in computer technology and documentation and to find new communication opportunities and techniques.

He says that the processes and practices that he uses aren't specific to the computer industry, although he suspects that many of them evolved into popular use from the computer field. Michael explains that because computers are in widespread use, this industry requires a great deal of "how-to" information. He believes that the use of audience and task analysis, task-oriented information formatting, and other common practices evolved because complex operations had to be communicated to an audience less interested in how something works than in how to use it.

Michael sees his future as working on the leading edge of information technology to bring his organization the latest and greatest methods for providing customers with the information they need, when they need it, anytime and anywhere. He observes that while this goal has remained the same for technical communicators over time, the means of achieving it are constantly and rapidly changing for the better, which keeps the job challenging and interesting.

He can foresee a time when the information engineering field will be so expansive that he won't be able to keep up with the advanced technology. He suspects that his ultimate role with the company will either be that of a specialist in one area of information product development or that of a consultant, designer, and planner for advanced projects, in which others do the actual development. He also recognizes that 10 years from now, technological advances may create challenging and enticing opportunities that even those who are now on the leading edge can't anticipate. Therefore, his approach will continue to be to learn all he can, be flexible, and remain alert for new opportunities.

He believes that customer satisfaction is probably the most important area in which technical communicators add value to the products they support. Effective, usable information product suites, which may contain reference manuals, user guides, online help facilities, user tutorials, electronic bulletin board access, and other user help tools, result in products that are easy to use and quick to master. This ease of use reduces training expenses and shortens the learning curve that users might go through. It also increases user efficiency and capability, satisfies customers, and results in positive customer perception of the specific product and of the company providing it.

APPENDIX

FURTHER INFORMATION
Organizations

When beginning your search for a job in this field, you should investigate at least the following professional societies. As you gain experience in the field, you will discover many other, less well-known organizations.

Association of Computing Machinery
Special Interest Group for Computer Documentation (ACM/SIGDOC)
11 West 42nd Street
New York, NY 10036

The smallest of the three most relevant organizations but the first to focus on technical communication in the computer industry. Quarterly journal and yearly international conference. No local chapters.

Institute of Electrical and Electronics Engineers
  Professional Communication Society (IEEE/PCS)
345 East 47th Street
New York, NY 10017
(212) 705-7900

Smaller than STC. Quarterly journal and yearly international conference. No local chapters.

Society for Technical Communication (STC)
901 North Stuart Street, Suite 904
Arlington, VA 22203-1854
(703) 522-4114
www.clark.net/pub/stc/www

With over 20,000 members, the largest of the professional organizations of technical communicators. Large, excellent, yearly international conference, a quarterly journal, and 141 local chapters. Local chapters post employment opportunities. Consulting a chapter job list is an excellent way to find career opportunities.

Usability Professionals' Association (UPA)
10875 Plano Road, Suite 115
Dallas, TX 75238

(214) 349-8841
Fax: (214) 349-7946
E-mail: UPADallas@aol.com

A relatively small organization with approximately 450 members, but its growth is steady. According to UPA's bylaws, "the purposes of the association include providing a network and opportunities through which usability professionals can communicate and share information about skills and skill development, methodology used and/or proposed in the profession [of usability], tools used in the profession, technology, and organizational issues."

REFERENCE

1997 Technical communicator salary survey. (1997) Arlington, VA: Society for Technical Communication.

chapter 7

Science Writing

Ricki Lewis
Freelance Science Writer
Scotia, New York

Jobs

- Writer/editor for newspapers, magazines, encyclopedias, textbooks, and on-line outlets.
- Public information officer/writer for universities, medical centers, private corporations, or public relations firms representing clients in technical fields.
- Writer/editor for science publications of government agencies, such as the National Institutes of Health, the U.S. Department of Agriculture, and state health and environmental conservation departments.
- Editor/writer for publications of scientific organizations, such as the American Association for the Advancement of Science or the American Chemical Society.
- Editor/writer for general science journals, such as *Nature* or *Science,* or for more specialized journals, such as *Cell* or *Inorganic Chemistry.*
- Editor/writer for newspapers for scientists, such as *The Scientist* and *Genetic Engineering News.*
- Trainer or independent writing consultant.

Responsibilities

Establish and maintain media contacts. Select story topics, do background research, interview scientists. Plan, write, and edit articles, newsletters, tip sheets, press releases, and backgrounders. Oversee editing of scientist-written research reports submitted to technical journals.

Outlook

Excellent and expanding.

Salary Range

$20,000 to $65,000 and up. Part-time is an option.

INTRODUCTION

The field of science writing is as diverse and broad as science itself. It includes science journalism—writing for the non-scientist—as well as writing news and feature articles for scientists. Pure scientific writing—the writing of scientific research articles, papers, and grant proposals—is usually done by scientists themselves. However, science writers may work as editors for a variety of scientific publications, or as trainers helping scientists to improve their writing skills.

YOUR LIFE AS A SCIENCE WRITER

As a science writer, you might face any one of the challenges posed by the following situations:

- The National Institutes of Health (NIH) plans to drastically cut funds to one branch. How will you describe these cuts and their implications in an article for the readers of your magazine, who are academic scientists whose careers depend upon NIH funding?
- At Arizona State University, a team of researchers analyzes the Sycamore Creek drainage basin, from the microscopic diatoms in the 14 incoming streams, to the food web branching from fallen leaves, to the geology of the region. How can you best describe the work in the university's research magazine, and interest the alumni readers enough, perhaps, to send a donation?
- An animal supply company is introducing a new breed of mini-pig for cardiovascular research. How do you describe in a bulletin to scientist clients how a lab should be built to house the animals?
- You are the editor of a quarterly newsletter for an organization whose members have a rare genetic disease. When a researcher identifies the gene that causes the disorder, how do you tell your sensitive readers just what the discovery means—and doesn't mean?
- A young researcher dies from infection by a herpes virus, contracted when a monkey with which she was working spit in her eyes. How do you explain to the readers of your consumer magazine that this tragedy differs markedly from inflection by move familiar herpes viruses?
- A well-respected and well-known scientist is accused by a former student of reporting the results of experiments that were never conducted. It is your job to interview both sides and write a balanced news story.

- As a feature writer for a medical newsletter, you are asked to compare the relative merits of two versions of a drug used to boost red blood cell supplies. The editor sends you 18 technical papers to read and digest, from which you must write a 500-word summary.

As you can see from this list, science writers address both nonspecialists and specialists, and these different audiences dictate different approaches. Like technical papers and most articles for specialists, science journalism for the scientist includes not only facts, but depth and analysis. However, an article on a scientific topic for the general public in a weekly news magazine is broader in scope and more superficial than a piece written for scientists to read. What are the implications of the information? How will it affect ordinary people? Moreover, if a topic isn't obviously relevant, the science journalist must present it in so fascinating a way that the reader is enticed beyond the first paragraph. Liberal use of anecdotes and statistics can do the trick.

A story on gene therapy illustrates the difference in tone and scope between science journalism and science writing for a scientific readership. For example, newspaper article told the story of Laura Cay Boren, the first child to receive a new gene-based treatment for her inherited immune deficiency. However, the same topic covered as research news in a general weekly publication for scientists was vastly different. It detailed the biochemical steps of how deficiency of the enzyme adenosine deaminase kills T cells, which, in turn, inhibits the function of B cells, effectively shutting down immunity. Jargon that is out of place in a newspaper—*DNA, T cells,* and *antibodies*—is part of the basic lexicon of the scientist reader. Still, some explanation is needed in news and features written for scientists to help readers who want to learn about a field that is new to them, such as a biologist reading an article on the Hubble telescope.

The primary skill you'll need as a science writer is the ability to adapt your material to your readers, whether the reader is your parent or the president of the National Academy of Sciences. You'll also have to know your audience's needs. Do not expect readers of popular magazines to know how a hormone works, and do not call a hormone a "body messenger" in the pages of a journal whose readers are biochemists. Finally, you'll need to develop and hone skills for dealing with details in order to be effective at your job. As a science writer, you'll have to do research to get the facts right. Verifying whether a researcher has a PhD or MD degree or is an assistant or associate professor are oft-encountered problems. Moreover, you'll need to double-and-triple check numbers, results, conclusions, names, and affiliations.

Another research skill you'll need to have is knowledge of where to get ideas and information. Web searches can get you started. *Science* and *Nature* are two of the most widely read publications for scientists. Therefore, science writers scan them weekly to find story ideas, to stay up to date, and to learn who in the scientific community is doing what. These and other journals regularly send out electronic press releases to writers a week or two before publication, or maintain searchable web sites. The ideal place to get story ideas is to attend a scientific conference where researchers may present their work before it is published. Some conferences hold sessions especially for the press and will usually waive registration fees.

Other traits you'll need to be a good science writer match those of a good scientist—curiosity, logic, and persistence. You must like people, and be driven to understand why things happen and how things work. Your work won't stop, however, with finding an interesting story and a researcher to interview. You'll need to sharpen special skills to get the information you need from scientists.

DEALING WITH THE SCIENTIST

The ability to draw scientists out is perhaps the most critical skill for a good science writer. It would be nice to think that scientists publish because they are anxious to get out word of their work simply for the good of humankind. But this is an idealistic view. In reality, grant funding, promotion and tenure, and the ability to switch jobs are heavily dependent on a scientist's publication record, and these are often more compelling reasons to communicate. Industrial scientists might be unable to provide some information because of trade secrets or pending patents.

Whatever their motivation for publication, scientists are often difficult to approach. As a consequence, you'll need to learn how to deal with scientists by addressing all of the following issues when interviewing scientists.

Because much of science uses unusual vocabulary and sometimes complex concepts, it helps to come to an interview prepared. Even interviewing a movie star requires prior background work, but studying up on metal vapor chemistry or superconductivity may entail a bit more effort. The formula for pre-interview preparation: "read, read, read, and then read some more," says Conrad Storad, director of research publications at Arizona State University. "I search out other writing (popular science type, preferably) on the subject," adds Bill Austin, specialist in public information at General Electric's Research and Development Center in Schenectady, New York. Austin does enough background reading so that he can rough out the press release or article before the interview, using the interview to flesh things out and correct errors. You might also attempt to read technical papers by the interviewee (you wouldn't interview a rock band without hearing the music first), especially if he or she sends them to you ahead of time.

Once talking to a scientist, do not be afraid to ask questions—it's your job! And remember that no question is too simple to ask. Gradually build to more complex questions. Also, try not to let a scientist's reputation intimidate you—he or she is a person too.

A thorny area is whether or not to send a draft of an article to a scientist whose work you describe. Editors at many magazines and journals absolutely forbid this practice, because some scientists, being human, attempt to change too much of an article. Newspapers and weeklies simply do not have the luxury of time to send articles out for review. However, if the editor approves and the interviewee is willing, a review of your article can often spot errors before publication.

Most scientists are not exactly knocking on writers' doors, offering to share their wisdom. Many scientists are particularly turned off by "gee-whiz" reporting (such as writer-originated claims of research one day curing birth defects or cancer, as if there is no other reason to investigate something), misquoting, hype, and quotes taken out of context. They are especially defensive about a writer uncovering a misdeed. Many scientists recall *Chicago Tribune* writer John Crewdsden's 1990 exposé of AIDS researcher Robert Gallo's claim to having discovered HIV before the French. Crewdsden's accusation led to investigations by the National Institutes of Health and by Congress. Media play in 1991 of prominent biologist David Baltimore's role in covering up fudged data by a colleague has also made many a scientist press-shy.

Finally, solid science writing requires familiarity with the scientific method, the modus operandi behind the way scientists think and work. You can learn this in any science course, or by reading technical articles and following the reasoning of making observations, posing testable hypotheses, conducting experiments, compiling results, drawing conclusions—and posing new questions.

Understanding the scientific method enables you to regard research with a critical eye. You might even think of a conclusion other than the one that a researcher came to that the data support, or you might identify questionable studies. For example, a medical study based on fewer than 30 participants, or lacking appropriate controls, is not scientifically rigorous. (If you don't know what a control group or a sample size is, you're not ready for science writing.)

THE UPS AND DOWNS OF SCIENCE WRITING

In sum, science writing is a challenging and varied profession, but like any other profession, it has its ups and downs. Below is a summary of what practicing writers say they like and dislike about their jobs.

What Science Writers Like . . .
- constantly changing topics
- opportunity to develop and shape a product
- contact with the best and brightest students, teachers, researchers, and journalists
- travel
- intellectual challenge of learning
- freedom to choose topics to cover
- talking to researchers about their work, and to government officials who make things happen
- learning about the technologies of tomorrow

. . . and Dislike About Their Jobs.
- following directives of administrators, politicians, and company executives
- having editors change what writers write to fit a particular publication's style
- always too much to do
- deadlines
- readers who don't understand deadlines and space constraints
- dealing with scientists who cannot explain their work in lucid terms
- lack of respect from egotistical doctors and scientists

WHERE YOU MAY WORK

Science writers work in a variety of settings. For example, as a science writer, you may write articles on science for newspapers or magazines, or entries on science for encyclopedias and textbooks. You may also write or edit science-related publications for a university, private corporation, hospital, or public relations firm, or do the same for a scientific professional association or government agency. Finally, you might edit scientists' writing for a scientific journal or proceedings or a grant proposal, or you could work as a private consultant or trainer, helping scientists to improve their writing.

Newspapers and Magazines

Newspapers are including more science stories, as discoveries such as those from the human genome project impact directly on peoples' lives. Although newspapers usually obtain their science stories from wire services or staff writers, you might approach a managing editor with a story idea and nab a freelance assignment. Or try writing a letter to the editor or an opinion piece on a science topic.

Similarly, you might freelance science articles for popular magazines. Many of these publications use science stories written by nonstaff. To get an assignment at a magazine, you must convince an editor that your idea is great, that you are the one to write it, and that the magazine's readers will care. This means being very familiar with the publications. The readers of *Ladies' Home Journal* would not be terribly fascinated by a report on transferring a growth hormone gene from rainbow trout to catfish to create gigantic catfish, but readers of *Field and Stream* would love it.

Some science writers at newspapers and magazines follow a well-defined "beat," such as covering biotechnology for a business magazine, the "Genome Watch" column for *Genetic Engineering News* on the worldwide effort to sequence all human genes, or physics for *Science News*. But many science writers switch hats often, interviewing a behavioral scientist one day, researching an environmental story the next, then perhaps attending a chemistry conference. When disaster strikes, the science writer with an appropriate specialty is in great demand. When nuclear reactors malfunctioned at Three Mile Island in 1979 and at Chernobyl a decade later, the media scrambled to find those few writers with physics backgrounds. The transfer of a deadly flu virus from chickens to people in Hong Kong called forth writers with knowledge of epidemiology.

Encyclopedias and Textbooks

An excellent source of assignments for science writers is the encyclopedia market, both for standard entries and specialized articles for yearbooks focusing on medicine, health, science, and technology. Encyclopedia articles are perhaps the easiest types of science articles to write because they require library research, rather than interviews with scientists. Besides, encyclopedia editors often provide so much guidance, in the form of outlines and reference materials, that your job may feel like just filling in the blanks.

Encyclopedia writing sticks to facts, with less emphasis on interpretation than other science writing, but requiring attention to details about when and where events occurred. For several years I wrote the entry on weight control for *World Book*. I spent a few hours in the medical library and on the Web gathering information on studies published in the relevant time period, then summarized them. I wrote one paragraph per study, or sometimes grouped similar studies in one section, and presto, there was the article. A long special feature for the *World Book Health and Medical Annual* on food supplements required considerably greater effort. Still, the editor's outline helped immeasurably.

Similar to encyclopedia writing is contributing bits and pieces to textbooks. Perhaps an author is too busy to crank out a chapter on microorganisms: A science writer might write a first draft, to which the author adds his or her special style. Textbooks at all levels have high-interest boxes often penned by writers other than the author. Send some of your clips to an academic publisher, and these assignments may result.

Universities, Corporations, Hospitals and Medical Centers, Research Institutes, and Firms

Universities, corporations, and hospitals have public information departments that employ writers, or they hire public relations firms to represent their organizations to the public. These public relations firms also employ writers.

As a science writer working in the public information department of a university, a corporation that develops and/or markets scientific products, or a hospital, you would serve as a go-between connecting the institution with the media. You would present information, research results, or products and services, and you would develop a network of recipients for press packages, including press releases about newsworthy events.

Working for a university might require you to know something about the many topics university researchers investigate, while working for a private corporation might require more in-depth knowledge of a specific area. For example, a director of news services at a technical university might write a press release about new polymers in the morning, then edit a story on robotics in the afternoon. In contrast, a science writer at a private research laboratory that provides laboratory animals might write technical bulletins and newsletters.

Biotechnology companies, which have proliferated like rabbits since the 1970s, need writers with savvy in biology and chemistry to transform technical endeavors into readable publications that will attract investor interest. This is especially challenging work because the readership includes both lay people (with an interest in business) and scientists.

A science writer at a hospital or medical center is in the exciting position of announcing breakthroughs to the media. This job might entail writing a press release to precede publication of a new development or discovery. The release would summarize experimental findings, provide background and perspective, and include quotes from the researchers.

Research Institutes often hire freelance science writers to produce newsletters or annual reports that present the work of the facility in an interesting way. For example, I write the annual report for The Trudeau Institute in Saranac Lake, NY. Formerly a tuberculosis sanitorium, the Institute today focuses on basic immunology research.

Science writers at public relations firms, like writers at universities, deal with the media. Says the president of such a firm, the company's role is "deciphering what our clients are doing so that newspaper and television reporters can understand and explain it to the readers."

Scientific Organizations, Government Agencies, and Funding Agencies

Professional scientific organizations, such as the American Chemical Society, the American Association for the Advancement of Science, the American Physical Society, and the American Institute of Biological Sciences, publish magazines targeting lay audiences, teachers, industrial and academic scientists, and students at all levels. Writing news articles for science magazines and journals that scientists read means less translation of jargon, but it requires an ability to recognize interesting and important information and put it into context with work in the field.

Government agencies and private granting agencies, such as the Howard Hughes Medical Institute (HHMI), produce beautiful, glossy magazines that publicize the research they support and strive to highlight the importance and relevance of the work. For example, the Office of Technology Assessment of the U.S. Congress published a long booklet entitled *Cystic Fibrosis and DNA Tests: Implications for Carrier Screening*. The publication addresses the question of whether the entire population should be screened for carrying the gene that causes cystic fibrosis, now that technology makes this screening possible. Although much of the material was written by experts, editors ensured consistency in style, reading level, and clarity.

Editing for Scientific Journals and Proceedings

Science writers do not write the scientific, technical papers that report research results to the scientific community unless they actually help conduct the research. I learned how to write such articles as a graduate student working for my doctorate in genetics. Scientific research is so specific, and the language, acronyms, and symbols so different from regular English, that a person who does not work directly in the field could not be of much assistance. However, editors at the journal to which such papers are sent may have some input by keeping tenses consistent, correcting misspellings, and breaking up the megapage paragraphs that many scientists produce.

Science writers can find work at the many technical journals to which scientists send their papers, but the job is more editorial than literary. An editor at a scientific journal coordinates a paper's progress in the peer-review process, which means sending it to other scientists actively working in the specific area and helping the author implement suggested changes. Such a job might include light copyediting, correcting grammar, and making minor stylistic changes to meet the journal's specifications. But the science writer doesn't question or alter content without the author's approval, which is quite different from the role of a science journalist. An editor with a degree in journalism, for example, could not comment on the content of a paper entitled "Tetranuclear osmium complexes as catalyst precursors in the hydrogenation of styrene"—unless he or she made a habit of hydrogenating styrene.

In a role similar to journal editing, I served as a technical editor for the proceedings of a conference on birth defects. I was handed a pile of papers presented at the meeting, and I edited them for grammar and consistency from paper to paper. Similarly, the copyeditor who worked on the college biology text I authored had no training in science, but she would spot undefined terms, vagueness, inconsistencies, and contradictions.

Training Scientists to Write About Their Work

It is a fact of the scientific life that one must write—to present data, to advise management, and to obtain funding. But what if a researcher cannot construct a readable sentence? This is where a trainer can help. A trainer is an experienced writer or editor who can identify problems in scientists' writing and show the scientist-authors how to improve. This process entails teaching the scientists to organize data, decide what to include and what not to include, and how to conform with the required style and format of a particular publication.

EMPLOYMENT OUTLOOK

The employment options for a science writer are vast and varied: They include industry, the media, hospitals, research institutions, textbook publishing, encyclopedias—or freelancing and thus sampling them all! Salaries start in the mid-twenties, and climbing the pay ladder requires years of productive work. Top salaries are in the mid-fifties to sixties, but of course, if you freelance or author books, the limits extend. As in science itself, pay is higher in industry than academia. "The university setting is great, but you can't eat the ivy," says Cornell University's news services' Roger Segelken.

Advancement in a science writing staff position usually means broadening responsibility. A staffer at *The Journal of NIH Research,* for example, began by editing freelancers' work. After a few months and a growing familiarity with the various sections of the magazine, she moved up to writing news (straight reporting) and then to the more interpretive feature articles. This is a common career trajectory.

For freelancers, a track record is critical to advancement. An impressive collection of clips plus a long list of sources and contacts spells success. Advancement means editors calling you with more and more lucrative assignments. "The ultimate product of the journalist is, by definition, totally visible. It must show ability, experience, and proven performance," says Michael Heylin, editor-in-chief of *Chemical & Engineering News.* At *The Scientist,* "you need to demonstrate writing and interviewing skills, and the ability to reshape disjointed, dry, or confusing copy into a smoothly flowing, interesting, relevant article," says one editor. Other factors in getting ahead successful science writers cite include luck, ability to work with a variety of personalities, willingness to take on assignments that will build new skills, dependability, problem-solving skill, and networking with others in the field.

The future for science writers in government, academia, and the corporate sector is bright, as our society depends more on technology. The human genome project, for example, is an international effort to sequence each of the 100,000 genes in our own species. It has already precipitated an avalanche of books, press releases, and articles. On another front, legislators rely on scientist advisors to understand such complex issues as global warming and pesticide risks, and often need skilled science writers to bridge the communication gap by extracting the important points from what these advisors report.

Ironically, the future at science magazines directed at the layperson is less rosy. Despite our increasing reliance on technology and the trendiness of environmental science, publications face an upward battle because the advertisers that support them are concerned about a science-scared and technophobic public. Many science magazines for general consumption have come, gone, and sometimes coalesced since the early 1980s. The few enduring popular science magazines, such as *Discover* and *Scientific American,* tend to have small, long-lasting staffs, and regular, well-known contributors.

You will find more opportunities, both as a freelancer and a staff writer, at the publications that scientists read, perhaps because not many writers know science in depth sufficiently to handle this market. *Nature* and *Science* in particular have extensive news and features sections that science writers contribute. In fact, *Nature* has grown so large that it has spun off several other journals, such as *Nature Genetics* and *Nature Medicine*. Many contributors to *Science* and the *Nature* publications have extensive science backgrounds.

PREPARATION

Ask 10 science writers to describe their academic backgrounds, and you'll probably get 10 different answers. In general, though, it's a good idea to take science courses and English or journalism courses. Particularly valuable science courses include:

- Introductory courses in each of the major areas of science: physics, chemistry, geology, and biology. These should include laboratory work.
- Computer science.
- Introductory psychology and physiological psychology. These will prepare you to cover the huge field of neurobiology and to better understand how people tick—valuable for interviewing.
- Statistics. A science writer must interpret experimental results that often include statistical tests.
- Bioethics. When science is applied to people, ethical questions often arise. Familiarity with this growing field will help you ask scientists important questions on the potential impact of their work that they may have overlooked.
- Doing research—what better way to learn how scientists work!

Should you major in science and take writing and editing courses on the side, or vice versa? A general consensus among writers seems to be that those planning to write for the layperson should earn a degree in journalism, communications, or English (especially technical and scientific communication), with several science courses. But if you want to write for scientists and physicians, or cover both lay and professional readerships, you should major in a science. An ad in *Nature* announcing an editorship, for example, requires "an excellent university education in some field of biology; experience in research or perhaps scientific journalism (writing technical papers); a lively interest in biology as a whole; ability to work under pressure." Adds a former editor of *Chemical & Engineering News,* "To work on a science newsmagazine like ours, you should definitely major in science, chemistry in particular. We're writing primarily for an audience of scientists. It's easier to learn the journalism than the science on-the-job."

Julie Ann Miller, former editor of *BioScience*, read mostly by academic biologists, agrees. "I'd advise [training in] science to develop the skills and confidence to evaluate scientific work, and not be scared by jargon, and to learn how scientists behave. But I also think courses in journalism and copyediting are important."

If you have already majored in French or economics, the door isn't closed on a career in science writing. One writer, who covers lab animals, majored in history and took lots of Latin and Greek, which she says helps greatly with "medicalese." And an editor at *The Scientist* came there following editorial stints at a Jewish weekly newspaper and a quilting magazine.

Even though science writers follow different academic routes, what many have in common is experience writing for a school newspaper. A good college newspaper is a microcosm of the real thing, and you can accumulate clips of as high quality as a piece in the *Washington Post* or *Chicago Tribune*. If your college days are long gone, try writing letters to the editor of your hometown newspaper or contacting an editor to see if you can write occasional freelance articles. A common place to start is to offer your services in reviewing books or writing opinion pieces. The goal is to get published—anywhere.

CONTINUING EDUCATION FOR THE SCIENCE WRITER

Once you land a job, you'll find that learning about science never ends, for the scientist or the science writer. How can you keep on top of an ever-changing field? "Hang out with scientists, go to seminars and meetings, and pay attention to the questions people ask," says Miller. Do science for a while. "Work in a laboratory. Have an idea of what doing experiments is like, how people get from actual results to the nice clear lines on graphs that are published," she adds.

Segelken agrees: "Learn first-hand how science happens by working on research projects, from initial proposals and laboratory drudgery to reporting of results." To get this first-hand knowledge, you might work at national labs, universities, research institutions, or facilities such as the Jackson Lab in Bar Harbor, Maine, famous for its mice, or the Woods Hole Oceanographic Institute on Cape Cod, Massachusetts. Spend a vacation on a research jaunt with EARTHWATCH. Freelance writer Alice Jacklet got several articles out of her three-week stay with orangutans in Borneo, thanks to this program.

FINDING A JOB

Just as photographers show what they can do by displaying their photographs in portfolios, science writers land jobs with clips—samples of published work, from anywhere. Clips snowball. I began by sending my articles from the *Indiana Daily Student* to the local newspaper. I sent articles from the local paper to the *Cincinnati Enquirer,* and when I did a cover story for their Sunday magazine on the breaking story of toxic shock syndrome, I sent that to a brand-new women's magazine, *Self,* and was soon writing for them. Clips likewise lead to regular jobs at publications.

"Try to get some freelance writing assignments in publications that are as close as possible to the ones you aspire to work for, so you have clips to show potential employers. Editors like to see that you have experience writing in the same style as that of their publication. The fact that you have written before, in and of itself, often isn't enough," advises an editor at *The Scientist,* where those competing for editor jobs are given a first-draft article to get into shape. The one who comes up with the clearest, crispest piece gets the job. Similarly, a job at *Nature* requires submitting a sample for their "News and Views" column.

Once you've published at least three science articles and can find a member to sponsor you, join the National Association of Science Writers. Their quarterly newsletter is filled with job tips and announcements.

Talk to science writers. "I talk to lots of prospective science writers each year, and I'm happy to steer them to opportunities I know of. Most other science writers are too," says Roger Segelken. Like Segelken, I've referred many beginning writers to editors I know and sometimes co-author articles with beginners to get them that first byline.

An internship is a great way to make job contacts. For job or internship announcements, scan ads in *Science* and *Nature.* Apply in medical center and university PR offices and government agencies. Be aggressive. Says GE's Bill Austin, "The best way to get a job here might be simply to show a keen interest. Write a letter to the communications manager expressing your interest and enclose a resume and a few samples. Then follow up on the phone, asking if any openings are in the offing and, if so, possibly requesting an informal get-together. If the credentials are right, this sort of an aggressive approach could pay dividends—immediately or eventually."

Finally, polish your craft with practice. Says Segelken, "Keep writing, even if you're not getting published. It's good exercise." That's good advice for any writer.

PROFESSIONAL PROFILES

This section highlights the work of two science writers in very different areas of the profession. Conrad Storad is the director of research publications at Arizona State University; Nancy Thornton is a consultant who teaches scientists in businesses, government agencies, and universities to write more effectively.

Conrad Storad

If there is such a thing as a perfect job, Conrad Storad thinks he has it. He is the director of research publications at Arizona State University in Tempe, the nation's fifth largest university. Storad's five years at ASU cap two years as a feature/science writer at Kent State University, which followed a year as a science/medical writer at the National Cancer Institute. Before that he spent two years as a graduate teaching assistant in reporting and editing while earning his MA in journalism with a concentration in science journalism. And sandwiched between undergraduate work in journalism and environmental biology and graduate work, Storad spent three years at a weekly newspaper, as editor and general manager.

The job of director of a university's news bureau or research publications office is challenging and diverse. "I write, edit, and supervise production of *ASU Research Magazine*, a tri-annual, four-color magazine distributed worldwide to a readership in excess of 40,000," Storad says. He does the same for a 450-page annual report, plus brochures and pamphlets for such varied university centers as the technology transfer office, the scanning tunneling microscopy group, and an industrial associates program.

What Storad likes best about his job is his almost complete control over the publications. And his products reflect his skill at spotting the most interesting stories and ensuring that they are reported well and attractively laid out and illustrated.

Nancy Thornton

Nancy Thornton of Schenectady, New York, has built a unique and thriving business teaching scientists to communicate clearly. "Scientists have to sell today," she says. "Twenty years ago, you wouldn't find salesmanship in writing. Today, if a scientist doesn't sell [in industry or in writing grant proposals], he or she will be unemployed."

Universities, large corporations, and government agencies hire Thornton to teach effective writing. Although her advice is tailored to specific types of scientific publications, a common lesson is that the very best writing reads as if it was effortless to write. "People don't realize it takes a long time and a lot of work to master clear writing. Companies say to me, 'Our people are very smart. Could you teach them how to write effectively in an hour?'"

Nancy Thornton's business literally grew on its own. Her background is eclectic—three years in college as a physics major, ending up with an English major and history minor. She worked for the civil rights movement, then began teaching a course at Union College (Schenectady, New York) in effective writing. A student working at the nearby General Electric Research and Development Center learned so much from Thornton that he arranged for her to develop a similar course for GE. Word spread. "People would take my course, leave GE, and recommend it to other companies. Before I knew it, I had a substantial business."

The first lesson in a Thornton effective writing course is to identify the audience, which sets the style and format. "Is it a progress report for a manager, or is it going to a scientific journal? That will affect how you do the opening. For in-house reports, the writer often starts with the "Five Ws" [who, what, where, when, and why] so that the reader can focus on where the article is headed. A scientific paper requires a different type of opening."

Thornton asks her students to step back from their work to "see the larger structure." Are data presented in the clearest possible way? She urges writers to be factual and objective, taking out "I think" and "I feel." Finally, she advises students to edit their work, then have someone else read it or read it aloud themselves.

"Teaching effective writing to industrial physicists one day and academic biologists the next isn't as difficult as it might sound, because the requirements are the same," Thornton says. She adapts one program to different clients, rather than developing individualized programs. "The basic things my clients need to recognize are who the audience is, the intent of the article, what to include and exclude, and how to be factual and objective. Every kind of writing requires these basic preliminaries and principles."

However, the format does vary somewhat from client to client. "A researcher at a university might spend more time on experimental papers, whereas a state health agency inspector might write reports on environmental waste sites, " she adds.

Thornton's career reflects science writing in general—applying a set of skills to a rich variety of situations.

APPENDIX

FURTHER INFORMATION

Where to Look for Jobs

- newspapers
- lay, professional, news, and consumer magazines
- television
- radio
- the internet
- disease foundations
- government science funding agencies (National Institutes of Health, Centers for Disease Control and Prevention, U.S. Department of Agriculture, state environmental conservation and health departments, National Science Foundation, Department of Energy.
- public affairs offices in industry, medical centers, universities, pharmaceutical companies, other private industry and granting agencies
- scientific/research institutions
- zoos and botanical gardens
- science policy organizations, such as the National Academy of Sciences and the U.S. Congress
- public relations firms
- environmental groups
- academic publishers
- encyclopedias
- advertising agencies
- public service organizations
- consulting firms

Where Science Writers Write for Scientists

- General science journals covering all fields of science, or one field broadly (*Nature, Science, Chemical & Engineering News, The Journal of NIH Research*)
- Newspapers for scientists, from general (*The Scientist*) to specific (*Genetic Engineering News*
- Technical journals (*Cell, Proceedings of the National Academy of Sciences, Inorganic Chemistry*), which consist exclusively of research reports that scientists write, but that science writers may edit.

Organizations and Publications

National Association of Science Writers
P. O. Box 294
Greenlawn, NY 11740

American Association for the Advancement of Science
1333 H Street, NW
Washington, DC 20005
(Publishes the weekly journal *Science*)

EARTHWATCH Expeditions, Inc.
680 Mount Auburn Street
P. O. Box 403
Watertown, MA 02272
(Publishes the magazine *Earthwatch*)

Science News
1719 N Street, NW
Washington, DC 20036
(Excellent weekly science news briefs and features)

Inquiry
Science Journalism Center
University of Missouri
P. O. Box 838
Columbia, MO 65205
(Newsletter of the science journalism center)

Morbidity and Mortality Weekly Report
Superintendent of Documents
U.S. Government Printing Office
Washington, DC 20402
(The *MMWR* is a weekly record of the nation's health and a wonderful
source of interesting statistics and ideas.)

chapter 8

Writing in Medical and Health Care Environments

Patricia L. Cornett
MedWrite Associates
Birmingham, Michigan

Jobs[1]

Medical writer, senior medical writer, freelance writer, author's editor, copy editor, assistant editor, managing editor, publications editor, proofreader, publications manager, publications coordinator, medical project manager, medical journalist, medical meeting reporter, medical abstractor, medical indexer, medical marketing or public relations specialist, medical translator.

Responsibilities

- Write, edit, or manage the publication of scientific manuscripts, articles, books, documentation for medical equipment or medically directed computer programs, newsletters, journals.
- Write or edit grant proposals, scientific reports, abstracts, posters for presentation at medical meetings, scripts for slide/videotape productions.
- Conduct research on medical and health care subjects.
- Interview physicians, scientists, technicians, patients, health care professionals.
- Search medical databases.
- Prepare data analyses/summaries.
- Manage medical projects and publications.

Employment Outlook

Fair to good until at least 2010.

Salary Range[2]

Entry-level positions range from $25,000 to $35,000, depending on the employer, the nature of the position, and the qualifications of the individual. At the upper end, as medical communicators move into managerial positions, the salary range varies more widely, from about $60,000 to $85,000, depending on the same variables as for entry-level positions.

INTRODUCTION

More than some writing professions described in this book, medical writing employs editors as frequently as writers, and it's important to understand the differences between them as you prepare for a career in what is often called the *medical communication* field.[3] Throughout this chapter, I will use the term *medical communicator* to include medical writers and editors. Perhaps the most important thing to know is that if you come into medical communication, as I did, without any background, experience, or academic training in medicine, health care, or biomedical science, it is easier to start your career, as I did, as a medical editor rather than as a medical writer.

YOUR LIFE AS A MEDICAL COMMUNICATOR[4]

Medical editors, like their counterparts in nonmedical settings, are fixers: They improve, correct, modify, build, shape, and nurture the writing of others. Medical writers are creators who start at the beginning of the process, often with only an idea. While the medical editor starts with a text already on paper or online electronically, the medical writer starts with an idea, interview notes, document guidelines, or an assignment from a client and shapes a text from embryonic beginnings, whether it is an article, book, manual, or some other kind of document. If writers gestate and give birth to a document, editors are the wetnurses who nurture and sustain its existence.

Despite this distinction, in many job settings, the lines of distinction between writer and editor are blurred. In some cases, the jobs are almost indistinguishable—because the same settings (for example, hospitals and medical publications) employ both writers and editors to work on the same material, or because the same person may be expected to write or edit as the needs of the job demand.

Here, for example, is a job ad for a publications editor at the Yale University School of Medicine:

> Writes, edits, designs and produces diverse materials, including alumni magazine, publications and news articles. Experienced writer/editor must handle complex medical topics accurately, write and edit news and feature-length articles clearly for internal and external audiences. Layout/design, production and desktop-publishing skills needed. Required bachelor's degree in English, Biological Sciences or a related field; master's preferred. Minimum 4 years' experience (American Medical Writers Association [AMWA], July/August, 1993).

Clearly, despite the title of publications editor, this position requires both writing and editing skills in equal measure.

Who Are the Audiences for Medical Writing and Editing?

The audiences for medical and health care writing are diverse. Here is a list of the most common types, although they are by no means mutually exclusive:

- doctors, nurses, and physicians' assistants
- medical and allied health personnel
- biomedical scientists and researchers
- laboratory and medical technicians
- government agencies (for example, the Food and Drug Administration and Centers for Disease Control)
- manufacturers of health care products and equipment
- drug manufacturers and providers (for example, pharmacists)
- providers of health care services (for example, medical insurance)
- health care consumers
- patients
- donors

In spite of this long list, there are only two types of audiences broadly defined: technical or general. All but the last three groups in the above list generally fall into the technical category (that is, an audience of technically trained individuals). If you work in the editorial or research department of a hospital, you will be writing and editing for a technical peer audience (that is, other scientists, physicians, and technicians), even though your job title may vary from clinical editor to editorial assistant to publications coordinator.

By contrast, health care consumers, patients, and donors constitute the great majority of the general or lay audience. If you work in the public relations and marketing department of a hospital, you will most likely write for a general audience, and your job will be to translate complex technical medical terminology and concepts into a language and form understandable to the broader public. You might, for example, write or produce promotional materials for hospital patients or donors. These materials might include brochures, reports, newsletters, videotape scripts, or press releases.

Donors are a special group of this audience—health care benefactors who are cultivated by hospitals and health care organizations because they support a variety of health care efforts with their gifts and money. A donor may be a private individual who gives money in memory of a loved one, or the donor may be a large corporation, such as the Ford Motor Company, that underwrites the building and development of a major research unit, such as the Edsel B. Ford Research and Development Center at Henry Ford Hospital. Today major hospital corporations have a development office or a marketing department responsible for identifying and cultivating donors through systematic, aggressive fund-raising campaigns.

Where Do All the Medical Writers and Editors Go?

Medical writers and editors work in settings almost as diverse as the audiences outlined above. But two common denominators define the field: (a) All the organizations employing medical writers are involved with some aspect of health care, and (b) they all use writers and editors to help them fulfill their mission of communicating with their clients, patients, or consumers.

Here is a comprehensive, but not exhaustive, list of the types of organizations where you may find employment as a medical writer/editor:

1. teaching hospitals
2. medical schools and universities
3. medical publications—for example, books, journals, and newspapers
4. medical societies and associations
5. medical research or service laboratories
6. medical public relations, marketing, or communication agencies
7. others:

   - private physicians and clinics
   - medical abstracting services
   - medical legal services
   - health care insurance companies and managed health care providers
   - health care and social service organizations
   - government health agencies
   - pharmaceutical companies
   - contract research organizations

Some of these organizations are more important to the job-seeker than others, either because they are responsible for more of the types of writing and media produced by medical writers and editors or because they employ medical writers in greater numbers. I will limit my discussion to only a few organizations in order to convey the range and variety of jobs, media, and audiences that the medical writer or editor may encounter. Sandra Lobbestael's chapter on "Pharmaceutical Writing" in this book discusses careers for writers in pharmaceutical companies.

1. **Teaching hospitals.** Large teaching hospitals (over 500 beds)[5] are usually found in major metropolitan areas and are usually affiliated with a university medical school engaged in clinical and basic biomedical research. The Cleveland Clinic, The Mayo Clinic (Rochester, Minnesota), Massachusetts General Hospital (Boston), Johns Hopkins Hospital (Baltimore), and Henry Ford Hospital (Detroit) are a few of the larger such institutions. Typically, these hospitals will have one or more of the following departments where medical writers and editors may find employment. However, not every large hospital has all of these departments, and in some institutions the departments may be combined.

Editorial department. Responsible for producing scientific publications and editing grant proposals, reports, and other scientific publications.

Clinical departments. Physicians, scientists, and technicians prepare manuscripts for publication; research grant proposals; and abstracts, posters, and slides for presentations at medical or scientific meetings. Henry Ford Hospital, for example, has several large research/clinical labs that employ editors to prepare these communications.

Marketing and public relations department. Responsible for producing publications and other media (videotapes, and TV spots and interviews, for example) aimed at a general audience of patients and health care consumers. This department usually produces the hospital's annual report, employee newsletters, patient information brochures, and other similar publications.

Medical or health education department. Produces publications relating to the education and work of medical students, residents, and interns. For example, St. John Hospital and Medical Center in Detroit has a Health Education Department that produces the *St. John Hospital Medical Bulletin.* This annual publication contains the best manuscripts prepared each year by residents as part of their residency training.

In addition, large teaching hospitals may have a separate art or photography department that, among other tasks, prepares posters and slides for meeting presentations by physicians and scientists, as well as medical illustrations, art work, photos, or computerized graphics for medical publications and presentations by the hospital staff.

2. **Medical schools and universities.** The work environment and job opportunities for medical writers and editors in a medical school or university setting mirror those found in large hospitals in most respects. Clinical departments (especially large ones like internal medicine or surgery), public relations and development offices, and medical education departments all may employ medical communicators. Likewise, depending on where in a medical school a writer or editor works, he or she may prepare publications for physician audiences, training manuals for medical students and residents, grant proposals for funding agencies, or a variety of print and media materials for the general public. About 10 percent of full-time medical writers and editors currently work in a medical school or university medical center, according to the results of a 1994 salary survey conducted by the American Medical Writers Association (Hermes, 1994).

Perhaps because of the close relationship of a medical school with its parent university or college, medical school departments and offices have a large, talented pool of student writers and editors to draw from. As a result, most hiring for writers and editors in medical schools takes place internally; thus, fewer such jobs are advertised in external sources, such as the AMWA *Job Market Sheet*. For example, after searching through eight separate 1995 issues of this publication, I was able to find only one ad that called for a writer in a medical school setting:

Science Writer Wanted. The University of Alabama at Birmingham, one of the nation's preeminent academic health centers, is seeking an experienced science writer to join its young, aggressive media relations staff. Beats include clinical trials, psychiatry, cardiovascular disease, nutrition sciences and geriatrics. Prefer someone with seven years of science writing experience, and background working with media helpful. UAB has nearly $200 million in grants, and is frequently rated as one of the nation's best medical facilities. Salary range is $35,000 to $38,000 (AMWA, February, 1995).

3. **Medical publications**. Just as the general public's appetite and demand for health care information has grown continually in the last 30 years, so have the number and types of medical publications. Medical publications generally fall into three broad categories: (a) books, monographs, and magazines; (b) newspapers or tabloids; and (c) periodically published medical or scientific journals. Newsletters also fall into the broad category of medical publications, but I do not discuss these below.

As you investigate these employment opportunities, you will quickly realize that medical publications are big business. Large medical book publishers like Elsevier, Mosby, or Excerpta Medica produce medical books for physicians, patients, nurses, other health care practitioners, medical students, and the general public. These may be reference or text books, practical health care manuals, or clinical guides, or they may be collections of articles by different authors on various aspects of medicine, from Alzheimer's disease to Zollinger-Ellison syndrome.[6] Medical and specialty societies, government agencies, private medical publications firms, and pharmaceutical companies also produce books, monographs, and magazines regularly and in large numbers. In addition, general publications such as large daily newspapers and broad circulation magazines may have columns, departments, or regular articles on medicine and health care.

All of these organizations employ writers, journalists, editors, and managers for many aspects of their operations. If you are a writer for a general circulation publication, you will write for general audiences, as a rule, rather than for technical or medical audiences, but you will still need a solid knowledge of medicine and health information. You must also be up-to-date on health care issues. As an editor, you might work on articles, books, and stories for general or technical audiences, depending on the publication.

For example, here is an ad for a medical editor for a general circulation publication:

Growing bimonthly magazine for health care professionals seeks an associate editor with a demonstrated interest in the medical field for a full-time staff position. Responsibilities include writing, editing, and proofing as well as administrative duties. Ideal candidate will have a degree in journalism or communications and a minimum of 4 years' experience writing news and feature articles, preferably for a medical or science-oriented publication. Knowledge of neuroscience a plus. Must have sharp eye for detail, be highly organized, and able to work independently. Macintosh experience desirable but not mandatory. (AMWA, July/August, 1993)

Medical journals are also a major source of work for medical writers and editors. Two of them are the must-read *New England Journal of Medicine*, published by the Massachusetts Medical Society (Boston), and *JAMA*, the *Journal of the American Medical Association* (Chicago). *Index Medicus*, a publication of the National Library of Medicine

(NLM) in Washington, DC, describes hundreds of medical journals of every conceivable type on every conceivable medical subject by every conceivable type of organization. Nor are these journals published only in English-speaking countries. For sheer numbers, probably more medical journals are produced for non-English-speaking audiences than for North American or Western European audiences.

You can learn a lot about these medical journals by going to the nearest medical library and becoming familiar with *Index Medicus* and other NLM resources. These are available electronically in computerized databases as well as in reference volumes. Some medical journals, as well as many services of the NLM itself, are also available online through the Internet and the World Wide Web. Besides the medical libraries attached to large university medical schools, some large hospitals and pharmaceutical companies also maintain medical libraries for their staffs. Although these are not usually open to the public, you might be able to gain access to their resources through the good will or connections of your college library.

You should know about one unusual feature of the editorial operation of most medical journals: These journals have a dual organizational structure, one part scientific, one part editorial or managerial. Even before you look for your first job, start to read one or two major medical journals regularly. Most university libraries and some large public libraries will carry *JAMA* or the *New England Journal of Medicine*. Pay special attention to the masthead page to learn how their editorial operations are organized and how many people are involved in producing the publication. The editor of the journal is usually a physician or scientist hired or appointed to that position for his or her knowledge of the medical field. This person may or may not be involved in actual hands-on editing, but other possible responsibilities will include overseeing the review process and serving as liaison among the reviewers, authors, and other editorial staff. The other side of the operation consists of the professional editorial staff, which may include the managing editor, copy editor, editorial assistants, proofreaders, and others. Often, medical journals employ part-time, freelance, or contract editors and writers for many or most of these tasks. This editorial part of the organization is where you are likely to find work as a medical editor.

4. **Medical societies and associations**. The American Medical Association (AMA) regularly produces about a dozen periodical publications, of which the most notable are *JAMA*, its weekly medical

journal (325,000 circulation), and the *American Medical News* (362,200 circulation), a weekly tabloid. The AMA also publishes the *AMA Manual of Style* (1998), a basic reference tool for medical communicators. The AMA, with 271,000 members, is the largest medical association that employs medical communicators to work on its many publications.

After the AMA, many specialty medical societies and associations use the services of writers and editors, often on a freelance or contract basis. The 1994 *Encyclopedia of Associations*[7] lists over 2,300 medical and health care organizations. Typically, these societies produce publications, brochures, newsletters, and other materials for their members. Larger medical organizations and professional societies may also have regular meetings or conventions, which require posters and slide-tape presentations. These organizations include: (a) specialty societies representing a large medical specialty—such as the American Academy of Pediatrics or the American Academy of Ophthalmology—which usually publish their own medical journals; (b) medical societies devoted to a particular disease or disorder, such as the American Diabetes Association or the National Multiple Sclerosis Society; (c) professional societies representing the interests of health care professionals, such as nurses, dentists, and laboratory technicians. Nurses, for example, may belong to one of more than 70 professional groups, ranging all the way from the American Nurses' Association, with more than 200,000 members, to small specialty groups with no more than a few hundred members, organized according to ethnic origin, professional specialty, or special interests. My favorite is the 300-member Nurses for Laughter, whose motto is "Warning—humor may be hazardous to your illness."

The *Encyclopedia of Associations*, published yearly, is an excellent source of information for medical communicators looking for possible employment opportunities. You will learn a lot about what's available in the field by browsing through the medical and health care society section of this multiple volume work. Each listing consists of a profile of the organization. Besides the address, phone number, and name of a top-ranking official, the listing contains the number of members, size of the staff, activities, events, and publications. Look for this indispensable resource in the reference or business section of any major public or university library.

5. **Research and service laboratories.**[8] Research and service labs generally process data that have been produced as a result of testing

new products, equipment, or drugs. The data may be incorporated in technical manuals, reviews, editorials, case reports, in-depth scientific studies, medical presentations, and manuscripts. If you are a medical writer working in this environment, you should be proficient with the standardized format for writing abstracts and technical scientific manuscripts, as well as with the procedures for submitting these materials to medical societies like the American Society of Clinical Pathologists, medical journals like the *Journal of Clinical Cytology and Cytopathology*, and other medical publishers.

Research laboratories are also involved in extensive reporting procedures, especially if they work with federal agencies such as the Centers for Disease Control in Atlanta or the Department of Health and Human Services. These laboratories are bound by federal regulations and guidelines, as set out in the Clinical Laboratory Improvements Amendments of 1988, called "CLIA 88."

Service laboratories, on the other hand, perform quality control and testing of equipment, chemicals, and devices for a variety of clients, such as hospitals, government agencies, private companies, other labs, or pharmaceutical companies. A medical writer working in this environment should be well-versed in the criteria for preparing procedure manuals, instruction guides, and technical reports to meet the needs of specific clients. Private companies that use the services of a testing laboratory may range from chemical supply companies to high-tech equipment and supply firms.

Research labs are more likely to employ medical writers than service labs, since research labs typically produce more publications and presentations. However, if service labs have elaborate reporting procedures, they may need qualified medical writers.

6. **Medical public relations, marketing, or communications agencies.** These firms are usually smaller, satellite organizations that provide services for the giants of the health care industry, such as pharmaceutical companies, government agencies, and large hospital or managed health care corporations. Those firms specializing in marketing, advertising, and public relations employ medical communicators whose backgrounds and training are strong in these areas. For these kinds of organizations, often your technical knowledge or medical training are less important than your skills in communication, advertising, and public relations. Also, because such firms may have a broad client base, you will have a better chance of

being hired if you have a general background in several areas of medicine or health care, rather than a technical specialist background in one field. The two ads below for medical communications companies are typical:

Dynamic, growing New York City medical communications company seeks highly qualified experienced candidate who can edit manuscripts and assist in managing editorial department. Frequent interaction is necessary with freelance writers/editors, clients, and physicians, pharmacists, and nurses. This position requires a highly motivated individual who is flexible, can operate within tight deadlines, and works well with people. Must be strong in a number of clinical areas, especially anti-infectives, cardiovascular, psychiatry, and diabetes (AMWA, September 1993).

We help improve cost, quality and access for health care payers and consumers . . . we seek a concise Medical Technical Writer to create newsletters, tracking reports, program manuals and other drug information publications for our Diversified Pharmaceutical Services. You will work closely with both internal and external clients, researching methods for maximizing the delivery of therapeutically appropriate and economically sound pharmacotherapy to members. You must possess a degree in English, Journalism or Technical Communications, or the equivalent, and 2–4 years' technical writing experience, preferably in medical technical writing. Word processing/desktop publishing and the ability to read and understand medical literature are essential (AMWA, July/August 1993).

7. **Other prospective employers and medical settings.** While not as visible as some of the employers mentioned above, the ones mentioned below can provide rewarding careers. Moreover, jobs with these kinds of employers are becoming increasingly available.

Private physicians and clinics. Some physician groups, although not very many, will employ medical writers (usually on a contract basis rather than as permanent employees) for ad hoc projects. A writer's responsibilities might include preparing manuscripts for publication or presentation at medical meetings, writing physician or clinic-based newsletters aimed at patients, producing patient education materials (for example, patient brochures), ghostwriting newspaper articles and speeches, or scripting radio and TV programs for physicians.

Medical abstracting services. As the computerized database industry expands its markets, publishers that provide abstracting services through electronic media will be a small but growing source of employment. This ad for a major database and information services publisher outlines the skills needed:

> Position available for an experienced writer to abstract and index professional and consumer-oriented medical and health magazine articles for our online and CD-ROM databases. Relevant work experience such as medical-related technical writing and a college degree in Nursing, Life Sciences or related area preferred. Qualified candidates will possess excellent writing skills, the ability to translate technical information into nontechnical language, and the ability to meet deadlines in a production-oriented environment (AMWA, May 1993).

Medical-legal services. Traditionally, medicine and the law mix as well as oil and water, but as medicine has become a more complex, technologically oriented field, the need for protection by and from the law has grown. As a result, some law firms are now beginning to specialize in medical law, and a few medical communicators in recent years have begun to work in this area. I have met several medical writers who were hired by law firms to prepare briefs for medical cases or to interpret information from expert medical witnesses.

The arcane legal-medical-ethical complexities of the biotechnology field are also providing new employment opportunities for medical writers, as this recent ad indicates: "Will train experienced science writer with biotechnology degree to write and prosecute patent applications for small, internationally known biotech/chemical patent law firm" (AMWA, May 1993).

EMPLOYMENT OUTLOOK

For medical communicators, the employment outlook is fair to good, well into the next century. Except in the pharmaceutical industry, the current demand for medical communicators has remained steady throughout the 1990's and will even grow somewhat in the years beyond the turn of the next century. Although the American economy has performed unevenly in the recent past, with companies "downsizing" and "outsourcing" faster than these terms can be included in new dictionaries, you can remain optimistic about job opportunities in this field for the next decade.

There are several reasons for this optimism. As the globalization of medicine that began in the 1980s continues, the demand for medical communicators to disseminate medical information globally will expand. Moreover, medical communicators, like their counterparts in other fields, can take advantage of technological advances in the Internet and the World Wide Web, online database services, laptop computers, facsimile machines, CD-ROM reference tools, and other electronic communication devices now readily available on the commercial market. These developments make it possible for medical writers and editors to remain in daily contact with clients throughout the world and to research and communicate the latest medical advances from their homes and offices.

Nevertheless, while medical communicators will find employment without difficulty into the first decade of the next century, distinct changes in the type of employer and form of employment are already evident. Pharmaceutical companies no longer absorb large numbers of medical writers as they have in the past. Since the early 1990's, drug companies and their subsidiaries have reduced or eliminated whole departments of employees, including medical writers. Today, more medical writers are employed in smaller, entrepreneurial firms, often on a contract basis rather than as employees.

The medical communications field has traditionally had a sizable contingent of freelance writers and editors, as evidenced by results from two salary and job surveys conducted in the last six years by the American Medical Writers Association. In the 1994 AMWA salary survey (Hermes, 1994), 18.7 percent (230/1229) of respondents working full time identified themselves as self-employed or consultants, and 55 percent of part-time workers were self-employed as freelancers or consultants. Only the pharmaceutical industry employs more medical communicators on a full-time basis: 27.3 percent of those surveyed (335/1229). In the 1989 job survey (Robie, 1990), with 886 AMWA members responding, 17.8 percent had full-time freelance work, and 19.9 percent reported income from freelance work in addition to a full-time salaried job. By comparison, 19.6 percent of the respondents worked primarily for pharmaceutical companies, and 18.9 percent worked for universities, medical schools, or hospitals. However, as writers are dismissed from drug companies or are offered early retirement, the trend to become self-employed or to seek work in smaller firms will grow.

But you may not fancy the freelance life. Not all medical writers want to be self-employed or to become independent freelance writers. If this sounds like you, then small biotechnology companies, communications firms, medical device manufacturers, public relations and marketing firms, managed health care organizations, computer software developers, and contract research organizations may offer you an alternative career choice. These companies tend to be smaller, newer, and more entrepreneurial in their corporate style and outlook than the traditional employers of medical writers and editors, the mega-pharmaceutical companies and major teaching hospitals.

PREPARATION

As a senior medical writer and editor with over 20 years' professional experience, I am sometimes asked how to break into the field. If you are a young college student interested in a career as a medical communicator or an older adult contemplating a career change, keep in mind one important feature that distinguishes this profession from most other writing careers—there is no well-charted, recognizable, or accepted career path to becoming a medical communicator. If you want to become a Pulitzer Prize-winning newspaper reporter or the next great American novelist, you can easily find academic programs, even whole schools, devoted exclusively to journalism or creative writing. But if you want to become a medical writer, you will have to plot your own course.

This somewhat daunting fact was a theme of my inaugural address when I became President of the American Medical Writers Association in 1988 (Cornett, 1988). What I said 10 years ago is still true today:

> Almost none of us started our [medical writing] careers with this particular career path in mind. All of us started out to be something else. . . . But somewhere along the way, in the last 10 or 15 years, we have all fallen somewhat accidentally into our present careers. . . . We have had to define our own careers, write our own job descriptions in many cases, at the same time as we have had to defend our professional credentials and convince our superiors, our colleagues, even our friends and family, of our professional value (Cornett, 1988).

Few colleges and universities offer degree-granting programs in medical communication. Even schools with technical communication programs have been slow to develop medical communication tracks. Nor are medical schools a good option in most cases, since historically they have not been receptive to courses or programs in medical communication within the medical school curriculum.

Several years ago, the AMWA surveyed academic institutions about the existing medical communication modules, courses, programs, or majors at their schools (Haneline & Turpin, 1991). The survey was prepared and carried out by Douglas Haneline and Elizabeth R. Turpin, two AMWA members who have taught in a technical communication program at Ferris State University in Big Rapids, Michigan; they developed a medical writing course as part of their program for students in pharmacy, allied health sciences, optometry, and medical technology.

Of 283 college-level institutions queried in the AMWA survey, 57 offered courses and 29 had programs in medical communication; 19 of these were graduate programs, 26 were undergraduate, and 3 were continuing education programs. Of the 29 programs, 22 were affiliated with arts and sciences colleges, mainly in English and communication departments, two with journalism, one with pharmacy, and four with medical schools. In general, the survey results offered grounds for cautious optimism about the growth of medical communications courses and programs in colleges and universities. AMWA and its Education Department continue to take the lead in nurturing such growth. At present, however, you will probably have to design your own course of study in medical communication rather than expect to find one ready-made for you in the college curriculum.

Keeping that fact in mind, you could prepare for a career in medical communication by gaining three types of experience: (a) academic course work, (b) on-the-job training, and (c) professional training and continuing education.

Academic Course Work

Despite the widespread lack of recognition for medical writing within the academic curriculum, you can still prepare yourself effectively by selecting your courses with this career goal in mind. Here are the courses I recommend:

- writing, especially technical writing or communication
- speech or oral presentations
- journalism or newspaper reporting
- life sciences—for example, biology, zoology, physiology, and anatomy
- chemistry or biochemistry
- pharmacology
- algebra
- calculus
- statistics or biostatistics
- research methods
- logic
- rhetoric
- computer applications
- desktop publishing
- computer graphics

In sum, medical communication is a hybrid career, joining in partnership medicine and communication. Therefore, your course work should also concentrate on both these areas. As the above list suggests, to improve your communication skills, you should take as many writing courses as you can fit into your program, especially technical writing or communication courses, and one or more courses in journalism or newspaper reporting, especially if you are interested in a nontechnical career track in medical communication. From the medicine and science partner, courses in the life sciences are essential. At least one chemistry course, especially biochemistry, is also important. If your school has a pharmacy program, an introductory pharmacology course is a good idea. From the math and physics curriculum, besides algebra and calculus, you should take an introductory statistics course if it is offered. If you can take a biostatistics course, so much the better. Biostatistics has heavily infiltrated the field of medicine in the last 10 years, and medical writers must have a nonmathematical working knowledge of statistics (Eastman, Smith, & Klein, 1990; Krauhs, 1994).

Courses in research methods and logic are also important, especially if you want to work as a medical writer for a research institution or a pharmaceutical company. Depending on your school and choice of major, these two courses may be taught in a liberal arts department or as part of the science curriculum. When I was an undergraduate, I took a nonmathematical logic course taught by the philosophy department in order to fulfill a math requirement; at other schools, logic may be taught in the math department. Training in research methods was part of my preparation for graduate work in English. Both these courses taught me how to recognize, establish, and test a hypothesis and substantiate the results through logical deduction and the use of objective evidence.

Computer skills also are essential for any medical communicator in today's job market. Whether your chosen school offers computer courses or not, you should learn to use at least one word processing software package (for example, WordPerfect or Microsoft Word), gain hands-on experience with desktop publishing, and know about computerized graphics programs, World Wide Web development, and multimedia authoring tools. Writers have traditionally been slow to adopt technological tools to aid their writing, but medical writers and editors cannot afford that luxury since we work in a very technologically oriented industry.

While it is possible to break into entry-level positions in medical communication with a major in English or the life sciences, you are going to be better prepared and a more attractive job prospect if you combine these two. You might, for example, pursue a double major in science and technical communication, or major in English, communications, or journalism and minor in a life science, such as biology or biochemistry.

If you have to choose between the two, major in one of the life sciences and take as many courses as possible in English and communication. From my own experience and that of others, I know that many employers in this field will look first and hardest at the science component of your college preparation. If you major in English, as I did, and are not heavily fortified with a battery of life science courses, as I was not, you will have a more difficult time selling your credentials to an employer. A friend of mine with a PhD in English from the University of Michigan and a good deal of experience as a business writer was turned down for a job as a copyeditor at the journal *Radiology* because she did not have a strong science background. The medical editor of this journal, himself a published radiologist, refused to hire anyone but a "scientist" for editorial work at his journal.

On-the-Job Training

This form of education may be as formal as student internships and employee training programs or as informal as the age-old learn-by-doing method. Much of my practical training in medical editing and writing came from the latter, but the former options may be easier to find. Especially as a student, you should take advantage of internships wherever they are available. When you are choosing a school or program, ask about student internships in your field. Many schools with undergraduate technical communications programs offer internships during the junior or senior year. For example, several students in the technical communication program at Ferris State University in Big Rapids, Michigan, performed paid internships at the Warner Lambert-Parke Davis company in Ann Arbor, largely because Douglas Haneline, the students' academic adviser, knew about the internship program and its sponsors through his contacts in AMWA. Warner Lambert-Parke Davis is a large pharmaceutical manufacturer, and its research division in Ann Arbor has developed a strong internship program. During their internships in the Clinical Communications department there, the Ferris State students gained practical experience helping to prepare technical reports. One of the students was hired as a full-time medical writer after she graduated.

If you are already working for a company, take advantage of company training courses or programs. These courses may be given on-site at the company headquarters; they may be provided by in-house training personnel or other qualified employees; or they may be offered at outside locations, conferences, or training centers. At the Warner Lambert-

Parke Davis Pharmaceutical Division, the Clinical Communications department regularly offers its writers and editors training workshops, like the workshop on biomedical statistics that AMWA regularly conducts for medical writers.

Even if you are not yet in the medical communications field, look for related training that can help prepare you for the transition or the opportunity when it arises. You may already have your college degree, and it may even be in communication, but your practical education is still ahead of you. A college education is only the first step in a lifelong educational process. Be aggressive in ferreting out these training opportunities. Scan bulletin boards for postings and announcements, read the company newsletter, and talk to staff in other departments. The human resources department may be an especially good place to find information about these offerings. Besides the educational value of on-the-job training, you'll meet others with similar professional interests, and these contacts may help you in your job search and career development. You can also add such training courses to your resume to show a prospective employer that you are serious about becoming a qualified professional in your chosen field.

Professional Training and Continuing Education

Like professionals in many other fields, the successful medical communicator makes career learning and preparation a lifelong experience. But unlike many other professional fields, continuing education, both formal and informal, is absolutely essential in medical communication. This is true partly because there are relatively few full-fledged academic programs, especially at the graduate level, to provide the beginning writer with the tools of the trade and the requisite body of knowledge in medical communications, and partly because the continually changing nature of modern medicine demands that we constantly keep up with the latest developments in medical technology and scientific discovery.

Although there are many ways to continue your education throughout your career, look first to professional organizations and societies for courses, workshops, and continuing education programs. For medical communicators, there are at least three organizations you should investigate: the American Medical Writers Association, the Council of Biology Editors, and the Society for Technical Communication. All three have vigorous, well established educational programs and yearly conferences where a wide range of workshops and courses is offered. You can find out more about these organizations by contacting their national offices at the addresses listed in the Appendix at the end of this chapter.

The education program of AMWA is the one I am most familiar with. Not only have I taken and taught workshops in this program for many years, but for two years I was the Director of the AMWA Education Department. Started about 20 years ago, the AMWA program has developed two levels of course offerings: the Core Curriculum program, with over 60 courses in six specialty areas of biomedical communication, and an Advanced Curriculum for experienced medical communicators. At each level, the participant may complete a course of study to earn a certificate in one of these specialty areas: audiovisual techniques, editing/writing, freelance writing, pharmaceutical writing, writing for public relations/advertising/marketing, and teaching. A multidisciplinary certificate is also available in two or more specialty areas. Core and Advanced Curriculum courses are offered at the AMWA conference each year in the late fall, as well as at selected regional sites and by state and local chapters.

In 1995, at the annual conference in Baltimore, Maryland, 73 courses were given: 42 Core Curriculum courses (for example, Writing Abstracts, Preparing Tables and Graphs, and Scope of Medical Communications) and nine Advanced Curriculum courses (for example, Microediting, Macroediting, and Computer Searching the Medical Literature). In addition, 22 special interest workshops were given on topics as wide-ranging as Medical Reference Resources on the Internet and Anatomy and Physiology for Poets.

If you are interested in learning more about the AMWA education program, contact the AMWA national office for a brochure outlining the requirements and course offerings. For more detailed information about the course content of specific Core Curriculum workshops, I recommend a 1994 AMWA publication, *Biomedical Communication: Selected AMWA Workshops* (Minick, 1994). Subtitled "A Practical Guide for Writers, Editors, and Presenters of Health Science Information," this book contains chapters based on over 20 long-standing Core and Advanced Curriculum workshops, each written by an AMWA member who has given that workshop.

AMWA workshops are taught by experienced medical communicators, who volunteer their time at the annual conference to share their expertise with other professionals. The courses and workshop leaders are regularly evaluated, reviewed, and graded through course evaluations filled out by participants and by means of monitoring procedures developed in the AMWA Education Department. While you needn't be an AMWA member to take courses in this program, you must be a member to earn a certificate.

Gaining certification or accreditation in your profession is a primary goal of many who participate in continuing education programs. To practice as a medical writer or editor, you do not have to be licensed by law or accredited by any professional organization or licensing agency. However, many medical writers and editors consider it important for professional recognition and career promotion to have some form of professional certification. One purpose of the AMWA education program is to allow members to earn a certificate as a biomedical communicator. This certificate, however, represents only AMWA approval; it is not the same as a license or the kind of board certification that physicians must obtain in order to practice medicine.

If you are specializing in biomedical editing, you should also know about the certification program of the Board of Editors in the Life Sciences (BELS). Developed over the last decade primarily through the Council of Biology Editors (CBE) but with support and input from AMWA as well, this board is now an independent agency that provides certification for manuscript editors in the life sciences through examination and credential review modeled on the certification procedures of other scientific and medical professions. Karen F. Phillips' 1993 article in the *AMWA Journal* describes the development of the BELS program. Besides CBE and AMWA, the European Association of Science Editors also supports BELS.

Beyond these professional societies for medical, scientific, and technical writers and editors, other organizations and institutions offer a vast array of training opportunities. Continuing adult education is big business for many groups and a way of life for many individuals. Possibilities for continuing education range all the way from local community educational offerings—I regularly receive mailings for at least three of these every fall and spring—to Elder Hostel programs for the over-50 set—I'm on that mailing list too. To help you focus your search, I recommend the *Directory of Publications Resources,* a biennial publication from Editorial Experts, Inc. (EEI). In its own words, EEI "publishes professional books for editors and writers and *The Editorial Eye,* a subscription newsletter focusing on standards and practices of excellence in publications." The 1993-94 *Directory,* subtitled "Selected Books, Software, Periodicals, Organizations, Courses, Contests, Grammar Hotlines, and Tools," contains 10 pages that describe training opportunities; these are divided into three sections, one for 41 single-location programs (most of which are affiliated with universities), 10 programs with various locations, and 4 that offer correspondence courses.

Desirable Personality Traits for a Medical Communicator

The academic skills needed to be a good medical communicator are relatively easy to come by if you plan carefully, choose wisely, and follow through. But what kind of personal attributes make a good medical communicator? Look again at the job ads from the AMWA *Job Market Sheet* in the section on "Your Life as a Medical Communicator." Many of these spell out the attributes desired in a medical communicator. Communication skills, of course, are a given, including the so-called "people" or interpersonal skills, especially if you are going to be a medical editor working in publications or an author's editor. For these jobs, you need infinite quantities of patience, tact, and persistence. Intellectually, I give special emphasis to a love of language and fascination with words; curiosity and an unflagging passion for learning something new; and a logical, analytical mind. It helps, too, if you have excellent organizational abilities, an underrated talent in the business world. You should be able to work independently or cooperatively with a team, since both situations will present themselves regularly. The ability to compromise and negotiate solutions is also vital, whether those are editorial (that is, changing sentences or language in a manuscript when the author doesn't understand what is wrong with the original version) or human (persuading team members to cooperate on project deadlines or meeting times).

The ability to work independently also implies the ability to work under deadline pressure or meet deadlines effectively. In fact, a deadline mentality is absolutely essential in medical communication, probably even more so than in other forms of writing and editing work. Not only must you be able to tolerate deadlines, often unreasonably short ones, but you must actually thrive on them. Unless your adrenaline level is pumped over the top by the race to the deadline, you should probably consider a less stressful line of work.

Finally, you should have a strong, confident sense of self but not need or desire to be a superstar. Medical communication is a support service in a high-powered industry with more than its share of big egos and scientific superstars. Physicians are used to giving orders and getting their way. You won't find too many Walter Mittys in medicine and the biomedical research community. To work effectively with such people, you must be able to walk a narrow tightrope between mild-mannered compliance with the demands of others and a strong-minded determination to assert and protect your own professional standards. If you are going to function effectively as a medical editor or writer in this highly charged environment, you need confidence in your skills and the value of the service you provide; those skills and your service may be challenged or dismissed as unnecessary by those who are not used to having their writing questioned or corrected. At the same time, remember that you are providing a support service. If your ego is easily wounded when your expertise is questioned, or if you are offended when your writing is changed (just as physicians or scientists may be when you change their writing) or your editorial suggestions are ignored, then you may do better in a communication field where you can claim direct ownership for your writing.

FINDING A JOB

My recommendations for getting a job in medical communication are much the same as my advice to students trying to break into any professional field:

- go where the jobs are,
- get practical job experience through an internship or part-time job,
- network with anyone who may be a possible job contact,
- join professional organizations.

All of these recommendations are equally important, and none of them takes precedence over the others. You should follow all of them in some fashion and more than one of them at the same time. Here are a few specific guidelines for each of these recommendations.

Go Where the Jobs Are

In medical communications, the greatest concentration of job opportunities geographically is on the eastern seaboard. By the eastern seaboard, I mean the whole area from Maryland and Washington, DC up to Massachusetts and Connecticut, but especially the area around New York City and New Jersey. Many pharmaceutical companies, in particular, are located in New Jersey. Other good areas are in northern California—in particular, the Bay Area around San Francisco, which is the home base of some pharmaceutical companies and biotechnology firms. In the Midwest, the best place is the Chicago metropolitan area and the lower Midwest, since, like the area around New York City, Chicago is the base for a large number of medically related industries. In the South, Atlanta, Georgia, is the home of the Centers for Disease Control, and Chapel Hill and Research Triangle Park in North Carolina have emerged as a growth area for medical communicators in the last few years.

To get an idea of the geographical concentration of jobs in medical communication, check out a few issues of the AMWA *Job Market Sheet* I've mentioned before. For example, when I scanned the July/August 1995 issue, 13 of 19 want ads for medical writers or editors were for jobs on the eastern seaboard: four in New York, three in Pennsylvania, and two each in New Jersey, Connecticut, and Maryland. As you're doing your job search, keep in mind that support services for any industry tend to concentrate in or near that industry's headquarters, although this fact may be changing somewhat in today's global marketplace, networked with fax machines and wired by the electronic superhighway.

How do you find out more about the companies in these locations? Go to your college placement office or library and ask for business directories that list companies by geographical location and their type of business. These directories are usually published or updated annually, and some contain brief descriptions of the type of work or kind of employment opportunities these companies offer.

If you don't already live in one of the central locations I've mentioned, or if you have no desire or ability to move, you can still find a good job. Any city or metropolitan area with a large medical center or several major hospital and health care systems will provide job opportunities in medical communication. If the area is also home to a university with a good medical school, so much the better for your job prospects. In fact, the two usually exist in a symbiotic, interdependent relationship: If the location has a large medical center, it is also likely to have a respectable medical school, or vice versa.

The Detroit metropolitan area, for example, where I have lived for more than 30 years, has both these features. Besides the Henry Ford Hospital system with its network of satellite medical facilities, there are at least three or four other competing, hospital-based, health care systems in the Detroit metropolitan area. These health care giants are also the major teaching hospitals for interns and residents training in medical schools at Wayne State University in Detroit and the University of Michigan in Ann Arbor. All of these hospital and academic medical centers employ medical communicators in one capacity or another.

Get Practical Experience

It's a catch-22 dilemma for anyone (regardless of age or previous academic credentials) that when you start out in a new field, your chances of getting a good job are much better if you have at least a year or two of practical experience in that field. But how do you get the practical experience until you get that first job? Here is where student internships are especially valuable. Another recourse for novice medical communicators is to take a part-time job or freelance project with the company or industry you are targeting. If you can't break into your target company immediately, look for similar jobs or projects in other companies that are like your target or do business with your target. Offering to take on a freelance project for a prospective employer may seem self-defeating when you really want full-time employment, but it's an excellent way to gain practical experience. Companies may be more willing to give you a chance on a freelance project or a short-term basis since they are limiting their risk and their financial investment. Once you have proven your ability, you may be able to negotiate a permanent job or long-term arrangement. If all else fails, you've gained practical experience to add to your resume.

It's also important to define your previous work broadly rather than narrowly, and positively rather than negatively, especially if you are changing careers rather than just starting out after college graduation. This was one technique I used when I applied for my first job in medical communication. Although I had never worked as a medical editor, I had been a freelance editor for the Wayne State University Press and a part-time copy editor at the Bureau of Business Research at the University of Michigan Graduate School of Business Administration. I had also done some typing and proofreading of medical articles for a local allergist when I was an undergraduate English major. With these experiences, coupled with my PhD in English, I was able to persuade my prospective employer that I had the qualifications to be a medical editor. Needless to say, I did not emphasize the fact that I had no academic training in medicine, health care, or the life sciences; and I certainly did not mention that the only science courses I had taken in college were botany and geology.

Network With Possible Job Contacts

Business networking has become a cliché for today's college graduates. The axiom that it's not what you know but who you know has been parlayed into books, careers, courses, workshops, and even movies. But it's still true, especially in a relatively small field like medical communication. Networking breaks down into several tasks: meeting people ("contacts"), gathering information, and following up on leads. Gather information about possible jobs from everyone you know—your parents, your parents' friends, your friends, your friends' parents, your college instructors, your neighbors, your past and current employers—you get the idea. Attend professional meetings and workshops where you are likely to meet prospective employers or make contacts with other professionals. Be polite but assertive in introducing yourself and your credentials. Don't ask for a job outright, but make it clear that you are looking for a job as a medical writer or editor. Ask for information about jobs in your contact's company or field.

If the prospects seem promising and you get a positive response from your contact, ask for a business card and the name of someone in that company you should contact about job openings. Then follow up any such leads with a phone call or letter within two weeks. Even if the contact is a dud and nothing comes of it, a short thank-you letter to the original contact is a good idea. If you do get a job interview or, best of all, a job offer as a result of the networking contact, send a thank-you letter to everyone you contacted. When you begin networking, you are building goodwill among your contacts as much as you are looking for a job. Professional courtesy, in the form of follow-up calls and thank-you letters, is more than good manners—it's good business sense as well.

Networking has another aspect that eager new job-seekers sometimes neglect. Think of it as the house that Jill (or Jack) built. While you are developing your own network of job information contacts, you are also tapping into a well-established network of contacts among experienced professionals in that field. Each person in that network has his or her own contacts in turn. They work together, they dine together, they play together (bridge or golf are favored), they commute together, they attend meetings together, they may even live together. So when you meet an experienced professional, you are potentially also making contact with everyone in that person's network. A good network is as sensitive as a finely-tuned musical instrument. For the gifted player, it is as valuable as a rare Stradivarius violin.

Join Professional Organizations

From my own experience, I cannot emphasize enough the value of becoming involved in a professional organization. As I mentioned earlier, the most prominent and largest organizations for medical communicators are the American Medical Writers Association, the Council of Biology Editors, and the Society for Technical Communication. Joining a professional organization is important for many reasons already discussed in this chapter, such as professional training and educational programs or job contacts and a job information network. Membership benefits in these organizations usually include access to their job search or employment services. AMWA distributes to members its bimonthly *Job Market Sheet*, which lists job openings throughout the industry, including freelance opportunities. This publication alone may be worth the price of AMWA membership to you. At the AMWA annual conference each year, an active job information exchange service and facilities are available for job-seekers and prospective employers so that they can easily meet and interview each other face-to-face in an informal setting.

Less tangible but equally important reasons to belong to a professional organization include the camaraderie and support of sharing experiences or "war stories" with others. Over the years, I have learned as much from my AMWA colleagues informally over dinner, in long-distance phone conversations, or at the theater or opera performances we attended together as in formal workshops and training sessions. A professional organization like AMWA can also provide you with opportunities for professional growth and development beyond the boundaries of your regular job. Because of my involvement in AMWA, I was able to develop my administrative and leadership skills in a way not possible to me at Henry Ford Hospital or in my own medical publications business. Kelley Williams, whose career is profiled in this chapter, has been able to blossom as an AMWA workshop leader in an educational setting more congenial to her talents than her daily workplace provided.

PROFESSIONAL PROFILES

The following profiles of two medical writers will give you some idea of the work these professionals do. Marilyn Citron is a freelance medical writer, while Kelley Williams is a medical editor at a large teaching hospital in the Midwest.

Marilyn Citron

Marilyn Citron has been a full-time freelance medical writer for the past 17 years. In 1991, she formed her own medical writing firm, Citron Communications, in Birmingham, Michigan. Before 1991, she was a freelance writer in Toronto, Ontario. During her eight years as a Canadian resident, she wrote articles, brochures, newsletters, monographs, press kits, historical pieces, and slide/tape packages for a variety of clients. In addition, Marilyn periodically worked on short contracts for the Canadian Cancer Society as a publication coordinator.

Marilyn has a strong interest in writing and producing materials on medical conditions that the general public can read and understand. She strives to translate complicated medical information and lingo into the language, style, and format that patients, health care consumers, and providers can understand. Marilyn believes that health care information should be clearly written and free of gobbledygook and technical jargon.

Her client list runs the whole gamut of organizations and institutions that employ medical writers: hospitals like Detroit's Henry Ford Health Systems, publication offices like the Cleveland Clinic Foundation Office of Scientific Publications, health care organizations like the Canadian Diabetes Association and the Canadian Cancer Society, government agencies like the Ontario Ministry of Health, biological companies conducting research like Connaught Laboratories in Toronto, diagnostic product manufacturers like the Diagnostics Division of Miles Canada, and managed health care organizations like the Health Alliance Plan of Michigan.

She has written articles on health care subjects for special interest magazines such as *Family Practice*, *HAPlines*, *Hospital News*, *Arthritis News*, and *Pharmacy Review*. In 1992, her article "A Fertile Prospect for Infertility," written for *Pharmacy Practice* (Canada) won the Distinguished Technical Communication Award for a technical publication from the Southeastern Michigan Chapter of the Society for Technical Communication. Other articles Marilyn has written include "High Anxiety: The Terror of Panic Disorder" for *Family Practice*; "Promoting Wellness in the Workplace" for *The Detroiter*; "AIDS Scorecard: Facts You Should Know" for *HAPLines*; and "Dialysis Decisions: Whose Choice Is It Anyway?" for *Renal Family*.

Marilyn researches articles like these by interviewing physicians and research scientists. She also spends hours, if not days, in the medical libraries of Wayne State University and the University of Michigan gathering the most up-to-date information on new diagnostic and therapeutic treatments for old medical problems like infertility or carpel tunnel syndrome. Armed with her tape recorder and laptop computer, she attends medical meetings, such as hospital grand rounds and seminars on specific conditions like osteoporosis or women's health issues. She records speakers presenting recent developments or describing the newest procedures for diagnosing and treating diabetes, inflammatory bowel disease, or panic disorder. She meets with graphic artists, designers, typesetters, photographers, and printers to coordinate the production of publications, such as *Urinalysis News*.

As sole proprietor of her own business, Marilyn also performs the myriad of day-to-day management tasks that any single business owner must handle—setting budgets, keeping books and accounting records, billing clients, tracking and managing project time, promoting her business to new clients, following up with old clients, and bidding on new projects. To build a client base, she recommends that the would-be freelancer make lists of health care organizations, communication and public relations agencies that have such organizations as clients, and medical and scientific journals. A freelance writer should also identify the person who assigns projects, write a letter enclosing samples of published work, and follow the letter in two weeks with a phone call.

Much of Marilyn's expertise in medicine and health care was gleaned from her education and experience as a medical technologist. She holds a bachelor of science degree in medical technology from the University of Michigan in Ann Arbor, a master of science degree in medical technology administration from Wayne State University, and a master of arts degree in adult and continuing education, and certificate in biomedical communications from the University of Nebraska. She worked for more than 10 years as a medical technologist, including a stint as chief technologist. After earning her MS, she started and directed a medical laboratory technician program at a Detroit community college. Upon completing her MA, she became a writer/producer for Business Marketing at Michigan Bell in Detroit. Like other medical writers who have adapted their education to careers other than the one they originally intended, Marilyn used her medical training and experience as a springboard to a career in medical writing.

Marilyn is also active in several professional and nonprofit, health-related associations. Like many medical writers, Marilyn belongs to the American Medical Writers Association, and she has appeared on the program at the AMWA National Conference on several occasions. From 1993–1995, she was President of the Michigan Chapter of AMWA. She is a board member of the Michigan Affiliate of the American Diabetes Association, a member of its Public Relations Committee, and a frequent speaker representing the organization's interests and goals. She is also a support group leader and speaker for the Alzheimer's Association—Detroit Area Chapter.

Where does a freelance medical writer like Marilyn Citron go from here professionally? Freelance medical writing is a satisfying career, even though sustaining it as a business is a constant challenge. In five years, Marilyn has established Citron Communications on a solid foundation. Now, as she strives to expand her client base, her goals are to increase her financial stability and gain greater professional recognition as a medical writer.

Carolyn Kelley Williams

Kelley Williams has been the medical editor in the Department of Obstetrics and Gynecology at Northwestern Memorial Hospital since 1975. Her present title is Senior Editor of Publications for Northwestern University Medical School. She also serves as the managing editor of the *International Journal of Gynecology and Obstetrics,* published by Elsevier, and the quarterly journal *Advances in Contraception,* published by Kluwer. Like my position as medical editor at Henry Ford Hospital, Kelley's position at Northwestern involves her in a wide range of writing, editing, and publications management tasks. She is, first of all, the department editor, and in this capacity, she edits, writes, and manages a variety of medical publications, including medical monographs and journal articles for specialty publications, as well as brochures, fund-raising publications, and journal articles for specialty publications. Her job also involves coordinating the efforts of authors, the publisher, other editors, designers, illustrators, other production personnel, and the printer in producing materials for publication.

A significant part of her responsibility as department editor is producing the Annual Report of the Department of Obstetrics and Gynecology, which contains a description of all publications, presentations, and research produced each year by physicians and scientists in the department. Since Northwestern Memorial Hospital is a teaching hospital for the Northwestern University Medical School, this report is an important vehicle for disseminating research results, as well as for documenting teaching and patient care accomplishments and innovations. Widely distributed to faculty, alumni, obstetrics/gynecology departments nationwide, and others interested in the teaching, research, and patient care activities of the department, the report is also used in faculty recruitment and fundraising. Kelley collects the information to be included, writes and edits all copy, and coordinates the production of the report, including design, printing, and distribution.

Kelley is also an author's editor and works directly with department authors to evaluate and edit their manuscripts (abstracts, journal articles, book chapters) for content, logic, stylistic consistency, correct grammar, punctuation, and clarity of expression. Beyond the actual manuscript itself, Kelley represents and champions the cause of the author in contacts with the publisher, whether that publisher is a medical journal, book publisher, medical society, or some other publishing entity. Over the years, she has developed a worldwide network of contacts in the medical publishing industry to help her represent the interests of the author and of her department.

Her final area of responsibility involves being managing editor and publication consultant for monographs and reference texts in gynecology and obstetrics, such as the six-volume annual reference series, *Gynecology and Obstetrics*, published by Lippincott/Kluwer, which she has helped produce since 1975. Between 1975 and 1986, she was managing editor of publications for the Program for Applied Research in Fertility Regulation (PARFR), located at Northwestern University. In this capacity, Kelley co-edited the 10 reference volumes comprising the PARFR

Series on Fertility Regulation and was managing editor of a monograph series on advances in the field of contraception.

Even before she took her present job at Northwestern, Kelley was a medical writer. Almost as soon as she graduated from college, she became the editorial assistant to Dr. Walter C. Alvarez, the editor-in-chief of *Modern Medicine and Geriatrics* and an internationally syndicated newspaper columnist, best-selling author, and radio/TV personality. She worked for him for 14 years until his retirement in 1975. Kelley credits Dr. Alvarez with teaching her the language of medicine and much that she needed to know about medical editing and writing.

Kelley's academic background includes a bachelor of arts in English literature and theatre from Northwestern University and graduate studies at the University of Illinois, Roosevelt University, and the Art Institute of Chicago. Her degree in English is an important qualification for someone pursuing a career in technical or medical writing and editing. Although she had no academic training in medicine or science beyond basic courses required of English majors, she has always been a writer and editor.

Kelley's first love, in fact, is writing poetry. She is an accomplished poet who published poetry in several poetry magazines (*Primavera, Silo, Poet Lore*) long before she became a medical editor. Nor have her demanding responsibilities in the Department of Obstetrics and Gynecology at Northwestern Medical School dimmed her interest in poetry and dramatic performance. Quite the opposite. She has become well known in the Chicago area for the performances of poetry, song, and dance she produces with other poets and performance artists. Besides public performances of a choreographic production of her poem "Arriving at Onion" and programs of poetry performance and song that Kelley and her performing group, World Enough and Time, have produced and performed in the Midwest, she has also produced two poetry and music videotapes. Kelley is presently completing her novel, *The Realm of Persephone*, a mythopoetic story of healing set in Chicago and Amsterdam.

Kelley's unflagging energy and creativity have extended into other areas of her professional life as well. She has been active in the American Medical Writers Association for many years and became its president in 1986–87. She is an outstanding workshop leader and has given many educational AMWA workshops in the last ten years. In 1989, her teaching abilities earned her the AMWA Golden Apple Award, the highest award AMWA bestows on educators in the organization. In 1993, she also received the Swanberg Award, the highest honor given by AMWA to one of its members. Kelley has developed and presented numerous workshops and seminars for writers and editors on such topics as goal setting, negotiation, and making effective presentations.

Since 1985, Kelley's teaching talents have taken her on a new journey, launching her on the Intensive Journal program founded by psychologist Dr. Ira Progoff. After studying with Dr. Progoff, she became a registered Journal Consultant in 1991; she gives workshops throughout the Midwest on keeping a structured journal by means of the Intensive Journal process.

Medical editor/writer, poet, novelist, performance artist, publications consultant, educator, organizer, leader—Kelley's kaleidoscopic talents have taken her to the top of her profession and brought her rewards and recognition. During her undergraduate years at Northwestern, her ambition was to be a dancer and actress. She could not have predicted where her writing talents would lead her. When Kelley began in 1962 as an editorial assistant for Dr. Alvarez, the career of a medical writer/editor was uncharted territory. In some ways, it still is. But because of accomplished professionals like Kelley, young medical writers and communicators today have role models to admire, mentors to guide them, and more clearly defined opportunities to pursue their goals, both in college programs and in professional settings.

APPENDIX

FURTHER INFORMATION

For a more comprehensive annotated listing of organizations and other resources for writers and editors, see the 1996 edition of *My big sourcebook: For people who work with words and pictures*, listed below.

Professional Organizations

American Medical Writers Association (AMWA)
9650 Rockville Pike
Bethesda, MD 20814
(301) 493-0003
Fax: (301) 493-0005

Council of Biology Editors
111 East Wacker Drive, Suite 200
Chicago IL 60601

(312) 616-0800

Society for Technical Communication
901 North Stuart Street, Suite 904
Arlington, VA 22203-1854
(703) 522-4114
Fax: (703) 522-2075

Style Manuals, Guides, and Dictionaries

American Medical Association manual of style (9th ed.). (1998). C. Iverson, Chair. Baltimore: Williams and Wilkins.

Dorland's illustrated medical dictionary (26th ed.). (1985). Philadelphia: WB Saunders.

Encyclopedia of Associations (1993) (27th ed.), Vol. 1, Part 2. Detroit, MI: Gale Research.

Haubrich, W. (1984). *Medical meanings: A glossary of word origins.* New York: Harcourt Brace Jovanovich.

Huth, E. (1987). *Medical style and format: An international manual for authors, editors, and publishers.* Philadelphia: ISI Press.

Style Manual Committee: Council of Biology Editors. (1994). *Scientific style and format: The CBE style manual* (6th ed.). Cambridge, England: Cambridge University Press.

Reference Publications for Medical and Scientific Writing

Bailar, J. C. and F. Mosteller. (1988). Guidelines for statistical reporting in articles for medical journals: Amplifications and explanations. *Annals of Internal Medicine, 108,* 266–73.

Day, R. A. (1988). *How to write and publish a scientific paper* (3rd ed.). Phoenix, AZ: Oryx Press.

International Committee of Medical Journal Editors. (1997). Uniform requirements for manuscripts submitted to biomedical journals. *JAMA, 227,* 927–34.

Kirkham, E. B. (1992). *Career opportunities in healthcare/pharmaceutical communications.* Cupertino, CA: Technical Communications Dept., De Anza College.

Minick, P. (Ed.). (1994). *Biomedical communications: Selected AMWA workshops.* Bethesda, MD: American Medical Writers Association.

O'Connor, Maeve. (1991). *Writing successfully in science.* Chapman & Hall.

Schwager, Edith. (1991). *Medical English usage and abusage.* Phoenix, AZ: Oryx Press.

Witte, F. and N.D. Taylor. (Ed.). (1997). *Essays for Biomedical Communicators: Volume 2 of Selected AMWA Workshops.* Bethesda, MD: American Medical Writers Association.

Ziegler, Mimi. (1991). *Essentials of writing biomedical research papers.* New York: McGraw-Hill.

Professional Journals and Newsletters

American Medical Writers Association Journal
9650 Rockville Pike
Bethesda, MD 20814
Quarterly journal published by the American Medical Writers Association.

The Editorial Eye
66 Canal Center Plaza, Suite 200
Alexandria, VA 2314-5507
Newsletter published monthly by Editorial Experts, Inc.

Journal of Technical Writing and Communication
26 Austin Avenue, Box 337
Amityville, NY 11701
Quarterly journal published by Baywood Publishing Co.

STC Intercom
901 North Stuart Street, Suite 904
Arlington, VA 22203-1854
Bimonthly newsletter published by the Society for Technical Communication.

Technical Communication
Arlington, VA
Quarterly journal published by the Society for
Technical Communication.

Technical Communication Quarterly
The University of Minnesota
Department of Rhetoric
202 Haecker Hall
1364 Eckles Avenue
St. Paul, MN 55108-6122
Quarterly journal published by the Rhetoric Department at the
University of Minnesota for the Association of Teachers of
Technical Writing.

Directories

My big sourcebook: For people who work with words or pictures. (1996).
Alexandria, VA: EEI Press.

1997–1998 freelance directory of medical communication services (14th edition). (1997). Bethesda, MD: American Medical Writers Association.

NOTES

[1]See the *Freelance directory of medical communication services* (14th ed.). Bethesda, MD: American Medical Writers Association, 1997, pp. 3 ff. for a comprehensive "Services Index" of types of medical writing services, from abstracting to writing.

[2]For a detailed analysis of 1994 salaries for medical communicators in various job categories, see the article by K. E. Hermes on the 1994 AMWA Salary Survey in the *American Medical Writers Association Journal*, 10, No. 2 (1995), 88–92.

[3]Besides writing and editing, medical communications encompasses medical art, illustration, and photography; desktop publishing; slide and video scriptwriting and production; and even computer software development.

[4]In the following discussion, I will illustrate my points with typical job ads for medical communicators taken from the AMWA Job Market Sheet, a bimonthly publication for members of the American Medical Writers Association. These ads specify the types of settings and organizations and the qualifications that jobseekers in this field should have. See the sections in this chapter on "Preparation" and "Additional Resources" for more information about the American Medical Writers Association.

[5]One common way to define the size of a hospital is by the number of beds it has available for patients.

[6]"A rare condition characterized by severe and recurrent peptic ulcers in the stomach, duodenum, and upper small intestine." *The American Medical Association Encyclopedia of Medicine*, ed. Charles B. Clayman, New York: Random House, 1989, p. 1088.

[7]Developments in making NLM resources available electronically through the Internet were discussed at the 1995 Annual Conference of The American Medical Writers Association, in a plenary session entitled "Using Information Technology in Teaching Medical Communications."

[8]I'd like to thank Jane Smith-Purslow, C.T., B.S., Supervisor of the Cytopathology Laboratory at Henry Ford Hospital (Detroit), for her advice and suggestions for this section.

REFERENCES

American Medical Writers Association. (May 1993). *Job Market Sheet.*

American Medical Writers Association. (July/August 1993). *Job Market Sheet.*

American Medical Writers Association. (September 1993). *Job Market Sheet.*

American Medical Writers Association. (February 1995). *Job Market Sheet.*

Cornett, P. (1988). AMWA and the biomedical communicator: From here to the year 2000: Challenges and opportunities for the future. *American Medical Writers Association Journal, 3,* (4), 24–25.

Eastman, J. D., Smith E. O., & Klein, E. R. (1990). Medical writers and editors should learn fundamentals of statistical principles. *American Medical Writers Association Journal, 5,* (1), 14–17.

Encyclopedia of Associations (1993) (27th ed.), Vol. 1, Part 2. Detroit, MI: Gale Research.

Haneline, D. & Turpin, E. R. (1991). Results of the higher education survey demonstrate increasing link with academia. *American Medical Writers Association Journal, 6,* (3), 10–16.

Hermes, K. E. (1994). AMWA salary survey: A brief report. *American Medical Writers Association Journal, 10,* (1), 88–92.

Krauhs, J. M. (1994). Statistics for medical writers and editors: Meeting the guidelines for statistical reporting. In P. Minick (Ed.), *Biomedical communications: Selected AMWA Workshops* (pp. 48–56). Bethesda, MD: American Medical Writers Association.

Minick, P. (Ed.). (1994). *Biomedical communications: Selected AMWA Workshops.* Bethesda, MD: American Medical Writers Association.

Phillips. K. F. (1993). The BELS program: Certification for manuscript editors in the life sciences. *American Medical Writers Association Journal, 8* (2), 56–58.

chapter 9

Pharmaceutical Writing

Sandra J. Lobbestael
AZTECH Communications
Dexter, Michigan

Jobs

- *Staff*: (bio)medical writer, clinical writer, medical editor, senior medical writer.
- *Management*: group leader, supervisor, manager, director.

Responsibilities

- *Writer and editor*: write documents according to specified guidelines, summarize large amounts of clinical data, distribute draft documents for others' review, conduct meetings to discuss draft document review, edit draft documents to reflect consensus, prepare manuscripts for publication of data in peer-reviewed journals, participate on project teams. Participate in miscellaneous projects, such as preparing abstracts, poster presentations, review articles, copy for slides or videos, handbooks, standard operating procedures, newsletters, and educational materials.
- *Supervisor*: interview, hire, and train other writers; conduct meetings; allocate resources; set policy; plan and monitor progress of writing projects; evaluate performance; prepare budgets; contract with outside resources; and participate on project teams.

Employment Outlook

Rapidly changing environment that requires skill in writing and information technology, as well as the ability to function effectively in teams.

Salary Range

For writers, $25,000 to $60,000; for supervisors, $50,000 to $85,000, plus stock options and bonuses.

INTRODUCTION

If you write in the pharmaceutical industry, your main work will be to produce documents that are included in various submissions to regulatory authorities worldwide. In fact, since most of your writing will be communications that are submitted to the U.S. Food and Drug Administration (FDA), your job as a writer will be to present scientific concepts to this target audience. In this work, excellence in communication is assumed, computer skills are fundamental, organizational and analytical skills are essential, and impossible deadlines are routine. Knowledge of governmental regulations and guidelines, as well as the specialized terminology used in them, is beneficial. The rate of change in the pharmaceutical industry is rapid. And no one survives without flexibility and a sense of humor. The following section will give you an appreciation for why this is so.

The Drug Development Process

The pharmaceutical industry is regulated by the FDA, which was formally included as a unit of the Department of Health and Human Services in 1988. The FDA's mandate is consumer protection, and it has three branches that regulate drugs, biologics, and medical devices, respectively. It derives its power from federal laws that have been enacted (and amended) since 1848 to address the purity, safety, and effectiveness of food and drugs. The Federal Food, Drug, and Cosmetic Act was originally enacted in 1938. In its presently amended form, generally referred to as the Act, it is the primary legislation for the pharmaceutical industry.

Like all government agencies, the FDA publishes its regulations in the *Code of Federal Regulations* (CFR) and amends them by periodic updates that appear in the *Federal Register*. Title 21 of the CFR contains the volumes with regulations pertaining to the Act. Regulations are numbered to correspond with the related federal laws.

For example, Parts 300-499 of Title 21 of the CFR (i.e., 21 CFR § 300-499) describe the regulations about drugs for human use—new drugs, new drug applications, and antibiotics. 21 CFR § 600-799 has equivalent regulations for biologics, diagnostics, and cosmetics, while 21 CFR § 800-1299 contains the regulations for medical devices.

In addition, government agencies issue guidelines for all parts of the CFR to help people comply with the requirements. Penalties for failure to comply with regulations are also detailed in the CFR.

The FDA's Center for Drug Evaluation and Research (CDER) regulates drugs, drug labeling, and drug advertising. It is integral to the work of the pharmaceutical industry. The other branches of the FDA are the Center for Biologic Evaluation and Research (CBER) and the Center for Devices and Radiological Health (CDRH).

The ever-increasing restrictions imposed by laws and regulations have significantly increased the time and cost to get drugs on the market. Initially, chemists synthesize new molecular entities (NMEs), which are drug substances (i.e., the active part of a drug) they hope will be promising in their company's *in vitro* (in an artificial environment outside a living organism, such as a test tube or petri dish) and *in vivo* (in a living organism, such as a mouse or a rat) laboratory tests. If the data from such preclinical testing support the hypothesis that the NME is both safe and effective for some human condition or disease, the company summarizes the available information and submits an Investigational New Drug Application (IND) to the FDA. An IND is effectively a request to start testing a drug product (i.e., a specific formulation of the drug) in humans. The formulation (e.g., tablet, capsule, solution) generally has components other than the active part.

If there is no response from the FDA within 30 days, the company can begin small-scale testing of the drug in a few subjects who do not have the condition or disease for which the drug may be used. These are called healthy subjects, and the safety of the drug is carefully monitored in them. Later, the drug is tested in restricted numbers of subjects who have the condition or disease for which the drug may be used. The company continues to monitor the drug's safety in these subjects, but also evaluates its effectiveness in them. If this testing confirms that the drug is effective, the company then tests it in clinical studies with hundreds of human subjects who have the condition or disease.

During these clinical studies, also called clinical trials, no one knows whether a subject is receiving a test drug or a placebo. This kind of study is called a double-blind clinical study. Results of each double-blind study are summarized as a Clinical Study Report (CSR). These individual reports are sent to the FDA, usually within a few months of when each study is completed.

Animal testing continues throughout this time. All testing—human and animal—is designed to answer whether or not the drug has the effect that researchers have predicted, based on the preclinical models they have used, and an acceptable safety profile at the dose used to produce the desired effect.

This drug development process takes, on average, 12 years—the time during which many people are collecting, analyzing, summarizing, and reporting data. During the entire development program, annual reports of progress are submitted to the FDA and the company works on the production process for the drug product it intends to sell (for example, oral contraceptive tablets or a solution of penicillin).

When the drug has been tested in a sufficient number of subjects (100–5,000), all data from all studies on the drug are summarized in a New Drug Application (NDA), which is a compilation of information to support the intended claim that the drug is safe and effective for something. An NDA contains copies of all the CSRs prepared for individual studies conducted with the drug as well as integrated summaries of data for selected subsets of studies and for all studies. The NDA must be submitted to the FDA for their review and approval before a drug can be marketed.

Restructuring the Drug Development Process

Because the drug development process is so expensive and takes so much time, all aspects of it have come under review.

For example, pharmaceutical firms recently have begun to evaluate the processes by which they perform their work, looking for opportunities to increase efficiency and reduce costs. This sort of process improvement is called re-engineering, and the resultant enhancements will be dictated by the type of clinical research the firm does. For example, one firm may be able to use electronic data entry from a remote location for one clinical trial; another may be able to design modules for paper data collection to be used in all clinical trials. Regardless of the particulars for each firm, re-engineering is likely to significantly change the way pharmaceutical business is done.

A second way in which the drug development process is changing concerns the increased role played by Contract Research Organizations (CROs), which provide a variety of services to the pharmaceutical industry—from conducting portions of clinical studies to writing entire NDAs. This partnering has reduced the time it requires to get a drug to market, since a pharmaceutical firm can expand its staff with a CRO staff that is already trained. Advances in information technology also have enabled NDA preparers to handle data more efficiently so NDAs can be prepared more quickly.

Third, pharmaceutical firms, represented through the Pharmaceutical Research and Manufacturers of America (PhRMA), have worked with the FDA to identify ways the FDA can help speed the drug review and approval process. This collaborative effort is crucial to the future of the pharmaceutical industry. All would stand to gain, since the structure of the bureaucratic FDA is ill-equipped to respond to the pace of change occurring in the pharmaceutical industry, and the agency has become the proverbial bottleneck in the drug development process.

Evaluation of the drug development process has also included addressing insufficient resources at the FDA, which delays evaluation of INDs and NDAs. In response, The Prescription Drug User Fee Act (1992) authorized the FDA to collect fees (for approximately 2,000 products and 250 establishments that produce products) to hire staff in order to speed the drug review and approval process. In addition, beginning in 1995, all NDAs had to have a portion that is available electronically. These applications are called CANDAs, computer-assisted NDAs. By using computer technology, reviewers have immediate access to at least some of the data. Thus, they can evaluate the NDA much more rapidly, thereby speeding the review and approval process

Other changes being discussed include restructuring the FDA, eliminating certain NDA requirements, and using non-FDA experts to review portions of NDAs. Throughout these discussions, the FDA remains committed to its original mandate of consumer protection and refuses to allow any change that may compromise the safety of the public.

Furthermore, there is a cooperative effort among regulatory authorities worldwide under the auspices of the International Conference on Harmonization (ICH). This body, of which the FDA is a member, is evaluating ways to introduce uniformity to drug applications. To this end, they have already published proposed rules to standardize many documents used in drug applications worldwide. Thus, one company eventually may be able to prepare one application for a drug and submit it to any regulatory authority, worldwide, to obtain marketing approval.

With this globalization, there is a trend to acquire, merge, or buy out competitors or to form marketing alliances with them. While all this change is exciting, it requires a great deal of flexibility, constant renewing of one's skills, and expertise in communication and information technology. Medical writing for the pharmaceutical industry is not for the faint of heart, but it affords exhilaration like no other job, for your work will be essential in bringing new drugs to patients who need them.

YOUR LIFE AS A WRITER
IN THE PHARMACEUTICAL INDUSTRY

There are employment opportunities for pharmaceutical writers in many places. To date, the traditional pharmaceutical firms, such as Parke-Davis or Eli Lilly, have been the major employers of pharmaceutical writers. However, that is changing. More and more writers are being hired by CROs. In addition, many writers elect to be self-employed and contract with pharmaceutical companies directly or with various agencies that contract with pharmaceutical manufacturers to provide ad hoc writing expertise.

Regardless of where you secure employment in the pharmaceutical industry, your work will be directly or indirectly governed by regulations, often known by acronyms. Some common ones are GMPs, GLPs, GCPs, and SOPs, which refer to Good Manufacturing Practices, Good Laboratory Practices, Good Clinical Practices, and Standard Operating Procedures. There are many more of these acronyms, and new ones appear regularly. You will need to become familiar with them to converse with others in the industry. A glossary of acronyms used in this chapter appears in Appendix B.

Moreover, all your documents will need to be prepared according to specified guidelines. Some of these guidelines are imposed by pharmaceutical companies to ensure that all documents supporting a regulatory submission have the same style and format. Others are imposed by the FDA and detail the format and content required by this agency. You will be expected to know these guidelines and apply them to all your writing. Furthermore, you will need to know when changes are made to them since these changes will affect the writing you do.

Your role as an entry-level pharmaceutical writer will vary, depending on the company that hires you. Some firms employ writers for their editorial skills alone. In these organizations, you will be required to edit draft reports for accuracy, consistency, and style. Other firms employ writers to prepare draft reports, based on information received from others.

With experience, you may be assigned to prepare entire documents or portions of INDs and NDAs that use data from more than one report. Instead of working with data from one study, you will evaluate data from many studies.

You will then distribute these draft clinical study reports for others' review. On occasion, you will convene meetings for reviewers to discuss these documents, especially the conclusions derived. You may be required to negotiate common ground for issues that arise, and, later, you will revise documents to reflect consensus. Distribution and final review will follow, and then the report will be issued.

You may have other writing assignments from time to time, but report writing for regulatory submission will take about 90 percent of your time. Additionally, you may be asked to prepare manuscripts designed to publish the results of clinical studies.

As a supervisor, you may continue to be involved in writing and editing, but generally you will devote your time to managerial responsibilities. These duties include such things as coordinating the efforts of other writers, planning and allocating resources, representing department interests at interdepartmental meetings, training staff writers, writing performance evaluations and recommending salary increases, and creating various proposals. The types of proposals vary with the company, and may range from optimizing procedures to re-designing the writing department.

Since the success of a pharmaceutical firm is related to getting new drugs to market as early as possible, you will need to complete your work within aggressive time frames established by senior management.

TYPICAL JOBS AND RESPONSIBILITIES

Depending on the company into which you are hired, your organizational assignment as an entry-level writer could be with technical operations, clinical research, or drug regulatory affairs departments. The structure and size of the company and the nature of its business will determine your typical job and responsibilities. For example, if you work for a small company, you may work in the drug regulatory affairs department and be instrumental in all aspects of IND or NDA production. You may help design the index or write the technical summaries for either of these documents, or edit summaries written by others, or you may participate in the compilation and pagination of these documents. Alternatively, if you work in a very large company, you may report to a physician who directs the clinical development program for one drug. In that capacity, you may write various documents for a period of years as the program progresses.

The audience for the vast majority of your writing will be review medical officers at the FDA. These are board certified or board eligible physicians who are experts in their disciplines, such as pediatrics, hematology, or metabolism. Your writing for all regulatory documents will have to be at the level of a peer-reviewed scientific journal.

When you start, your title may be assistant medical writer, associate medical writer, or biomedical writer. It generally takes two years to get basic training as a pharmaceutical writer. During this time, you will learn about clinical research and the names of documents that are prepared to summarize the data derived from this research for submission to the FDA or other regulatory authorities. You will become familiar with guidelines, including any style manuals and report guidelines your company uses to reflect their interpretation of the guidelines published by the FDA. You will also very likely work on the following kinds of tasks.

Early Assignments

Early assignments often will involve your summarizing the results of clinical studies, such as one that evaluates the safety and effectiveness of an investigational drug. Data may have been collected for 10 subjects or 500, according to the protocol designed by the clinical scientist. You will receive input from members of your team, among them physicians, biometricians, computer programmers, and clinical scientists. You will need to understand enough of their disciplines to interact intelligently and ultimately draft a report to summarize the data they have generated, tabulated, and interpreted.

Preparing Clinical Study Reports

In working on clinical study reports, you will describe the objectives of the study, the methods used to conduct it, which subjects were allowed or not allowed to enter the study, the results of research on the safety and effectiveness of the drug in the population studied, a literature review, which will serve as background to the current results, and the conclusions supported by the study results. An abstract or synopsis of the results and table of contents are also required. Although all clinical study reports contain the same elements, the complexity of the reports varies with the type of study that was conducted.

The length of these reports also varies—with the number of patients for whom data were collected, the amount of data collected for each one, and the number of analyses performed on the data. A clinical study report on a few subjects could be 25 pages long with 300 pages of appendices containing the supporting documentation. Appendices usually include supplemental tables and graphs, listings of patient data, and summary tables to describe group data. Larger reports could be 150 pages long with 2,500 pages of appendices.

You may have one week to prepare the draft for a small study, two to three weeks for large studies. Once you have prepared the draft, you will then distribute copies of it to members of your clinical study team for their review. Review comments generally are returned to you within days, and it will be your job to evaluate them. If you get conflicting comments, you may have to schedule a review meeting for discussion. You will then prepare the revised draft within one week and distribute it for review by the team as well as by upper management. The process repeats until consensus is achieved and the report is ready to be issued.

Often, a quality assurance audit is required before the report can be submitted to the FDA. Such an audit involves independent evaluation of the report to verify that study data have been analyzed, summarized, and reported accurately.

Clinical study reports are the bread and butter of pharmaceutical writing. They are the basis of many other documents, such as investigator's brochures and new drug applications. Indeed, you may write investigator's brochures in the early stages of your career.

Preparing Investigator's Brochures

An investigator's brochure ranges from 15 to 250 pages and describes the information a physician would need to safely administer an investigational drug (one that is being tested for its effects on people) to a human subject. You may be asked to prepare or revise such a brochure, which typically summarizes many studies for one investigational drug. For example, it may summarize data only from animal studies and *in vitro* studies or it may summarize data from *in vitro* studies, animal studies, and clinical trials (in humans). The investigator's brochure discusses known effects of the drug, conclusions from animal testing that may apply to humans, animal toxicity, what the body does to the drug (pharmacokinetics), and the study of the drug's action on living organisms (pharmacodynamics), such as animals and healthy subjects. The drug's effects on certain classes of subjects (those with kidney dysfunction, those in certain age ranges, and those who took the drug before or after eating) are also reported.

As with other documents in the pharmaceutical industry, the level of complexity in an investigator's brochure varies with the number of studies to be summarized and the number of parameters tested in each study. The first investigator's brochure is submitted with the IND for the drug. However, as more preclinical and clinical studies are completed, the investigator's brochure is revised to reflect the current knowledge about the drug. These revisions may occur at any interval, which is determined by the amount and timing of new information on the drug.

The review procedure used for investigator's brochures is similar to that used for a clinical study report. However, because the technical information in these brochures includes animal as well as human testing data, the reviewers come from all disciplines within the organization. Negotiating a consensus may require greater skill and more time, as vested interests may be in conflict. For example, when you revise an investigator's brochure, you may have to reduce the size of summaries for animal studies so you can keep the brochure to a reasonable number of pages while adding summaries for newly completed clinical trials. Laboratory scientists may believe their test results must remain as presented in the initial brochure; clinical scientists may believe that animal studies are not as relevant since the investigator now has the information available from human experience. How do you keep both of them happy and have a brochure of a size that an investigator can reasonably be expected to read, understand, and use?

Preparing Parts of Documents, Special Presentational Communications, and NDAs

You may also be assigned to prepare segments of larger documents. For example, you may be asked to prepare a tabular display of data that summarizes key information about all human pharmacokinetic studies. Your input would be the clinical study reports that had been issued. Having read and understood the reports, you would design an appropriate table with header information to indicate the types of information being presented. Then you would abstract the study information and enter it. The table would subsequently be reviewed for accuracy as well as consistency with other tables to be included in the same document.

Other kinds of assignments you may encounter early in your writing career include standard operating procedures, scientific publications, abstracts, posters, review articles, slides, handbooks, newsletters, video scripts, and other educational materials. Each type of document has a target audience that may or may not be the FDA. Accordingly, the focus must change to accommodate the intended reader. For example, standard operating procedures provide specific guidance to employees for routine activities (e.g., preparing a clinical study report) and allow for greater efficiency through standardization among employees. And they are required for much of the work done in the pharmaceutical industry. The audience for slides may be the FDA, as writers often assist in preparing slides for company presentations to the FDA or any of its Advisory Committees. Or the audience may be a group of physicians who specialize in a therapeutic field for which clinical research was performed by your company. The time to complete such assignments varies; however, rarely will any one take more than 10 percent of your time.

Preparing an NDA

The ultimate challenge, of course, is to prepare an NDA, the document that integrates all the data for a drug product. Since this assignment is critical in obtaining the approval required before a new drug can be marketed, it is usually reserved for writers with experience, often called medical writers or senior medical writers. Indeed, you may write for years and never have an opportunity to be involved in NDA preparation.

Most NDAs are enormous documents with many sections—all mandated by the FDA. The contents of an NDA are grouped by Item; the ones you are most likely to work on are described here. Item 1 is the NDA Index. Item 2, a 50–200-page summary of the entire NDA, contains information from all the other Items. Items 6, 7, and 8 contain various summary documents with (human) clinical data. Item 6 contains the pharmacokinetic and bioavailability data; Item 7 has microbiology data and is only submitted for antibiotics, and Item 8 contains summaries of clinical data in various documents that are described below.

One of the Item-8 documents presents an overview of the clinical investigations and is often referred to as the Background-Overview summary. It describes which studies were done, in what sequence, and why the development of the drug occurred as it did. It is a short document, usually fewer than 10 pages. However, it requires a lot of research and time to gather the necessary information.

Another Item 8 document, the clinical pharmacology summary (often called the "Clin-Pharm" summary), duplicates much of what is presented in Item 6. However, for Item 8, you will describe and analyze each clinical pharmacology study, comparing the study results with those obtained in animal studies. How you present your data and the analyses will be determined by the kinds of studies performed. Usually, however, presentation includes tabular displays with narrative to describe salient features and conclusions.

Two additional documents that you might have to create for Item 8 are the integrated summaries of effectiveness (ISE) and safety (ISS) for the drug. Because these two documents provide the basis on which you would be able to claim the drug's effectiveness and safety, they are crucial to the NDA. As such, they are high-visibility assignments, and the successive review cycles of their contents extend through the top management of the organization.

The Integrated Summary of Effectiveness contains data from all clinical studies that support the claimed indication—that is, the studies that let you prove that your drug will be effective in doing whatever you claim it will do. The ISE gives an overview of the demographics, effectiveness, and safety data from these studies, and includes those that provide evidence that you selected the right dose of the drug and the interval for prescribing it, as well as those that demonstrate modifications required for special populations, such as pediatric or elderly patients. An ISE can be 25 to 100 pages long. It may have appendices, particularly graphic and tabular supporting information. It always contains an abstract, which generally is confined to two pages, and a table of contents.

Its companion document, the Integrated Summary of Safety, summarizes all safety data obtained on the drug product in all studies. It is a summary and analysis that allows you to claim that the drug is safe to administer at the recommended dose and dosing interval. It may include discussions of safety data from animal studies as they apply to the use of the drug in humans. The ISS summarizes safety data in various ways, but not by individual studies. It looks at safety relative to the amount of drug to which a human is exposed and over what period; it analyzes safety on the per-subject basis as well as across all those who received the drug; it analyzes safety data from laboratory testing, electrocardiogram (ECG) data, X-ray data, and any other parameter by which safety has been measured during clinical trials; and it analyzes data by subsets of subjects stratified by age or sex. It, too, has an abstract, a table of contents, and appendices that contain supportive information.

The essence of the ISE and the ISS makes up the basis of the Benefit-to-Risk Statement, which is contained in Item 8 and duplicated in Item 2, the summary.

The major portion of the 50–200-page summary (Item 2) is clinical data. In fact, the clinical data contained in Items 6–8 are further condensed and incorporated into this summary. If the major summary documents were well prepared, portions of them can be lifted and placed into the summary. However, you may be required to edit them significantly to fit all of the relevant information into the pages allocated for the summary.

As with all documents, each NDA goes through a series of drafts and reviews until upper management is in full agreement with its contents. When all components are ready, the documentation is assembled as the NDA, according to FDA requirements. Depending on the size of the company and the size of the NDA, various people—usually in the drug regulatory affairs department—will check the NDA for quality and consistency of formatting. They will make certain that corporate style manuals have been adhered to so that the entire NDA has a uniform appearance. Also, they will ensure that pages, tables, and graphs are sequentially numbered and that graphs and other materials appear on the pages indicated in the table of contents. Many different kinds of edits are performed on an NDA before it is sent, and, because of all this activity, you may be required to revise an earlier clinical study report or edit selected pages of a summary document.

And just when you think you can relax from the hectic pace associated with NDA preparation, you must brace yourself for the various documents generally referred to as postsubmission documents. Four months after the submission of the NDA and whenever subsequently requested, you are required to submit updated safety information. If little additional safety data have been collected, the safety update is a short report to indicate that there has been no change in the safety profile of the drug. However, if the additional data are substantial, new written analyses may be required. Generally, the new information is compared with the safety data reported previously in the NDA. The validity of the NDA conclusions are subsequently substantiated or revised as appropriate.

Other postsubmission documents are called NDA Amendments and NDA Supplements. Amendments are documents that contain additional information about a new drug and are filed before an NDA is approved. Supplements are filed after approval. Each document is unique and can range from a few pages to the equivalent of an NDA in length, with entirely new analyses performed on an even larger database than that used for the NDA analyses.

Though few opportunities for management exist in medical writing, the management positions that are available generally require supervising the work of several writers, allocating resources, and planning with interdepartmental teams to be certain that needed writing expertise is available for projects. To supplement in-house writing expertise, managers may contract with freelance writers or CROs. Typical management titles are director, manager, supervisor, or group leader.

EMPLOYMENT OUTLOOK

Demand for pharmaceutical writers will continue; however, the type of employment may shift. Whereas most writers in this field are presently employed in major pharmaceutical firms, the trend in these firms is to replace permanent writers with temporary help. Some writing talent is secured through CROs; other writers are freelance talent employed on an ad hoc basis.

Salaries vary by region and by college degree, and they may be influenced by skills and experience. Starting salary for a BA or BS in the pharmaceutical industry in 1995 was $25,000-$30,000. For every five years of writing experience or for a higher college degree, you generally add $5,000 to the base salary. To this amount, one generally adds a corporate benefits package that is equal to one-fourth to one-third the base pay, so total remuneration is in the $30,000-$40,000 range. Some firms provide restricted stock options and an annual bonus.

Career advancement opportunities do exist, but not necessarily as a writer. You might advance along the line-management track, or you might move into other departments, such as quality assurance, clinical research, or drug regulatory affairs. As you are afforded visibility by the nature of your writing assignments, others will have an opportunity to see your talents and may offer you positions elsewhere in the company.

Future jobs will move toward preparing global registration documents and Standard Operating Procedures. They will generally entail much more computer expertise and technical proficiency. You will prepare drafts of documents and distribute them for review electronically. You will enter reviewers' comments online and make them available to other reviewers, replacing regular meetings with electronic "conversations." You will need to have access to and be able to use networks—local-area, wide-area, and Internet. And you can expect to move to paperless submissions in the next century.

If health care reform gains momentum, writers will need expertise in pharmaco-economic analyses, health economics, and quality-of-life issues. As the International Conference on Harmonization (ICH) continues with its recommendations, you will be required to extend your expertise in areas of international understanding and the ICH standard requirements for regulatory documents.

PREPARATION

Formal Training

Your preparation for a writing career may start even before you begin your undergraduate training. Indeed, you should develop your vocabulary, reading comprehension, and computer expertise early and pursue them throughout your education. Such skills are advantages in your career as a writer and editor in the pharmaceutical industry.

You can find initial employment if you have at least a bachelor's degree with a major in either the humanities or the sciences. However, if you major in English or one of the other humanities, try to take courses in the life sciences. Surveys of advertisements for pharmaceutical writers indicate that a background in any of the scientific disciplines (especially the life sciences) is an advantage, particularly when this knowledge is coupled with writing expertise. Courses in biology, pharmacology, anatomy, physiology, or medical terminology will help you understand the therapeutic areas for which you will write. Courses in math, especially logic and statistics, can also be valuable. If you major in the sciences, take additional courses in writing—and in the life sciences other than your major. Moreover, while a bachelor's degree will get you entry-level employment at many firms, advanced training (a master's degree or doctorate) will enhance your marketability.

On-the-Job Training

The pharmaceutical industry is changing so rapidly that you will be forced to redefine your knowledge base often to keep up with the changes. Much of this will be done while you are employed. In fact, your company will sponsor many programs in which you can get the required training. Internal experts may conduct workshops or seminars; consultants may be hired to prepare and present educational materials suited to the way your company does its business; or you may travel to a conference or training facility that sponsors relevant training. For example, several professional organizations conduct large training programs for pharmaceutical writers. Among them are the American Medical Writers Association (AMWA), the Drug Information Association (DIA), the Pharmaceutical Education and Research Institute (PERI), and the Institute for Applied Pharmaceutical Sciences (IAPS). In addition, you need to read the many publications that describe changes occurring in the industry. Some of them are *The Federal Register*, *The Pink Sheet*, and *Scrip*. *The Federal Register* is published by the federal government and supplements the CFR. It publishes proposed changes in federal drug regulations and allows for a period during which the companies can respond to them. Later, when the changes are finalized, it publishes what is required. The other two publications are privately owned magazines that monitor and report on changes in the pharmaceutical environment.

Other Skills and Abilities

In addition to the skills that relate to *what* you do on the job—write and edit documents to specification—you will be expected to have skills that relate to *how* you perform the job. Can you maintain a balance between demands of the job and other activities? How do you set priorities when you have many tasks that must be done now? Will you sacrifice quality for time? Can you influence others? Can you defend a scientifically tenable position in the face of opposition? Can you get others to do work? Can you work effectively in a team? Are you alert to changes in your environment, and can you respond quickly and appropriately? Can you envision solutions to problems and present these solutions in a convincing manner?

Pharmaceutical writing assignments occur in an environment that changes quickly. Working in it is much like trying to maintain your balance in the ocean, when the undercurrent is pulling and the sands are shifting rapidly. Your solid foundation five minutes earlier will not give you enough support to stand against these new forces of change. You will be called upon to respond instantly. If you are up to such kinds of exciting challenges, the rewards are many. Your satisfaction is knowing that your participation in the project was instrumental in getting a new drug on the market; it may be your best reward.

FINDING A JOB

How do you find the perfect job for you? The search begins with an inventory of yourself. You need to identify your interests as well as your strengths and weaknesses. You may wish to determine your preferences for the following:

- location (east or west, rural or metropolitan, large city or small, U.S. or Europe)
- compensation (less money with more autonomy, or the reverse)
- risk (lower or higher amounts),
- type of company (traditional pharmaceutical or biotechnology, small or large)

Once you have listed your preferences, ask yourself if each one is negotiable or not. For example, you may prefer not to work in a large metropolitan area; however, if big money and jobs for writers are located in New York, would you take a job there?

Now you need to identify potential employers. Getting a list of companies that employ writers may be easier than determining the companies on the list that are closest to meeting your specifications. To identify companies, you can consult the following publications. The American Medical Writers Association (AMWA) acknowledges all corporate sponsors in its annual *Membership Directory,* and this sponsor list represents the major pharmaceutical employers of writers. Current addresses of these firms can be found in the *Physicians' Desk Reference.* The Drug Information Association (DIA) publishes a *Register* that lists many prominent CROs that employ writers. *Med Ad News,* a publication for and about the pharmaceutical industry, publishes an annual (summer) listing of biotechnology firms and addresses. The process of narrowing this list will vary, depending upon your preferences. If location is your primary criterion, you will be able to prepare your list of companies to target with your resume relatively easily. If other criteria are important, you may need to get corporate annual reports from the library and read up on several companies. Or call the human resources department of companies you're interested in and request materials about the company.

If you want to know that an opening exists before you send a resume, networking among the membership of AMWA and DIA may provide your most direct and current information about job opportunities. The AMWA also distributes a quarterly Job Market Sheet that lists available jobs for medical and pharmaceutical writers. In addition, many search firms are hired by the various companies to fill positions, so you may want to monitor the ads in pharmaceutical publications or inquire about the availability of jobs.

Your resume and cover letter are your marketing tools for presenting your talents—for one job at one company at one time—and securing an interview. Make sure that relevant information, with emphasis on relevant, is on the first page. Include your name, how to contact you, training, skills, capabilities, and accomplishments. Make the presentation crisp. Do not fax your resume and cover letter: The U.S. Postal Service is still your best bet. Assume that the reader will decide in one minute whether or not to grant you an interview. During the interview, you can then determine if you are right for the company and if the company is right for you. This means you will want to bring all your unanswered questions, but don't ask questions for the mere exercise. Time is important in this industry, and you may reduce your employment chances by not respecting others' time.

If you aspire to the fulfillment enjoyed by a pharmaceutical writer, understand that it may take more than one or two resumes or interviews, but it will be well worth your time and effort.

PROFESSIONAL PROFILES

The following three profiles will give you an idea of what pharmaceutical writers do on the job. Gordon Penn is a writer with a pharmaceutical company; Sara Phelps supervises writers for a pharmaceutical company; and Ellen Graham is a manager of biomedical publications with a large pharmaceutical company in the South.

Gordon Penn

He surveyed the stacks of paper containing the data from the clinical study he was summarizing and shook his head. Gordon Penn's first writing assignment had been less than two years earlier; now he was faced with 3,000 pages of computer print, from which he was to write a report. No one could have described the pace of the writer's world he now knows.

Gordon, who has a PhD in pharmacology, had been doing university teaching and research. He had published much of his research in peer-reviewed journals, so he knew about writing fundamentals. Based on that experience, he answered an ad in the local paper and was hired as a writer for a pharmaceutical company. His first assignment was to summarize data for a Phase 1 clinical trial.

The study seemed simple, for it had just four subjects, each one of whom had received one dose of the medication being studied. However, just about everything had been monitored on each subject during the week before the dose was administered and for two weeks afterwards. The report ended up being 13 pages of text and 374 pages of appendices. Even though Gordon had plenty of time to prepare the report, doing so was a challenge because there were so many new things to think about. The report had to follow the company style manual. There were also FDA guidelines that he had to read. And his supervisor worked with him for two hours each week, discussing the way the department wrote clinical study reports.

Later assignments were larger as he proved that he was capable. Mostly, he wrote clinical study reports, but a few times he prepared manuscripts for medical journals based on the clinical study results he had summarized. In two years, he learned a lot while doing a significant amount of writing. More and more was expected of him—in less and less time.

When asked if he prefers university life, he smiles and says no. It was interesting and served as a solid foundation for what he is now doing. But he enjoys pharmaceutical writing. He likes the people he works with. Above all, he likes the sense of accomplishment he has when he completes each assignment. It makes up for the difficulties he sometimes encounters along the way. Gordon knows by looking at the stacks of paper on the desk that he has a few of them to face before this next report will be issued.

Sara Phelps

Sara Phelps supervises five medical writers at one of the largest pharmaceutical firms in the Midwest. Although she continues to write, it seems that she spends most of her time supervising her group or going to meetings.

Sara came to the company 12 years ago with a BS degree in medical technology and started working in the laboratories, where she performed high throughput screening of test compounds in cardiovascular research. A few years later, she responded to a job posting for a medical writer and was hired based on her knowledge of cardiovascular science. There was no writing department, as such, and policy was determined while she and the other writer had coffee breaks or lunch with the medical director, who also gave them their assignments.

All that changed in 1987 with the IND Rewrite. In these new federal regulations, the requirements for what a company needed to do to support an investigational new drug application were substantially changed. The new regulations required much more written documentation to support INDs. The company hired more writers during the following years and subsequently organized them into groups, according to therapeutic areas of clinical research. With her experience, Sara was assigned to manage the group of writers who worked primarily on drugs intended for cardiovascular indications.

As supervisor, Sara trains each writer who joins her group. It is important that the group's reports be written according to corporate standards in terms of style, content, and format, so Sara individualizes the training routine for each writer. For inexperienced writers, this training period can take two years or even longer.

She also decides which projects to assign to each writer. This requires that she know about any changes in the cardiovascular development program that will affect the dates by which her staff must complete drafts of documents. This management activity is a big challenge, particularly since priorities can change quickly. To keep abreast of the changes, she meets regularly with people from other departments who work on the same projects and with the cardiovascular medical director. In fact, the cardiovascular team often has coffee together when they cannot schedule a meeting during the day. If the changes are such that Sara needs to re-assign projects, she convenes staff meetings on short notice, in addition to the ones that occur each week. To date, she has been able to cover the assignments with her three writers, but it appears she needs to start interviewing for another. She knows she will need more help, because there is an NDA scheduled for submission at the end of next year. In fact, she and the other supervisors discuss project scheduling and resource requirements at weekly breakfast meetings with their director.

Sara also evaluates all draft documents that her staff prepares. By doing these reviews, she maintains consistency across all documents and can make suggestions individually and assist writers in conducting review meetings if they must be held. She also gains information with which to complete the performance evaluations of her staff, which she must prepare annually.

Perhaps her biggest concern at present is trying to anticipate the changes that may occur in the pharmaceutical industry and plan for how such changes may affect her work. To get the information to help her plan, she goes to two conferences each year, one a writers' convention and one that is specific to cardiovascular research. She also reads the major publications for the industry.

Sara's biggest satisfaction came when she heard that the NDA she had worked on was approved by the FDA. That she looks forward to experiencing such feelings again is what sustains her drive for excellence in view of the daunting challenges ahead.

Ellen Graham

Ellen Graham was recently hired as the manager of biomedical publications at a large pharmaceutical company in the South. She is responsible for all journal publications based on their clinical research.

After she got her MA in English studies, Ellen went to work as a writer for a large university medical school, where she prepared manuscripts based on researchers' biomedical data. From there, she became an assistant editor for a major medical publishing house, and while there, she was recruited for her present job.

Initially, she was asked to design a plan that would allow the company to publish the results of its clinical research at times that would coincide with approval of various drugs. In fact, she has been at her new company for almost a year and is still trying to refine the plan. One obstacle to her progress has been her lack of computer skills. She has taken a few training classes at work, but has finally decided she needs to go to a nearby university for more rigorous training. She knows that she is expected to access the data from clinical trials via computer and that these data summaries are to be the bases of the publications she prepares. Her immediate solution had been to hire an assistant who is expert with computers. But this has been a temporary fix.

Ellen also wishes she had taken more science courses, for she has learned that her knowledge of grammar and editing are merely a start. She will eventually take more science courses, and she looks forward to seeing journal articles that she has written appear in print. Having one of her own articles in print would represent not only years of dedication by many people who worked on the project, but also would be a personal accomplishment.

APPENDIX A

FURTHER INFORMATION

Professional Organizations

The American Medical Writers Association (AMWA) and the Drug Information Association (DIA) are the two professional organizations that most pharmaceutical writers join. In addition to the fine educational programs and conferences offered, they can provide you with opportunities to know others in the industry.

American Medical Writers Association
9650 Rockville Pike
Bethesda, MD 20814
(301) 493-0003
Fax: (301) 493-6384
E-mail: amwa@amwa.org

Drug Information Association
321 Norristown Road, Suite 225
Ambler, PA 19002-2755
(215) 628-2288,
Fax: (215) 641-1229
http://www.diahome.org

Government Publications, Electronic Services

The FDA provides numerous publications, many of them free of charge, to assist organizations in the preparation of regulatory submissions. The ones listed below are representative of the types of guidelines you will use when you write for the pharmaceutical industry. In addition, the FDA maintains a home page on the Internet that includes information on topics, other than drugs, over which it has jurisdiction (for example, biologics).

U.S. Food and Drug Administration. (1988). *Guidelines for the format and content of the clinical and statistical sections of an application.*

U.S. Department of Health and Human Services, U.S. Public Health Service, U.S. Food and Drug Administration. (1992). *CANDA guidance manual.*

U.S. Food and Drug Administration. *Clinical guidelines.* General and by therapeutic area (publication dates vary).

For a free copy of these FDA publications, contact:

CDER Executive Secretariat HFD-8
Food and Drug Administration
7500 Standish Place
Rockville MD 20855
(301) 594-1012

Code of Federal Regulations (CFR) volumes are available for various prices. Call the Government Printing Office order desk at (202) 512-1800 for current prices and availability.

FDA Bulletin Board Service, a menu-driven electronic newsletter, is a free service available through the "More Choices" button on the FDA's Internet Home Page (http://www.fda.gov/). If you are using a package with modem (PCPLUS, CompuServ, DialogLink), dial 1 (800) 222-0185.

Books

The following books are general discussions about the pharmaceutical industry, the changes it has experienced, and the regulated environment in which it operates.

Mathieu, M. P. (Ed.). (1994). *New drug development: A regulatory overview.* PAREXEL International, Inc., Cambridge, Mass.

Smith, C. G. (1992). *The process of new drug discovery and development.* CRC Press.

Snyder, D. E. (Ed.). (1992). *FDA-speak. Interpharm Press, Inc.*

Articles

The following articles were based on a survey from the FDA's Office of Planning and Evaluation and give suggestions for preparing good NDAs.

Cook, J. (1990, December). Plain and simple advice for improving NDAs. *Pharmaceutical Executive.*
(Gives advice on NDA indexing systems.)

Cook, J. & Meyer, G. F. (1992, June). Structure for success: Speeding NDA reviews. *Pharmaceutical Executive.*
(Describes NDA organization and structure.)

Mitchell, C. J. & Meyer, G. F. (1992, October). Charting a path to NDA approval. *Pharmaceutical Executive.*
(Explains development of NDA tables and graphs)

Directories and Continuing Education

Pharmaceutical Contract Support Organizations (PCSO) register. (1995). Contact the Drug Information Association at (215) 628-2288 or fax (215) 641-1229.

The American Medical Writers Association, the Drug Information Association, the Pharmaceutical Education and Research Institute (PERI), and the Institute for Applied Pharmaceutical Sciences offer courses, often at conferences, in which you can enroll to continue your professional development. AMWA and DIA contact numbers are included above; the PERI and IAPS addresses and numbers are below.

Pharmaceutical Education and Research Institute
1616 North Fort Myer Drive, Suite 1430
Arlington, VA 22209
(703) 276-0178
Fax: (703) 276-0069
http://www.peri.org

The Institute for Applied Pharmaceutical Sciences
Division of the Center for Professional Advancement
P.O. Box 1052
East Brunswick, NJ 08816-1052
(908) 613-4535

APPENDIX B

GLOSSARY

Like many professionals today, pharmaceutical writers must master an alphabet soup of acronyms and initialisms that identify organizations, regulations, and communications they typically encounter in their work. Here are some of those abbreviations, all of which are discussed in this chapter.

AMWA	American Medical Writers Association
CANDA	Computer-Assisted New Drug Application
CBER	Center for Biologic Evaluation and Research (a branch of the FDA)
CDER	Center for Drug Evaluation and Research (a branch of the FDA)
CDRH	Center for Devices and Radiological Health (a branch of the FDA)
CFR	Code of Federal Regulations
CRO	Contract Research Organization
CSR	Clinical Study Report
DIA	Drug Information Association
FDA	U.S. Food and Drug Administration
GCP	Good Clinical Practices
GLP	Good Laboratory Practices
GMP	Good Manufacturing Practices
IAPS	Institute for Applied Pharmaceutical Sciences
ICH	International Conference on Harmonization
IND	Investigational New Drug Application
ISE	Integrated Summary of Effectiveness
ISS	Integrated Summary of Safety
NDA	New Drug Application
NME	New Molecular Entity
PERI	Pharmaceutical Education and Research Institute
PhRMA	Pharmaceutical Research and Manufacturers of America
SOP	Standard Operating Procedure

chapter 10

Writing for Government and Nonprofit Social Service Agencies

Lisa Meeder Turnbull
Yale Divinity School
New Haven, Connecticut

Jobs

Technical writer or editor in a federal, state, or local government agency. Development officer or communication manager in a nonprofit organization.

Responsibilities

- *Technical writer:* gather information and prepare text for pamphlets, reports, and handbooks addressing a broad range of governmental activities and research. Editors perform traditional editorial functions, oversee production, and supervise the work of writers.
- *Development officer:* develop campaigns and manage activities and communications (including formal proposals and reports) to generate support for nonprofit organizations.

Employment Outlook

Positions in both government and nonprofit organizations are competitive, and job security depends upon which programs are favored by administrations and agencies that provide funding. In the nonprofit sector, job security also depends upon the programs each organization wishes to undertake and on the funding it can obtain for these programs.

Salary Range

$16,000 to $72,000.

INTRODUCTION

Social services are provided by federal, state, and local governments, and by private agencies, usually known as "nonprofit organizations." A career as a technical writer or editor in a government or nonprofit social service organization is an attractive alternative if you want to combine a career in communication with a desire to help people. To give you an idea of the role professional communicators play in social service organizations, this chapter describes the work done by writers and editors in some government agencies and by development officers in nonprofit organizations.

While work in government and the private sector may seem very different, the activities performed in each arena are, in fact, similar. On the one hand, writers in the public affairs offices of federal agencies have to communicate with a variety of audiences about the social services provided—or funded—by the federal government. For example, the National Institutes of Health must communicate information about diseases and related medical research to Congress, the medical community, and the public. The Department of Education must communicate with educators, parents who wish to help their children succeed in school, and students themselves. And the Social Security and Veterans Administrations have to make sure that individuals understand their rights to benefits and services provided by these agencies.

Similarly, in most nonprofit social service organizations, the development staff must promote the organization and its services to board members, supporters, volunteers, and clients. Development officers also work closely with administrative staff to decide how to expand the organization and how to raise money for this expansion.

One thing you should note is that this chapter only tells you what it is like to work in certain types of organizations. You may also want to read other chapters in this book that relate to your specific area of interest. For example, if you are interested in working for the National Institutes of Health, this chapter will give you information about working for government agencies, but you might also want to read Patricia Cornett's chapter on "Writing in Medical and Health Care Environments" to learn more about writing in the health care profession.

YOUR LIFE AS A WRITER OR EDITOR
IN A GOVERNMENT AGENCY

If you were to decide on a career in a federal government agency such as the National Institutes of Health, the Social Security Administration, the Veterans Administration, or one of the departments of the executive branch of government, you would probably begin as an entry-level editor with a title such as editorial assistant, assistant editor, copy editor, or production assistant. Your daily responsibilities might include reviewing copy for errors in grammar, punctuation, and spelling; reviewing manuscripts for readability, style, and agreement with editorial policy; adding or rearranging sentences to improve clarity; deleting incorrect or unnecessary information; researching and verifying facts, dates, and statistics; arranging page layouts; composing headlines; proofing galleys; and reading and evaluating quality and suitability or usefulness of manuscripts submitted by freelance writers.

The duties of experienced communicators are more varied. For example, Polly Onderak is a writer at the National Center for Research and Resources, one of 21 Institutes, Centers, and Divisions (ICDs) that make up the National Institutes of Health (NIH). Polly's office has only four people, but each ICD has its own public affairs office, making a total of 84 public affairs professionals in just one federal organization.

Polly has broad responsibilities, including developing an average of two new brochures each year and maintaining revisions on existing ones. She also prepares press kits and arranges news conferences, a major responsibility, given that the NIH is in the news nearly every day. Polly's Center has a major media event approximately six times per year. In nonmedia-related work, Polly prepares Congressional reports to inform members of Congress and their staffs about the Center's activities. She organizes conferences and exhibits, and she answers inquiries from media representatives and individual citizens.

WHERE YOU MAY WORK
IN A GOVERNMENT AGENCY

Whether you work as an entry-level editor or as a more experienced writer and project coordinator, your working conditions as a government employee will vary a good deal. You might work in the quiet of a private office, or you might be part of a large writing staff concentrated in a noisy, crowded, open area. Depending on the kind of research in which you are involved, you might travel to visit plants, factories, field sites, or laboratories. Most editors and writers work 35 to 40 hours per week, although your hours might vary with particular assignments and deadlines; you might occasionally work on weekends or work overtime during the week.

You might have the opportunity to work in a variety of locations, since public affairs jobs with the federal government exist throughout the

United States. The majority, however, are concentrated in New York, Chicago, Los Angeles, Boston, Philadelphia, San Francisco, and of course, Washington, DC. Regardless of where you work, you will probably be required to take a civil service examination. You might also have to undergo additional screening and security evaluations, depending on the agency you want to work for and the nature of the work you want to do.

If you do not wish to work in one of the cities listed above, you might consider state and local government organizations. Although opportunities might be limited, perhaps to part-time positions or freelance contracts, you would have the flexibility of choosing from among 50 state capitals and numerous county seats and local government offices.

One area at the state level in which you might find opportunities would be in the Department of Environmental Protection (DEP) publications office. In Connecticut, which has the most extensive publications office of any state's DEP, the manager of that office functions much like a commercial publisher, managing a staff of writers, editors, and artists, and overseeing business operations, such as working with printers and negotiating contracts. Regardless of its size and scope, each state's office produces publications and other information on the environment for various publics: specialists in all scientific and technological fields, public consultants and city planners, state and local elected officials, and the general public.

Another potential source of opportunities at the state level would be the State Department of Economic Development and its Tourism Division. Holly Nolan, Director of Trade Education and Development for the State of New York, Division of Tourism, describes her office's goal as "marketing tourism to increase visitation to the State of New York and providing information to help people travel to and within the state." Specifically, Holly was hired in 1978, after a 16-year career as a high school English teacher, to develop communications that would improve New York's negative image. In response to this challenge, Holly developed a training program to enable the 800,000 individuals employed in New York's $19-billion tourism industry to provide visitors with a more positive travel experience. Holly's program, entitled "New York Loves You," was piloted as the state prepared for the 1980 Lake Placid Olympics. The program consists partly of a *Handbook for Successful Customer Relations in the Tourism Industry*, which Holly developed and wrote. It also includes a video, for which Holly wrote and edited the script, cast and hired actors and technical personnel, and produced the final tape. She also developed training guides for leaders in individual cities and communities throughout the state.

Holly's department employs six writers, who research and write stories and press releases about attractions throughout the state, historic sites, and special events and festivals. In addition, the department employs two video producers, who also write scripts.

Opportunities for writers in local government may be limited by the size of the city, or they may be available only on a part-time or freelance basis. In Middletown, Ohio, with a population of approximately 50,000, for example, many of the communication and public affairs writing activities discussed in this chapter are included in the regular activities of the Planning and Economic Development Department. Communications such as commercial brochures promoting the city to a business audience, communications related to tourism, and business brochures are created by an outside agency. Members of the city planning staff develop grant applications to federal agencies and work in cooperation with businesses to write loan applications to state agencies for community projects.

As a member of the local government of this small midwestern city, Larry Wood, Principal Planning and Economic Development Specialist for Middletown, points out that even a city the size of Middletown would benefit from employing "someone who has the ability to focus on issues and communicate information to residents. . . . People don't think about the condition of their streets or the maintenance of their sewers until something goes wrong or until funding is needed. People need to feel good about where they live and support the quality of life in the city on an ongoing basis."

If you are interested in volunteer work, Larry also suggests that preparing communications for civic organizations, such as the publicity committees for local celebrations or art festivals, the city's Chamber of Commerce, and area professional and trade associations, is a good way to gain experience writing for public agencies.

YOUR LIFE AS A DEVELOPMENT OFFICER IN A NONPROFIT ORGANIZATION

If you find you are not interested in working for a government agency, you may be interested in a position on the communications and development staff of a nonprofit organization. As part of a development staff, your main goal would be to obtain funds to support the organization's activities and underwrite its operating expenses. Obtaining funding might include writing formal proposals to state and federal agencies for public funding or to foundations, corporations, and even individuals for private funding. You may also develop fund-raising campaigns and activities designed to attract individual supporters and work with a volunteer board of directors and staff to carry out the organization's mission. Once funding is obtained, you must report on the organization's activities, demonstrating that the organization did what it promised to do with the money it was given.

Kit Gillem, Director of Development and Communications in the Ohio Field Office of The Nature Conservancy, writes proposals to private foundations to secure resources for carrying out the organization's mission of preserving and protecting endangered species by protecting the best examples of ecosystems and communities. In addition to financial contributions, approximately 20 percent of the contributions Kit's programs secure are in-kind donations, such as professional services from media, public relations, and research firms; human resources, such as volunteers to work with the employees of a business or among members of civic organizations; and other non-cash resources, such as equipment, photographic images, and gifts of land.

Kit is also responsible for maintaining follow-up communications with the individuals and organizations making contributions to the Conservancy. Several times each year, Kit develops communications designed to demonstrate the program's success, show appreciation for the contributions it receives, and make the contributors feel as if they are active members of a partnership working toward a common goal. These communications include thank-you notes for each contribution, periodic progress reports on conservation efforts, and public recognition of major donors. As Director of the Development and Communications Department, Kit is fully responsible for planning and managing all of these communications.

All development officers and their staff members must not only possess outstanding communication skills but also be creative, congenial, and well organized. In addition, they must be intimately familiar with the organization's mission, its short- and long-term goals, and its activities.

Kit points out that a development officer must have a good working knowledge of basic tax laws that apply to charitable contributions and must understand the organization's procedures for arranging large contributions, bequests, and endowments (commonly known as "planned giving vehicles"). At the very least, he or she must be able to advise potential donors about how their money could be used by the organization and must know how and when to consult the organization's attorney to draw up the paper work.

WHERE YOU MAY WORK
IN A NONPROFIT ORGANIZATION

Opportunities for development personnel are as varied as the range of nonprofit organizations itself. Depending on your interests, you can work at the local, regional, state, or national levels; you can work part-time or full-time; and you can work as either a salaried or volunteer staff member. The Nature Conservancy, for example, has field offices in 50 states, regional offices that coordinate the work of a group of states, and a headquarters office in Arlington, Virginia, that coordinates the organization's activities in Latin America, the Caribbean, and the Pacific. In other organizations, such as Planned Parenthood or United Way, you will find offices in local communities as well. In general, you are more likely to find part-time and volunteer opportunities in your local community; many organizations centralize full-time career opportunities at the regional and national levels.

In general, the profession offers an environment in which people who believe in an organization's mission work hard to get the job done. You can count on being in an environment that is generally understaffed and where space is at a premium. Don't be surprised if you share an office, or even a desk, particularly as an entry-level or part-time employee.

EMPLOYMENT OUTLOOK

Even though the Department of Labor expects the employment of writers and editors to increase faster than average through the year 2000, opportunities in both government and private social service agencies are likely to become increasingly competitive as economic pressures force staff reductions and programming cutbacks. A discussion of this outlook in both kinds of agencies follows.

Writing and Editing in Federal Government Agencies

Demand for writers and editors in federal organizations is sporadic and depends a great deal on where you want to work. For example, in the Midwest, the Office of Personnel Management (OPM) in Dayton, Ohio, which serves a two-and-a-half-state region, might post an opening for a technical writer or editor every year to year and a half. In areas such as Washington, DC, on the other hand, openings occur more frequently.

As a sign of the generally depressed employment outlook for writers and editors in social services, the OPM does not currently offer the Public Information Examination, a national exam used to recruit and rank applicants for technical writing and editing positions in the federal government. The exam is not being given because there is not enough demand to justify developing a pool of qualified applicants. However, if you're really interested in working for a federal agency, there is limited opportunity for undergraduate students with at least a B+ average or who rank in the top 10 percent of their undergraduate class. Through the Outstanding Scholars Program, these individuals are permitted to apply directly to federal agencies. The OPM maintains a listing of agencies with openings for Outstanding Scholars in all professions.

Trends in federal employment, particularly in regard to the demand for technical writers and editors, are even more difficult to predict. On one hand, the federal government will always need to convey information to the public and will, therefore, always need technical communicators. On the other hand, political and social agendas are constantly changing, and the allocation of human and financial resources changes with each agenda.

For example, upheaval in Eastern Europe and Asia in the early 1990s caused dramatic changes in the Department of State. Education in the United States, particularly in science, engineering, and mathematics, has become a national priority, as has fighting illiteracy. AIDS and cancer are still at the forefront of public health concerns. These priorities, however, may change with each shift in international relations, with each administration, and with each breakthrough in medical research. Furthermore, the federal government's ability and willingness to hire writers also changes according to national economic factors.

Salaries for writers and editors in the federal government tend to be about the same as those for technical writers employed elsewhere. The Bureau of Labor Statistics indicates that in 1994, $42,524 was the average salary of writers and editors employed by the federal government. In the same year, the Society for Technical Communication reported the average salary of its members to be $42,469.

White collar federal employees, including technical writers and editors, are paid according to the General Pay Schedule (GS). This schedule is made up of 18 pay grades corresponding to job duties and responsibilities; within each grade, there are 10 steps. Thus there are 180 possible salaries that you could earn in the course of your career.

If you have a bachelor's degree and are hired as a technical writer or editor, you could begin at grade 5, 6, or 7 on the General Schedule. However, if you have a master's or a doctoral degree, or professional experience or training, you might begin at GS-9, 10, or 11. In 1997, the base pay for a Grade 5/step 1 employee was $19,520. The base pay at Grade 11/step 10 was $46,523.

Development Officers in Nonprofit Organizations

Demand for people willing to work in nonprofit organizations is expected to be strong throughout the 1990s because of the concern for problems such as AIDS, drug abuse, poverty, aging, crime, illiteracy, and the environment. However, the social service sector is not expanding as it should to meet the needs associated with these concerns, largely because of severe cutbacks in local, state, and federal funding. So while there is a tremendous amount of work that needs to be done, not much money is available to attract personnel, and the competition for the best jobs is intense.

If you decide on a job in the private sector, you may begin your affiliation with an organization through volunteer work or academic internship programs. Although you are not guaranteed subsequent employment, the contacts you cultivate through such programs often allow you to bypass the initial screening process when an opening occurs or provide you with information about career opportunity. Occasionally, an organization will invite you to join its staff based on its impression of your interest, dedication, and performance while a volunteer or intern.

However you break into the field, you will likely begin your career as an entry-level development staff member. You may then advance to a position as program manager, in which you manage one aspect of an organization's operations. Eventually, you may become a director of communication and development, responsible for all the organization's communication functions, or an executive director. Because each of these positions is likely to be available to you in the course of your career, all are discussed in this section.

At the entry level, you might be responsible for routine or regularly-scheduled communications, such as the organization's newsletter. In developing these communications, you would work in cooperation with a manager or other entry-level personnel. Your workload would be varied, consisting of a number of small- to medium-sized projects rather than larger, ongoing projects. For example, you may design and/or develop brochures, informational pieces, solicitations, and press packets; and you may support program managers in writing and editing funding proposals and preparing reports to funding agencies. Depending on the size and structure of the organization, you may interact with a board of directors, serve as staff liaison for certain board or volunteer activities, and assist with programs that directly serve the organization's clients.

As you gain experience, expertise, or a specialized interest, you will likely advance to the position of program assistant or program manager, at which point you will be responsible for a particular program or aspect of the services the organization offers. Again, depending on the size and structure of the organization, you will likely be under the supervision of a director of communication and development or under the direct supervision of an executive director; you may also have to coordinate your activities with managers of other programs within the organization. At this point, you may also supervise some portion of the development staff or volunteer corps. You might have a secretary or other support personnel, although you will probably share their time with another manager.

As a manager, you will quickly become the organization's most knowledgeable individual regarding the program or service you oversee. Therefore, it is likely that you will assist the executive director in reporting to the board of directors and that you will take a more active role in designing additional or expanded programs and developing more efficient mechanisms for delivering services. For example, if you work for a community service agency, you may notice that a large number of inquiries for transportation assistance come from a certain region of your city. You could then use this information to research funding sources and approach the local public transit authority or taxi service to develop a jointly sponsored program. You thus improve service to the community by working with existing resources. As you can see in this example, managers become more actively involved in developing and writing funding proposals, fulfilling obligations to funding agencies, and meeting accountability requirements.

As part of your managerial responsibilities, you might also plan and organize meetings, workshops, conferences, and tours for your organization's clientele as well as for individual donors. If, for example, you are involved in educational outreach and community development for a local zoo or botanical garden, you might plan a promotional week, during which you conduct afternoon activities for area school children, along with evening events that appeal to a variety of adult interests: walking tours narrated by a professional naturalist, workshops for home gardeners that allow them to learn from professional botanists, a more formal event for large donors attended by park administrators, family or all-adult scavenger hunts with park-related prizes and bonuses along the way, etc. Because nonprofit organizations tend to share programming ideas and successes with colleagues in other communities, you may also be called upon to attend conferences, make formal presentations, and perhaps conduct workshops on behalf of your organization. By participating in professional meetings, conferences, and workshops, you and your colleagues learn from one another's successes and frustrations; you are thus able to constantly improve upon the service your organization provides its various constituencies.

It is entirely possible that you could spend your entire career as a program manager. While you might not formally advance, you will find that as the program you manage becomes established, you will be able to focus on the development of new programs. You might even interview and hire additional managers and support staff for newly developed programs.

Depending on the exact nature of your management experience, advancement from this position could be to either director of communication and development or to executive director. Some large organizations have separate directors for their development and communications divisions; your promotion to one of these positions would, again, depend on your interest and experience.

As director of communication and development, you would be responsible for all of the organization's communication functions as well as all program development, fund raising, and long-range planning. You would work very closely with the executive director and board of directors to establish the organization's long-term goals and formulate specific operational and financial plans for achieving them.

As an executive director, you would be responsible for all aspects of the agency's operations and would be accountable to all of its constituent groups: clients, the board of directors, supporters, and the public. If you directed an office that was part of a larger organization, you would also be accountable to the state, regional, or national divisions in the organization's structure.

While you might hold each of the positions described at various points in your career, you might not spend your entire career in one organization. You will find that, partly because of the realities of nonprofit funding and partly because nonprofit staffs tend to be small and offer limited opportunities, communicators in nonprofit organizations tend to move from job to job. For example, an experienced program manager might leave an organization to become executive director of another, perhaps smaller, concern. In larger organizations, it is also possible to advance by moving among units. Within The Nature Conservancy, for example, a director of communications and development in one state-level field office might advance by becoming executive director of another state's chapter.

Two things about a career in nonprofit development are extremely important to remember. First, nonprofit organizations tend to be flexible in their employment policies and thus are attractive to those who want to work only part-time or limit their professional commitment. Second, a majority of the jobs are supported by grants or other "soft money." When these funds are no longer available to the organization, your employment will typically end.

As an entry-level staff member, you can expect a salary in the mid-teens. However, if you bring something unique to the organization or you accept increased responsibility, you might expect a salary in the mid-twenties. As you gain experience in both the profession and the organization, advancement to a management position could bring a salary in the low to mid-thirties. In a large organization, a director of development and communication could expect to earn $50,000 or more.

PREPARATION

In general, an effective development or public information officer is creative, innovative, far-sighted, and above all, flexible. He or she is able to examine a problem from many angles and devise a solution that represents the most effective compromise for people with different needs, as well as one that is politically realistic. Staff members must be team players, must be able to brainstorm, and must be able to appreciate and integrate a variety of viewpoints.

If you have these qualities, as well as good writing skills, the desire to write, and the ability to write a variety of communications, you are probably well-suited for a technical writing career in government or nonprofit agencies. Because the preparation for a writing career in both sectors is similar, the information in this section applies to both and is not broken into distinct subsections. Where possible, examples and illustrations point out the best preparation for working in one sector or the other.

The Department of Labor suggests that you take courses in English, journalism, public relations, and communication, as well as courses in a specialized field such as environmental studies, public health, medicine, art history, and/or curatorial studies. These courses will allow you to either specialize within the communication profession or change professions more easily should the employment outlook change drastically. In planning your major and elective coursework, it would be useful to begin as early as your sophomore year in college, reading employment notices and advertisements to get an idea of what qualifications employers will desire when they fill social service positions.

Employers in both the government and nonprofit sectors may expect you to have a degree in either journalism or public relations as part of your undergraduate background. Employers may also expect or prefer some specialized knowledge. This may take the form of strong "content knowledge" in an academic or professional field such as environmental science, public health administration, sociology, or gerontology. Specialized knowledge may also take the form of expertise in a certain type of writing. For example, if you have taken education and psychology electives, you may be well-suited for developing materials that successfully communicate with low-literate populations, while a business background, particularly in marketing, would be useful in a position that involves planning and managing public and corporate fund-raising campaigns.

Your technical or specialized knowledge need not be obtained through formal education. Take advantage of experiences available through extra-curricular activities or through your university's work-study program. You are also likely to gain a great deal of knowledge through an internship or apprenticeship as a technical editorial assistant or through on-the-job experience after you graduate. For example, over 80% of my time as an academic development officer was spent seeking government funding for educational programs. For this position, I applied my academic background in political science and government communication to become a specialist in reading and analyzing announcements in the *Federal Register* and specific program announcements sent out by individual government agencies. I also analyzed proposed and pending legislation, as well as daily news articles, to predict policies and social trends that would affect the availability of funding. In this way, I can assist my employer with short- and long-range planning.

Preparing for a career in a government agency or a nonprofit organization truly depends on what level and branch of government or what type of organization you hope to work for and what specific functions you wish to perform. While you need to be familiar with the mission and operations of the organization for which you work, the general and specific requirements vary. Some nonprofit organizations require excellent communication skills, an ability to motivate and supervise a volunteer staff, and experience with a variety of funding mechanisms. In other words, some organizations look for an effective communicator first and a subject specialist second. Other organizations require more specialized knowledge on subjects such as health care delivery, environmental management, and other specialized fields.

All organizations, however, are interested in your knowledge of their subject areas. Because specialized knowledge is so important in marketing yourself to potential employers, you should take communication courses related to your area of interest if they are offered. The School of Natural Resources at the Ohio State University, for example, offers a course in Environmental Communications.

Do not underestimate the value of an internship that will interest prospective employers, nor of volunteer work that will provide professional experience and demonstrate your interest in the field. Even with nine years of professional experience, my most recent career move was linked to a graduate internship I performed 10 years earlier and to volunteer

teer research I completed two years ago. Employers will also expect you to have a demonstrated ability to write on nonliterary subjects. To gain experience and collect published writing samples that demonstrate your abilities, you might work on your university's newspaper or participate in academic activities that lead to publication.

Whether your preparation emphasizes communication skills or technical skills will largely be determined by the type of job that interests you. For example, if you are on the development staff of a nonprofit organization concerned with preserving natural areas, and you are responsible for producing a quarterly newsletter, organizing the board of directors' annual meeting, and developing and updating a preserve guide, you will need mostly communication skills. On the other hand, if, you are responsible for organizing volunteers for nature preserve work trips and developing relevant communications, you will need to understand environmental management issues, be proficient in the techniques to be applied to a given site, and work effectively with volunteers to provide a pleasant and safe experience—all in addition to being an outstanding communicator.

Likewise, if you work for a broad-based community service organization, you will not only need good communication skills and thorough knowledge of funding mechanisms, you may also need an understanding of a particular issue, such as AIDS, and of ways of addressing related issues in the community.

Depending on the area of the country in which you work and the services offered by your organization, you should consider the value of foreign language proficiency. For example, Spanish would be a good language to learn if you planned to work in the Southwest, South Florida, or New York City. You might not use it regularly, but it would make you more attractive to prospective employers.

As you gain experience, and most likely an advanced degree in communication, administration, public relations, or your area of expertise, you will also want to prepare to advance to a management position or directorship. (The Schools of Management at Case Western Reserve University and Boston University offer master's degree programs focusing on nonprofit management; see the Appendix at the end of this chapter.) In these positions, you will work with others in research, administration, and community relations functions, but you will ultimately synthesize the ideas of others in order to move from an abstract idea to a concrete plan of action. In this process, you must be willing to revise, rework, and rewrite many times, sometimes incorporating ideas with which you do not agree. It is vital that you be able to promote an idea that you know to be right without becoming possessive of it or defensive toward its critics; you also must know when to defer to the ideas of others.

Regardless of your position or the sector in which you are employed, you must frequently read professional journals, material published by your office's parent agency or associations to which your organization belongs, and newsletters published by organizations similar to yours to maintain current knowledge the field. You also should be aware of the vital role that professional organizations play in your development.

Many organizations, such as the Public Relations Society of America, Women in Communications, and the National Society of Fund Raising Executives, appeal to a broad base of communication and development professionals. (The addresses and telephone numbers of these societies are provided in the Appendix at the end of this chapter.) Other societies address the needs and interests of a more narrowly defined professional constituency. Through local chapter meetings and regional and national conferences, such organizations offer valuable opportunities for networking, maintaining your knowledge through seminars and short courses, and professional certification. It would be to your advantage to find out about the activities of professional societies in your area; many offer student membership and meeting rates, and some have student chapters at colleges and universities.

Finally, Burton Nadler (1989) reminds us that "wanting to work with people is not enough to be successful at obtaining a job in human/social service. You must be prepared to state what specific abilities you possess to help others effectively and to work within the guidelines of particular services and programs. . . . Don't underestimate the power of a volunteer position to be a springboard into a challenging, professional opportunity. Also, don't let the stereotypical (and often accurate) image of low pay and long hours stop you from exploring job options. You can gain a great deal of experience and satisfaction in a few years in this field and then move to another, if you wish, later on."

FINDING A JOB

Writers and Editors in Federal Government Agencies

To find out about positions in federal government agencies, contact the Federal Job Information Center, maintained by the Office of Personnel Management (OPM), listed under "United States Government" in your local telephone book. Most offices will have a recorded listing of announcements and will allow you to leave a message requesting further information and application materials for the announcements that interest you. Some offices also offer the opportunity to leave your name, telephone number, and best time to be reached. An OPM representative will return your call the following business day, allowing you to speak with someone in greater detail about the types of positions that interest you. At some locations, this service may be subcontracted rather than operated by the OPM and may not be a fully reliable source of information. A placement officer in your university's career planning office may also be able to give you the name and direct telephone number of a contact person in a nearby OPM regional office.

In addition to contacting an OPM regional office, you can directly approach government agencies to inquire about technical writing and editing positions, particularly if you are seeking an internship or if you qualify for the Outstanding Scholars Program.

The *Career America College Directory* is a national listing of federal agencies published by the central office of the OPM. It outlines the current staffing needs of each agency listed and provides the name, address, and telephone number of the appropriate contact person.

An additional resource is *Opportunities in Public Affairs*, a biweekly publication announcing current openings in public affairs, including legislation, government and public relations, communications, and print and broadcast media on Capitol Hill, as well as in associations, corporations, and federal agencies.

The following is a list of federal government agencies, in addition to those already discussed, that are known to hire professional writers and editors. The reference librarian in your university or community library will be able to help you locate the addresses and telephone numbers of these organizations. All of these agencies maintain World Wide Web sites, and all have their headquarters in Washington, DC, unless otherwise noted:

- Consumer Products Safety Commission
- Department of Education
- Environmental Protection Agency
- Federal Trade Commission
- Government Printing Office
- Department of Health and Human Services: Administration on Aging, Office of Child Development, Office for Handicapped Individuals, National Institutes of Health
- Department of Labor
- Library of Congress
- National Foundation on the Arts and the Humanities
- Social Security Administration (Baltimore, MD)
- Vista

- Department of Justice
- Department of Veterans Affairs
- The Peace Corps
- Department of Agriculture
- Animal and Plant Health Inspection Service (Minneapolis, MN)
- Forest Service (Atlanta, GA)
- National Credit Union Administration

Development Officer in a Nonprofit Organization

Literally thousands of nonprofit organizations exist in the United States, many of which have opportunities for professional communicators at the local, regional, state, and national levels. The reference librarian of your university or community library will be able to show you a number of directories of nonprofit organizations that describe each organization's mission and activities and provide current addresses and telephone numbers, as well as the names of appropriate contact persons. (See the Appendix at the end of this chapter for a list of organizations that you might consider and the addresses of their national offices.)

You also should read publications in your field. For example, in the area of environmental concern, organizations such as The Nature Conservancy post openings in *Environmental Opportunities* and welcome applications from readers. You might also consider development or alumni relations positions in colleges and universities, private schools, and national headquarters of fraternities and sororities. In general, these organizations prefer to hire alumni, but they can be excellent sources of experience as you establish your career.

PROFESSIONAL PROFILES

The following two profiles will give you some additional insight into the work done by writers who work for government and private social service agencies.[1] Nancy Paulu is a writer for an office of the U.S. Department of Education, while Maureen Noe is Director of Community Services for the Middletown, Ohio, Area United Way organization.

Nancy Paulu

Nancy Paulu is a part-time writer/editor in the U.S. Department of Education's Office of Educational Research and Improvement (OERI). Nancy describes her job as "taking educational research, which tends to be very technical and rather academic, and translating it into language that normal mortals can understand." Before obtaining this position, Nancy was in a middle-management position, leading a team of Department of Education writers. Nancy chose to become a writer/editor because, for her, "management involved too much paperwork and not enough writing." She now writes on a wide range of education-related topics for a variety of audiences. Her goal is to provide information that will improve the quality of American education and influence educational policy.

One of Nancy's publications, *Dealing with Dropouts*, seeks to help policy makers in urban areas throughout the United States determine what they can do to decrease the high school dropout rate. The 75-page book is addressed to members of urban school boards, superintendents, state senators, and concerned citizens within urban communities. Nancy's tasks for this publication included gathering information from superintendents in urban areas and producing a coherent document that describes successful retention programs.

Improving Schools and Empowering Parents: Choice in American Education is another of Nancy's publications addressed to educational policy makers. This 50-page document is based on the White House Workshop on Choice in Education and presents information in a way that is understandable and useful to the nonexpert reader. Nancy describes her basic purpose in developing this document as "telling people, 'This is what we know about choice; here is where it's working; here are what the potential problems are.'"

Nancy also prepares documents for parents or other family members and caregivers. *Helping Your Child Learn Science* is a 58-page book Nancy wrote for parents of young children. One hundred fifty thousand copies of this book were printed, and because the book was so popular, it is now being reprinted in English and translated into Spanish.

The success of the science volume has also prompted OERI to expand the project into a series of *Helping Your Child . . .* books on such topics as math, staying healthy, and learning history. Nancy has just completed a volume entitled *Helping Your Child Get Ready for School*. She hopes the series will make quality educational enrichment materials available to a variety of parents, including the less affluent and less educated, who are generally less able to seek out supplementary educational information. With this goal in mind, the text for the books is written at about the tenth-grade reading level.

Nancy's responsibilities in preparing documents include not only writing, but a great deal of research, much of which entails reading research published by others and looking for material that can be adapted for a general audience. As a document progresses, Nancy also interviews experts in fields appropriate to the topic and solicits expert reviews of her drafts. After OERI's Publications Branch has completed its final editing of Nancy's drafts, she works closely with colleagues in graphics and production. Throughout all of these activities, Nancy draws heavily on her experience as a reporter for the *Minneapolis Star and Tribune*, as assistant editor of the *Harvard Education Letter*, and as business reporter for the Quincy, Massachusetts, *Patriot Ledger*.

Because some of the topics Nancy writes on are politically sensitive, her writing skills are complemented by her negotiating skills. In fact, Nancy finds that tact and diplomacy are vital as she develops documents that satisfy several audiences, many of whose members do not agree. In all her work, Nancy follows general conventions of ethical writing, looks for cultural balance and unbiased representations in words and images for publications, and is sensitive to her department's and office's responsible use of taxpayers' money.

Nancy's assignments are linked, in part, to the political agenda of the current administration. While interest in specific publications may wax and wane with changes in administration, OERI officials have been consistently committed to producing relevant publications over the past few years.

When asked to consider her future, Nancy is extremely positive, pointing out that hers is "not a dead-end field; the need for excellent communicators is always there." With what she believes is "a dearth of excellent communicators in the field," Nancy suggests that she could transfer her talents to the private sector, work for a publishing house, or become a public relations professional. Because she lives and works in Washington, DC, Nancy has access to professional and political networks which make career mobility possible during periods of economic stability or growth.

Nancy also points out that she would be happy to remain in her present position. She emphasizes that although her career causes her life to be hectic at times, writing and editing is an excellent profession for someone with a small child or other personal reasons for seeking flexible employment.

Maureen Noe

Maureen Noe is Director of Community Services for the Middletown Area United Way in Middletown, Ohio. Middletown Area United Way is a volunteer organization dedicated to uniting the community's people and resources to meet human needs and improve quality of life. Examples of United Way member organizations in Middletown include Family

Services, the Salvation Army, Red Cross, Junior Achievement, Big Brothers/Big Sisters, and the YWCA Battered Persons Shelter.

Written communications are critical to the success of United Way and the social service organizations it works with in the community. These communications are designed to gain community support, encourage community members to use social services, share information with other social service agencies, and ensure that volunteers understand their responsibilities.

Before joining the Middletown Area United Way, Maureen was a counselor in the teenage parenting program of family services in Middletown, Ohio. As director of community services, Maureen reports directly to the President of the Middletown Area United Way. In addition to managing the communications discussed in greater detail below, Maureen has continuing responsibility for coordinating and supervising three telephone services: PhoneFriend, an all-volunteer service for children in kindergarten through sixth grade; TeenTalk, a service for area teens staffed by volunteer professional counselors; and First Call for Help, a community information and referral line and a relay service for the hearing impaired, staffed by students from the Middletown campus of Miami University, who earn college credit in sociology and counseling for their voluntary service. Maureen also coordinates United Way's Voluntary Action Center, which places volunteers in community organizations that can best use their talents.

In describing the communication tasks she performs, Maureen points out that within the Middletown Area United Way, all professional staff have communication responsibilities, each managing the communications that pertain to his or her division. While this decentralization allows staff members to create communications that meet the needs of their divisions, it also causes a lack of uniformity among publications. To help solve this problem, Maureen and her colleagues are careful to ensure that all communications consistently convey the message that the Middletown Area United Way cares about its contributors, its member organizations and their clients, and its volunteers. Division directors also try to use the same colors, style, and other features to establish a visual identity for the organization's documents.

When Maureen discusses the types of communications she creates, we begin to see just how diverse the nonprofit professional's activities really are. In our conversation, Maureen chose to focus on videotapes, directories and handbooks, public presentations, and grant proposals, illustrating her conviction that community service professions are "good for a person who doesn't enjoy a stagnant lifestyle." Maureen further points out that in her field, "diversity challenges your skills and makes the job enjoyable; constant change is a good deterrent for burnout because you see successes within yourself."

Maureen recently developed two videos, one to promote PhoneFriend (a community hotline for latchkey children or any elementary-age children who need someone to talk with) and one to promote TeenTalk (a similar hotline for teenagers). The PhoneFriend video was distributed to area schools to encourage students to use the service and to gain support from teachers, who, in turn, recommend it to students. To develop the 10–12-minute PhoneFriend video, Maureen worked with students in the Middletown City School's program for gifted and talented students to brainstorm ideas and to help them draft a working script. She then worked with a professional promotions agency, which polished the script; a volunteer who held auditions, cast children in the various skits, and supervised rehearsals; a volunteer who filmed and edited the video; and another volunteer, who added music to the finished footage. Finally, Maureen organized a party to release the video and to recognize the students and volunteers who had been involved. The entire process took approximately six months.

The TeenTalk video was designed to appeal to a teenage audience. Although the video for TeenTalk had a longer running time (20 minutes), it took only two months to produce. Maureen again acted as a facilitator among a group of volunteers, but rather than allowing teens to write the script as the elementary students had, Maureen and a few volunteers wrote a first draft, then invited the teens to make revisions to reflect their speech habits and to make the interactions among peers and with adults more realistic.

Each year, Maureen develops, produces, and distributes a directory that gives information about United Way organizations and the services they provide. These directories are not comprehensive. Each is designed for use by a particular group of people in the community and is distributed accordingly. For example, a directory of services for senior citizens would be distributed to agencies which serve the senior population, to the senior citizens themselves, and to persons with aging parents. Maureen is presently developing a directory that will guide persons facing unemployment in the current economy to the agencies prepared to help them.

Grant funds support the development of one directory or handbook per year. Thus, Maureen must use her judgment and knowledge of the community's needs to identify each year's target population. Handbooks and directories average about 40 pages each, although the page count can be influenced by special needs of the target population, such as the need for large print among senior citizens. To produce handbooks and directories as cost-effectively as possible, Maureen relies heavily on

volunteers and on donations of materials and services from local business people. Maureen generally outlines the document herself, has a
volunteer write it, then checks the final draft before production.

Following an organizational policy that any activity beyond daily operations must be supported by a grant or be donated or underwritten by a
business or individual in the community, Maureen writes up to six grant
proposals each year. She begins by deciding what program or service she
wishes to propose; what financial, human, and material resources she
will need; what resources are already available; and what result she
hopes to see. She conducts research to be sure that what she proposes
can be done and will achieve the desired result. After reviewing her
plans with everyone in her office who might be affected by the new program, and after obtaining the director's approval, Maureen begins writing the proposal and developing the program budget. She also solicits
letters of support for the proposed project from persons who have been
involved in similar programs, persons who are familiar with United Way
and its programs, and persons who are likely to benefit if the proposed
program is funded. The purpose of such letters is to demonstrate to the
funding agency that the proposed service is needed and that Maureen's
organization is capable of efficiently and effectively meeting that need.
When the proposal is complete, Maureen must again obtain the director's approval before submitting it to a funding agency.

The development process tends to be similar for all proposals, but
other factors vary according to the requirements of the funding agency.
Community foundations, for example, tend to require only a two-page
letter with a budget. However, a proposal Maureen prepared for the
Points of Light Foundation in co-operation with United Way of America
totaled 10-20 pages. Proposals submitted to the State Department of
Human Services or the State Department of Health require yet more
detail about the proposed project and can total 30-40 pages.

Approximately once every two months, Maureen is called upon to
make a presentation that will help educate the public about the needs of
the community and the services United Way and its member organizations offer to meet those needs. Organizations such as the American
Association of Retired Persons (AARP), the American Association of University Women (AAUW), the Rotary and Kiwanis Clubs, church groups,
and other community groups invite Maureen to speak at their meetings.
Although these talks can be as short as 10 minutes or as long as an hour,
they generally average 20-25 minutes. In preparing to meet a community group, Maureen must plan her talk according to what the audience
has requested, prepare overhead transparencies and handouts, and plan
her schedule to include travel to and from the meeting.

While Maureen finds the diversity of activities in her job both challenging and rewarding, she looks forward, ultimately, to having responsibility for more than one division or for an entire organization. She may stay with the Middletown Area United Way or seek employment with another community service organization. In reflecting on her own career, the variety of projects she has worked on and responsibilities she has held, Maureen advises, "the more diverse you can become in your background and abilities, the better."

APPENDIX

FURTHER INFORMATION

Useful publications in the nonprofit and social service sector are too numerous to list completely. While your career advisor or someone in your area of interest will be able to direct you to specific publications, you may also find the following general-interest publications useful:

Books

Anzalone, J. (Ed.). (1985). *Good works: A guide to careers in social change* (3rd ed.). New York: Red Dembner Books.

Buell, B. & Hamerscheas, K. (1987). *Alternatives to the Peace Corps: Gaining Third World experience*. San Francisco: Food First Books.

Cohen, L. & Young, D. R. (1989). *Careers for dreamers and doers: A guide to management careers in the nonprofit sector*. New York: The Foundation Center.

Croner, H. B. (Ed.). (1990). *National directory of private social agencies*. Croner Publications, Inc.

Finding a job in the nonprofit sector. (1991). Rockville, MD: The Taft Group. Lewis, W. & Milano, C. (1987). *Profitable careers in nonprofit*. New York: John Wiley & Sons.

Parness, J. M. (Ed.) (1988). *The complete guide to Washington internships*. New York: JMP Enterprises.

Smith, D. C. (Ed.). (1990). *Great careers: The Fourth of July guide to careers, internships, and volunteer opportunities in the nonprofit sector* (2nd ed.). Garrett Park, MD: Garrett Park Press.

Newsletters and Directories

Community Jobs. A monthly publication of nationwide listings of socially responsible jobs and internships.

Current Jobs in Writing, Editing, and Communications. A newsletter published monthly by the National Employment Bulletin for the Communication Arts Profession. To subscribe, write or call

National Employment Bulletin for the Communication Arts Profession
P. O. Box 40550
5136 MacArthur Boulevard, NW
Washington, DC 20016
(703) 356-1683

Directory of Community Services. Published every five years by United Way. Lists organizations and the names and addresses of directors but does not announce openings.

The Job Seeker. A biweekly newsletter listing natural resources and environmental vacancies nationwide. A summer job special is also available. To subscribe, write or call

The Job Seeker
Rt. #2, Box 16
Warrens, WI 45666-9501
(608) 378-4290

Nonprofit Organizations

The Nature Conservancy
1815 North Lynn Street
Arlington, VA 22209
(703) 841-5300
http://www.tnc.org/welcome/
(Some state chapters also have World Wide Web sites.)

Goodwill Industries of America, Inc.
9200 Wisconsin Avenue
Bethesda, MD 20814-3896
(301) 530-6500
http://www.goodwill.org

Planned Parenthood Association
17 North State Street
Chicago, IL 60602-3315
(312) 781-9550
http://www.plannedparenthood.org

Alcoholics Anonymous World Services, Inc.
468 Park Avenue South
New York, NY 10016-6820
(212) 686-1100
http://www.alcoholics-anonymous.org

The Child Welfare League of America
440 First Street, NW, Suite 310
Washington, DC 20001-2085
(202) 638-2952
http://www./cwla.org

Center for Science in the Public Interest
1501 Sixteenth Street, NW
Washington, DC 20036-1499

Habitat for Humanity, Inc.
Habitat & Church Streets
Americus, GA 31709
(912) 924-6935
http://www.habitat.org

United Way of America
701 North Fairfax Street
Alexandria, VA 22314-2044
(703) 836-7100
http:www.unitedway.org
(Has an excellent training program for directors.)

B'Nai B'rith Youth Organization
1640 Rhode Island Avenue
Washington, DC 20036-3278
http://www.bbyo.org

Boy Scouts of America National Council
1325 Walnut Hill Lane
Irving, TX 75038-3096

(214) 580-2000
http://www.bsa.scouting.org

Boys and Girls Clubs of America
1230 West Peachtree Street N.W.
Atlanta, GA 30309
(404) 815-5700
http://www.bgca.org/html/home.html

Coro Foundation
609 South Grand Street 810
Los Angeles, CA 90017-3851
(213) 623-1234
http://www.coro.org

International Voluntary Services, Inc.
1424 16th Street, NW, Suite 204
Washington, DC 20036-2285

National Board of the YWCA of the USA
726 Broadway
New York, NY 10003-9511
http://www.ywca.org

Professional Societies

Public Relations Society of America
33 Irving Place, 3rd Floor
New York, NY 10003-2376
(212) 995-2230
http://www.prsa.org

Women in Communications
1244 Richie Highway, Suite 6
Arnold, MD 21012-1887
(410) 544-7442
http://ww.womcom.org

National Society of Fund Raising Executives
1101 King Street, Suite 700
Alexandria, VA 22314
(703) 684-0410
http://www.nsfre.org

Graduate Programs in Nonprofit Management

Many university-based schools of Business or Schools of Management offer courses and/or degree programs focusing on management in the nonprofit sector. The following are only a sample of the programs available.

Boston University School of Management
Boston, MA 02215
http://www.management.bu.edu/program/index.html
Select "MBA—Public and Nonprofit Management"

Mandel Center for Non-Profit Organizations
Case Western Reserve University
Cleveland, OH 44106
http://www.wru.edu/msass/mandel center/index.html

NOTE

[1] These profiles are based on interviews conducted in 1991 and 1992. Specific details of each interviewee's career are presumed to have changed in the interim, but the discussions reflect activities typical of their respective positions at the time.

REFERENCES

Career choices for the 90s: For students of political science & government. (1990). (pp. 38–43, 49–53). New York: Walker Publishing.

Career Information Center, Vol. 3: Communications and the arts, and Vol. 11: Public and community services. (4th ed.) (1990). Princeton, NJ: Visual Education Corporation. Mission Hills, CA: Glencoe Publishing.

Nadler, B. J. (1989). *Liberal arts jobs: What they are and how to get them* (2nd ed.). Princeton, NJ: Peterson's Guides.

Norback, C. (1980). *Careers Encyclopedia.* Homewood, IL: Dow Jones-Irwin.

U.S. Department of Labor, Bureau of Labor Statistics. (1990). *Occupational outlook handbook: 1990-91 edition.* Washington, DC: Government Printing Office.

United States code annotated, title 5: Government organization and employees, sections 5101-7100. St. Paul, MN: West Publishing.

chapter 11
Technical and Scientific Communicators in Advertising

Karen Levine
Adam Filippo and Associates
Pittsburgh, Pennsylvania

Jobs

- Junior copywriter, writer, senior copywriter, copy supervisor; technical or marketing communications specialist.
- Group creative director, executive creative director; account executive, account supervisor, vice president account services.
- Communications manager, communications director; advertising/marketing communications director, vice president advertising/marketing communications.
- Freelance technical writer, freelance marketing communications specialist.

Responsibilities

- *Entry level:* research, write, and edit marketing communications and advertising copy; collaborate with other members of the creative team.
- *Experienced:* (in addition to the above) analyze communication needs and write communication plans; develop copy strategies for marketing communication programs and ads; manage projects; supervise junior staff; handle account management activities; assist with new business development.

Employment Outlook

Highly dependent upon the general condition of the economy—not for the fainthearted. However, technical writers with talent, versatility, and a promotional flair will find an outlet for their skills. As organizations become more sophisticated in their promotional approaches, the need for professional communicators who can translate complex concepts into functional, persuasive marketing tools will increase.

Salary Range

Entry level: $20,000 to $30,000. Experienced: $60,000 and higher. As a freelancer, beginning: $25 to $45 per hour; established: $75 per hour and higher.

INTRODUCTION

Does the prospect of a career in advertising or marketing communications intrigue you? How can you know if your talent and temperament are suited to this industry?

If you're a person who

- thrives on challenges;
- understands marketing;
- relishes learning about new industries, products, processes, and services; and
- writes with extraordinary clarity, creativity, and exquisitely precise language,

then advertising might be an industry in which you'll find both job satisfaction and success.

You'll need to be able to handle uncertainty and perhaps even job insecurity. You must have the ability to work well under pressure, respond effectively to tight deadlines, and juggle multiple projects simultaneously.

If you have the disposition for it, technical communication in an advertising context can be a very exciting profession. It will keep your adrenaline going, and if you're good at it—and a quick study—technical advertising/marketing communication will allow you to tackle a diversity of assignments unlike any other technical communication job I know. As one copywriter put it, "Your future is bounded only by your ability, mitigated aggressiveness, and blind fate." Advertising is an exciting but unpredictable business.

Before we get started, here are a few working definitions for industry terms I've used throughout the chapter. They are not necessarily dictionary definitions. However, they do convey some of the distinctions which exist within the advertising and marketing communications community.

Advertising

A sales message delivered in a paid-for space (for example, in newspapers, popular magazines, trade publications, and on billboards) or time (such as radio or television). This definition makes a distinction between advertising and other forms of marketing communications such as corporate capabilities brochures, product literature, direct mail, point-of-purchase displays, sales promotions or incentive programs, promotional videos, and CD-ROMs and interactive media, to name just a few.

Marketing Communications

A term which encompasses a variety of communication specialties, all of which share a promotional intent, although their respective media of transmission and scope may vary greatly. Exactly what falls within the realm of marketing communications is a matter of some discussion within the profession. Any communication which helps an organization to

- create an image for itself (both internally, with its employees, and externally, among its many target audiences);
- boost awareness of its products and services;
- educate prospective customers about the benefits of those products and services; and
- generate increased demand for its products or services and results in higher sales,

falls within the category of marketing communications, even if not exclusively so. A company's annual report, for example, is generally considered an investor relations document and not a form of marketing communications. Yet every client company I have ever written for has used its annual report as a marketing tool.

Therefore, although some practitioners might disagree, the definition of marketing communications which I've offered is broad enough to include the specialized practices which form the basis for advertising, public relations, media relations, collateral promotional literature (including capabilities brochures, marketing brochures, product literature, technical literature, and special event support materials), and direct mail marketing. While differing in their specifics, these are all forms of marketing communications.

Business-to-Business Marketing

The marketing of products and services by one organization to other companies, the government, and not-for-profit institutions for their use in producing another product or service—or for resale to other organizations. Marketing of this type used to be called "industrial marketing," in contrast to "consumer" marketing. However, in the advertising community and among most marketers, the term industrial marketing has largely been replaced by "business-to-business." This change in terminology reflects two important changes in marketing communication practice. First, the practice has been expanded to encompass more than manufacturing companies. Second, it has adapted consumer marketing and advertising techniques to the business-to-business arena. The term business-to-business marketing thus blurs some of the old boundaries between promotional techniques once thought suitable for only one area or the other.

An example of business-to-business marketing is a company that produces a polymer and then sells it to a processing company, which injection molds that polymer into housings for computer monitors. The injection molder produces the housings as a custom product for a manufacturing company which assembles computer monitors. That company, in turn, may sell its computer monitors to wholesale distributors or to retailers. All of these transactions are considered business-to-business. It is not until you seek to purchase a computer monitor that this chain of transactions switches from being business-to-business to consumer marketing.

JOB DESCRIPTION

Technical advertising is a specialized form of advertising designed to help companies who offer technical products or services to market, promote, and sell these products or services, primarily to other companies that make something else. For example, a company that produces plastic resins may want to sell them to a manufacturer that custom molds these plastic resins for in-line skate boots and wheels. The communications which help sell the plastic resins to the skate manufacturer are an example of technical advertising or business-to-business advertising.

This form of advertising is very different from the advertising that the skate manufacturer—Rollerblade, for instance—uses to promote sales of its products to consumers. Occasionally, technical advertising is targeted at the general public (referred to by advertisers as "consumers"), but this segment is small compared to the overall technical advertising field and is not discussed further in this chapter.

Before we consider what a day in the life of a copywriter in business-to-business advertising might be like, let me try to describe the structure and environment within a typical advertising agency.

Where Technical Advertising Takes Place

Most technical advertising is created by advertising agencies or marketing communications consulting firms that specialize in serving business-to-business clients—that plastic resins company mentioned above, for example. Some technical advertising is also produced in-house by departments within corporations, such as advertising or marketing services departments within the plastic resins firm. I won't be focusing on these kinds of departments in this chapter, but you can find more information in the chapter on "Writing in Business and Manufacturing."

At one time, an advertising agency retained by a client virtually had a lock on all, or a very large part, of that client's advertising business. The agency would have a contract which designated it as "agency of record," and all advertising done by that client would be handled by the one agency. For example, a corporation might designate Agency A as agency of record for all of their corporate image advertising. Dow's advertising campaign, "Dow lets you do great things," is an example of corporate image advertising. However, today, companies may contract with different agencies to take care of different parts of their advertising business. For example, Dow might designate a separate agency to handle the advertising for one of its divisions. Within Bayer Corporation, different agencies handle individual product lines: Their polymer products, industrial coatings, agricultural chemicals, and pharmaceutical products are each assigned to a different agency. Within a division, different brands may even be assigned to different agencies to give each brand a unique image. This last situation is more common with consumer products than with business-to-business products or services, but it does occur in the business-to-business arena. Depending on the specific nature of each client company's corporate, divisional, and product line communications requirements—and the scope of work which has been awarded to the advertising agency—a technical writer may well be involved in writing corporate communications and a variety of marketing communications for a client.

Most advertising agencies are retained on an annual or multi-year contract basis that establishes an annual fee for professional services plus a commission on the value of the media placement. Agencies earn commissions (at a specified percentage) for placing television, radio, newspaper, and magazine/trade journal advertising for their clients. Since media placement costs can be considerable, particularly when broadcast media such as television and radio are involved, these commissions are often the lifeblood of an advertising agency's revenue stream. Commissions provide the incentive for advertising agencies to concentrate on advertising per se, rather than on other forms of marketing communications. That's why consumer products have traditionally been the mainstay of most major advertising agencies—because consumer products rely heavily on advertising in various media to promote their products.

Marketing communication consulting firms specializing in serving business-to-business clients have been born out of the specialized nature of technical product marketing. Most often, these firms are engaged for a particular assignment, an individual project or campaign, rather than on a retainer basis, and are paid according to the scope of services for that specific assignment. New work from a client is based on successfully delivering the current project and cultivating a strong relationship on a project-by-project basis with that client, rather than on an annual or multi-year contract. Marketing communication firms that are diligent in their efforts often enjoy long-standing client relationships that can very well outlast an agency relationship. Depending on the arrangements with the client, marketing communication firms may, or may not, receive a commission for media placement.

Some corporations use both advertising agencies and marketing communication firms, awarding their consumer advertising work to an agency and other marketing communication assignments to a consulting firm. By adopting this approach, companies often optimize their communications expenditures and retain flexibility.

The Structure of a Typical Advertising Agency

Most advertising agencies have two parallel structures within them: account management and creative services. These two groups have very different functions within an agency, but they must work together cooperatively to provide clients with the best possible integrated marketing communications or advertising solutions.

The account management team is generally responsible for

- seeking out and acquiring new clients;
- developing short-term and long-term communications plans for the client's corporate communications needs and individual product or service advertising;
- negotiating schedules and budgets with the client;
- being the client's advocate within the agency and accurately communicating client input to the creative department;

- being the agency's spokesperson with the client, providing day-to-day communication with the client, including progress reports on the status of campaigns and troubleshooting; and
- planning media selection and placement. (Most mid-sized or larger agencies have a separate media department to handle this function. In small agencies, the media planner usually works as part of the account management team.)

The creative services group is generally responsible for

- providing creative strategies to help acquire new business (for example, advertising campaign themes, slogans, graphic and photographic design approaches, "the look" of an advertising campaign);
- developing creative strategies for existing clients to address changes in the marketplace, to support new products or services, and to enhance a company's image in the marketplace;
- art directing all print, broadcast, and other electronic media;
- designing and writing copy;
- coordinating with outside vendors, such as photographers, illustrators, printers, publishers, video and electronic media producers; and
- assuring quality and on-time delivery of all materials produced.

Many agencies have a traffic department that coordinates production activities with outside vendors. The traffic department's function is to ensure timely delivery of finished products to clients or to the media.

The Structure of a Marketing Communication Consulting Firm

The same functions exist within marketing communication consulting firms. The difference is that they are usually organized and deployed differently. In my experience, professionals in marketing communication consulting firms often carry both account management and creative responsibilities. Who bears these responsibilities on a given project is determined by the expertise required to execute a specific assignment, rather than by predetermined roles (which is the norm in any agency environment).

YOUR LIFE AS A TECHNICAL WRITER IN ADVERTISING

What types of things will you do as a technical communicator in marketing communications or advertising? You'll write, of course, and rewrite and rewrite until you and the client are satisfied that the copy is just right. But what will you be writing? You can expect to write a variety of promotional materials, not just ads. Among these materials are marketing and product sales and technical literature, direct mail campaigns, marketing videos, interactive media—in fact, virtually any type of marketing communication can be fair game for a technical writer who writes with a promotional flair.

As with any effective communication, however, the process begins long before you start writing and entails far more than just successfully putting words on paper. You'll need to become knowledgeable about your clients' business. A spokesperson for the advertising agency of Bozell, Jacobs, Kenyon & Eckhardt once said, "If your advertising agency doesn't know your business, they don't know their business." Read everything you can find about your client company, their products and services, their industry, and their customers' industries. Your days of studying and reading won't be over when you graduate; to be successful in advertising, you'll have to be a lifelong learner.

If you didn't write your client's marketing and communication plans, you'll certainly want to read them to learn everything you can about the client's marketing strategies. Then, and only then, will you be reasonably well-prepared to embark on your current assignment.

As the writer on the project, you'll probably want to do your own copy content research by interviewing the appropriate client representatives to define your target audience, define the objectives and desired results of the communication, establish key points to be covered in the copy, and determine the context in which the communication will be delivered. Will it be an ad? A capabilities brochure? A marketing brochure for a product or service? A technical specification sheet? A complete program that consists of many separate but interrelated communications materials? Even if an account executive has done some of this prep work for you, it is usually helpful to talk with the client yourself. By initiating client contact, you can get answers directly and avoid the unintentional filtering which occurs when an intermediary is part of the communication process.

When audiences, objectives, and key messages have been defined and your preliminary questions have been answered, it's time to put these together in a copy platform for the specific project you'll be working on. A copy platform will also include your recommended theme, a working headline or title, the tone and style of the piece, and a brief outline of the copy content. These will be reviewed within your firm and then presented to the client. As an entry-level employee, you may or may not participate in these meetings. Your participation will vary depending on the culture within your particular agency. As you gain experience—and the confidence of your employer—you will, in all likelihood, be invited to attend client meetings and become an active presenter.

Setting creative strategies is another key element in developing effective advertising or marketing communications. Often, a brainstorming session is part of the process by which creative strategies are developed. These brainstorming sessions may occur before, at the same time as, or following the development of the copy platform. In all probability, you'll participate in these sessions. During them, the copywriters, art directors and graphic designers, creative supervisors, and account manager or supervisor explore ideas for the creative aspects of the assignment—a catchy headline or a powerful visual hook.

Television and movie depictions of these brainstorming sessions often portray them as adolescent free-for-alls. While it's true that brainstorming sessions can be fun, they are also hard work and put pressure on everyone to be creative on the spot. A truer portrait would show a talented team of individuals, hard at work, jointly exploring options for creative execution in a fairly disciplined fashion. Coming up with a creative execution that matches a client's objectives can be like giving birth—a long gestation period, a hard labor, and a deep sigh of relief when your baby is born.

Once the copy platform has been approved and the creative strategy is set, you may need to do some additional research to ferret out the fine points and subtleties of the information you need to cover. If understanding a manufacturing process is important to the copy, your client may arrange a plant tour for you. If knowing how a device operates will help you differentiate your client's product from their competitor's, the client may provide you with a live-product demonstration. If their product offers enhanced performance vis-à-vis their competitors, a client's technical staff may brief you on the product testing they did and the results they obtained so that you can include these meaningfully in the copy.

As a technical writer, you typically will handle "copy contact" with the client. This means that you'll talk with client representatives to research and resolve copy content issues as they arise and ultimately to help ensure the technical accuracy of the information you present.

Now, finally, you're ready to write. You may write preliminary ad copy in the morning and start on a companion brochure in the afternoon. You'll most certainly bounce back and forth among assignments for a single client or for several clients as copy goes out to a client for review and comment, then cycles back for revisions.

You will be interacting on an ongoing basis with the art director or graphic designer responsible for creative visualization of the design concept, layout, and finished camera-ready art. This step is essential to ensuring that the copy and design work together to support the objectives of the specific piece.

In addition to original copywriting, you may be asked to make suggestions about or edit copy written by another writer in your firm or copy supplied by your client. You will certainly be responsible for proofreading, not only the copy you submit to the client, but the typeset copy that goes to the printer and the "bluelines" the printer returns for your review and approval before putting the job on press.

If there's such a thing as a typical day in advertising, I've never had one. Every day is a new adventure. Clients drive the process. Things move at the clients' pace because they are the ultimate decision makers in advertising. As a technical writer in this field, you'll need to be responsive when the client is ready to take the next step—and patient when the client is not.

Clients are known to change their minds frequently—often at the whim of one key decision maker—after everything has been reviewed all the way up and down the decision-making ladder. So you'll need to be emotionally detached from the copy you've written and prepared to support your copywriting decisions with sound, objective rationales. More important, you must be willing to accommodate a client preference calmly and graciously when even your best efforts at persuasion do not prevail—despite the soundness of your copy recommendation.

You will also have some administrative duties. First among these is keeping track of your billable hours—the amount of time you spend each day on each project. This accounting helps your employers know if they have accurately estimated the amount of time it will take for you to do the work on the project and set the fee at a profitable level. Even if they have taken the project on a fixed-fee basis (and therefore cannot go back to the client and ask for additional money), knowing the hours it took you to complete a project sets a benchmark that can be useful in setting fees on similar projects in the future.

As you gain experience, you may also acquire project management responsibilities in addition to your copywriting duties. These project management responsibilities may include

- tracking and reporting overall progress on a project;
- coordinating the efforts of in-house individuals contributing to the project;
- handling client-directed project correspondence;
- negotiating initial budgets and schedules, and changes to these resulting from client-approved revisions to the project;
- contributing to photographic/illustrative art direction;

- managing details with outside vendors; and
- identifying opportunities for additional business with the client.

CAREER PATH OPTIONS

Your career track in an advertising agency or marketing communications firm will generally follow one of two career ladders, depending on whether you are interested in advancing on the creative side or the account management side of the business. Although job titles vary from firm to firm, a typical progression on the creative side would be from junior copywriter to writer, to senior copywriter, to copy supervisor, to creative director, to vice president of creative services. On the account management side, the progression might be from copywriter to account executive/copy contact, to account supervisor, to vice president of account services. Copywriters generally do not become senior executives without gaining considerable account management experience. If you aspire to someday join the ranks of senior management, you will have to, fairly early in your career, become not just a writer, but one of the "suits" (what the "creatives" in an agency call the account executives).

Another factor which will affect your career opportunities is the size of the firm for which you work. As the above progression suggests, medium-sized and large firms tend to be more highly structured. Small-to medium-sized firms tend to be more flexible in their approach to individual job descriptions and boundaries, often enabling a qualified technical communicator to handle both copywriting and account management responsibilities.

EMPLOYMENT OUTLOOK

Corporate "right-sizing" and structural changes in firms are creating new opportunities for technical writers. However, your employment opportunities in this field will be subject to the state of the overall economy. When the economy is strong, companies tend to do more advertising. Conversely, when the economy slows, businesses cut back on what they consider to be discretionary expenditures. Although this pattern runs counter to good marketing sense, advertising is considered by many companies to be a discretionary expenditure and is among the first things to be reduced significantly or eliminated when the economy takes a serious downturn.

Consequently, those advertising agencies whose revenue is highly dependent on the commissions they earn on media placements (i.e., on major ad campaigns running as TV commercials, radio spots, or in popular magazines) tend to be more vulnerable to economic fluctuations. When business is strong, agencies hire more staff to meet the demand. When business is off, agency personnel get downsized, and, unfortunately, those employees whose areas of expertise are perceived to be on the periphery of mainstream agency work are the most vulnerable.

Technical writers who do not also have extremely imaginative, creative, and versatile ad copywriting skills appropriate for the broad spectrum of their agency's clients may find their jobs in jeopardy should the economy turn soft. It's important, therefore, that you demonstrate early in your career that you have versatility in your writing style, the ability to adapt to any marketing communications genre, and the commitment to learn quickly what you need to know to be proficient in a client's industry (an industry about which you may have known nothing the day before your assignment).

Your employment opportunities in advertising will also vary considerably, depending upon each advertising agency's current client roster. The more business-to-business client companies an agency has (as distinct from its consumer products clients), the more likely the agency will be to have a need for a technical communicator. The long-term employment outlook for anyone on the staff of an advertising agency is always, to a large extent, dependent upon the agency's ability to attract and retain profitable businesses as clients.

Anecdotal evidence suggests that turnover rates in advertising agencies among all staff, not just copywriters, are higher than in the corporate arena. Recent trends in corporate right-sizing appear to be creating opportunities for talented technical copywriters in highly entrepreneurial marketing communications consulting firms and for technical copywriters willing to pursue a career in advertising as technical communications freelancers. In fact, the whole right-sizing phenomenon has spawned freelance careers for many corporate employees who found themselves right-sized right out of their jobs. These individuals have taken their talent, skills, and years of experience and turned consultant or freelancer. They often sell their services as independent contractors back to their previous employers on a more lucrative per-hour or per-day basis than they earned as full-time employees.

Unlike the specified salaries of corporate employees, the annual earnings of these self-employed individuals fluctuate. The fluctuations are a result of the volume of work they obtain and, consequently, the actual number of hours for which they can bill their services; their overhead expenses, such as office space, equipment, telephone, fax, supplies, even health benefits (once paid for by their corporate employer); and the miscellaneous other costs of doing business, such as self-employment taxes.

Freelancing in technical advertising, therefore, entails some financial risk you should be prepared to assume if you want to pay the rent and eat on a regular basis. To learn more about life as a freelance technical writer, see the chapter on "Freelancing or Consulting" in this book.

In addition to the right-sizing I have just discussed, the advertising and marketing communications industry is, itself, in the midst of some major structural changes. These changes are driven, in part, by the challenges of financial survival in economically constrained times. But they are also coupled with demands from increasingly astute clients for cost-efficient programs and high levels of measurable effectiveness for their advertising investment. The result of these pressures on the advertising community has been the emergence of a number of hybrid organizations. These hybrids often deviate from the classic model of advertising agency structure—and often in ways unique to a single agency, or just a handful of firms, that are responding to niche market opportunities.

For example, the firm for which I work is a hybrid organization. We are a corporate identity and marketing consulting firm that uses strategically oriented, problem-solving methodologies to help client companies create and maintain a strong, positive perception of their organization, its products, and its services among all of its external and internal target audiences. We use traditional media, such as print, radio, television, and outdoor advertising; video; collateral print; public relations; trade show exhibits; and point-of-purchase displays to create awareness, generate positive public perceptions, and build preference for our clients. We also use other media—such as interactive multimedia, CD-ROM and CDi, online catalogs, informational kiosks, and the World Wide Web—when they are effective in reaching our clients' target audiences.

The staff and management of the firm are all experienced, senior professionals, each with his or her unique area of specialization, such as strategic planning, market research, communications, graphic design, interior design, industrial design, and space planning. As a result, we have a very flat organizational structure and a fairly fluid, matrix-type reporting structure. Based on the overall needs of a particular client and the nature of a specific project, we assemble a project team with the appropriate areas of expertise, designate a project manager, and work collaboratively and synergistically over the life of the project. The next project for that same client may have a different project team assigned to it, depending on the nature of the work. In all cases, however, we attempt to maintain regular, thorough, in-house communication about the scope, content, intent, and status of client projects so that all personnel in the company know about all of our clients and are prepared to step into projects on an as-needed basis with minimal briefing time.

While the emergence of such hybrid organizations has been beneficial for client companies, it also has created confusion in the marketplace during this period of transition, especially in the ways in which advertising and marketing firms describe themselves. Therefore, simply contacting advertising agencies for available positions won't exhaust the universe of possibilities open to you in this field. Companies may also refer to themselves as corporate identity consultants, strategic planning consultants, marketing communications consulting firms, public relations firms, and direct mail marketers. Yet within them all are opportunities for you as a technical communicator if you know how to market yourself to best advantage.

In addition, despite corporate reductions in staff, some corporations include technical writers on their advertising staffs, and some hire technical writers into their marketing divisions to work in tandem with marketing personnel to develop promotional materials. If you have your heart set on this route, by all means explore it—but with realistic expectations and full knowledge of the current trends.

Typical Salaries

At the entry level in an advertising agency, you can expect a salary ranging between approximately $20,000 and $30,000 per year. Entry-level salaries may be affected by your educational accomplishments; your portfolio presentation; and your familiarity with the products, services, and industries of the agency's clients for whom you'll be writing copy. Other factors which may influence your starting salary are the geographic location of the job, the overall size of the agency, and the gross annual billings of the branch office in which you will work.

Experienced professionals—that is, copywriters with 10 years of solid, award-winning copywriting experience—can earn $80,000 to $90,000 per year in a large agency and sometimes far more. Those who also have account management responsibilities (because they are involved with account retention, growth, and new business development) are likely to have even higher earning potential during their careers.

Unlike the technical writer who is an employee of an advertising agency and, therefore, on salary, freelancers may charge by the hour or set a fixed fee for a defined project. A very wide range exists in billable hourly rates for freelancers: $25 to $45 per hour for a freelancer with good skills and minimal experience is not uncommon. A highly experienced freelancer with a proven track record, a reputation for delivering excellent work on time, and a well-developed network of contacts (both in advertising agencies and within advertisers' organizations) may well be able to charge $75 to $125 per hour as a standard rate and more than that on projects where some specialized industry expertise is required.

These may look like hefty per-hour fees. But, before you decide to travel at warp speed through the freelance universe, keep in mind that freelancers get paid only for the hours they actually work; only after they have satisfactorily delivered a finished product; and often, not until the advertising agency that subcontracted the work to them has been paid by the client. While the upside potential on the hourly rate may seem attractive, if you are considering freelancing you should also factor into your calculations the cost of those things which your employer would supply if you were working full-time at an agency. Among those items are the cost of the time you spend searching out the project and cultivating the client to award you the work, your overhead (e.g., equipment, supplies, phone calls, faxes, mileage), and the cost of your benefits (health insurance, holidays, and sick time).

PREPARATION

Many well-established technical communicators working in advertising today did not start out with that career path in mind. Some earned undergraduate degrees in technical, scientific, or business disciplines and, early in their careers, held positions which required a substantial amount of writing for project documentation, instructional materials, or marketing and promotional purposes. Other technical communicators in advertising hold degrees in English, journalism, or communications and have developed areas of technical expertise by completing course work in technical disciplines or by on-the-job collaboration with technical specialists within their industry.

With the growth of strong technical communication programs at the undergraduate and graduate levels over the past 10-15 years, technical writers in advertising can expect to face far more stringent standards for entry into the field than did their predecessors. This is because clients in the business-to-business arena have grown increasingly more sophisticated about marketing communications and are requiring their agencies to provide credentials on the personnel who will work on their account.

How then do you prepare yourself to be a technical writer in this field? You can take a number of undergraduate courses that would be helpful. By and large, however, the courses fall into three categories: writing and communication courses, business courses, and technical and scientific courses.

Writing and Communication Courses

Here are some of the writing and communication courses that would be well worth an investment of your time and energy:

- writing for advertising
- public relations—theory and practice
- communications planning
- marketing communications
- corporate communications
- employee communications
- organizational communications
- technical writing
- scientific writing
- business writing
- financial writing
- video scriptwriting
- introductory/advanced courses in video production
- writing for electronic and interactive media
- writing instructional materials, documentation, and manuals
- public speaking
- creative writing/fiction and non-fiction

Most of the above course suggestions are self-explanatory in terms of their usefulness to a technical writer interested in building fundamental skills. They are presented in somewhat random order, since the benefit of any individual course will depend, in part, upon your career aspirations.

Because the ability to present effectively to a client is essential to moving up in advertising, a course in public speaking can be invaluable. It will help you gain poise and boost your confidence in your ability to deliver a polished presentation to a group.

I've included a course in creative writing (which at first glance may seem out of place) because advertising—even business-to-business advertising—needs imagination and creativity to engage readers and be effective. Often, writing styles and devices common to creative writing can be adapted in technical advertising and enliven what might otherwise be dry prose. Further, advertising agencies demand not only a high degree of writing proficiency in a copywriter, but they want to see spark, finesse, a unique juxtaposition of words in a writer's copy that separates the mundane from the magnificent. A course in creative writing would enable you to practice marrying the precision required of technical writing with the stylized prose more characteristic of creative writing. The end result could help you produce award-winning copy.

Basic Business Classes

A number of basic business courses may help you understand the environment in which you'll be working. Among those I would strongly recommend are

- introduction to marketing
- advertising
- business-to-business (or industrial) marketing
- international marketing
- strategic planning
- market research
- cultural diversity in the business environment
- finance
- accounting.

Marketing courses will help you better understand how companies price their products, promote them, and distribute them to the marketplace. Since all these factors should be considered in developing effective promotional copy, marketing course work can be an excellent introduction to how to support those activities with appropriate communications products. Specialized courses in business-to-business marketing and international marketing can be particularly useful since the majority of technical copywriting opportunities in advertising are for clients who fall within these two areas.

Advertising classes will help you understand the structure of the industry you're contemplating and your place within that industry. These courses typically describe the agency environment, how an agency is structured and functions, how it is compensated for its services, and how the agency/client relationship works. Such classes also will give you an overview of the media advertising employs and the laws and statutes which control those media. Since the legal and regulatory environment affects the types of claims advertisers can legally make for their products, you'll do well to be familiar with restrictions in order to approach copy development appropriately. It is, of course, the responsibility of the client's legal counsel to review promotional copy for its conformity with legal and regulatory requirements, but you'll save yourself a lot of revision time if you understand these issues to start with. Most advertising classes will also touch upon patent and copyright law since they affect advertising content and ownership.

Being familiar with strategic planning concepts will help you see the relationships among a client company's overall goals and objectives, recognize how these translate into marketing strategies, and draw the connections between them and all the marketing communications you produce. In a similar manner, understanding the principles of market research will help you appreciate the significance of customer attitude, select data gathered through qualitative and quantitative market research, and learn how to use that market intelligence to good effect in writing copy.

In today's complex, multinational business environment, a course in multiculturalism can help sensitize you to issues of cultural diversity and to linguistic differences that you may need to accommodate in your work.

If balancing your checkbook is as far as your financial knowledge goes, a course in finance will teach you about the fundamental financial issues and principles of concern to business. Courses in both finance and accounting will be invaluable to you if you want to be able to write annual reports and be aware of the bottom line financial issues that are certain to emerge as you plan, write, and produce marketing communications. By applying sound financial principals, you'll help produce marketing communications and advertising more cost-effectively, thereby contributing more to the profitability of your client company and your employer.

Technical and Scientific Courses

As part of your technical writing education, you may be required to take one or more courses in technical and scientific disciplines that match your career interests. The specific courses will, of course, vary from person to person. What might help you make sound choices among the catalog of courses available to you is to think about the knowledge you could acquire to serve your future clients best. Let's imagine for a moment that you hope to work for an agency that has several health care clients, among them Big City University Hospital, Not-So-Generic Pharmaceuticals Company, and Haphazard Health Insurance Company. What types of technical and scientific course work might help you prepare to serve that agency's client mix? Here are some suggestions:

- introductory courses in public health
- epidemiology
- health administration
- chemistry, biochemistry, and toxicology
- anatomy and physiology

- risk management
- crisis communications

Basically, the idea is to supplement your training in writing with courses that have special relevance to the industry or industries you wish to serve. By thinking about the day-to-day business of your prospective clients, you'll be able to select course work that will help make you more marketable when it comes time to begin your job search.

Advanced Degrees

Advanced degrees can be helpful to a technical writer interested in advertising, particularly if you combine a degree in writing at one level with a degree in a technical discipline at the other. Whether or not advanced degrees will significantly increase the salary offer on your first job is probably a coin toss, because advertising agencies are a lot like the person from Missouri who takes a "show me" attitude. An advanced degree will, however, certainly help you establish credibility more quickly with your clients and your employer because you will go in better prepared. As a result, you may be able to advance your career—and your earnings—more rapidly.

On-the-Job Experience

Hands-on experience is invaluable to a technical writer in advertising. If you've worked in marketing or advertising before, that's a plus. Even more useful, however, is the knowledge you've gained if you've ever worked within a client's industry, regardless of whether it was on the technical or the marketing side of the business. While there, you probably learned the vocabulary, methodologies, and processes relevant to that industry, and the needs and expectations of the industry's customers.

Essential Skills and Personal Attributes

What are essential skills for a technical communicator working in advertising? Be computer literate. Know a variety of word processing and desktop publishing software programs. Understand principles of good design and print production processes.

Learn about video and audio production and keep on top of developments in the electronic media as they continue to evolve. CD-ROM, electronic information kiosks, online catalogs, interactive media, and marketing via the World Wide Web and commercial online services are just a few of the media you'll want to know to serve your clients well.

As for personal attributes, there are many which would be useful to you in this field. Be a voracious reader. Reading will not only increase your knowledge—and provide you with useful quotes—it will also help you improve your writing. Be curious, open to new ideas. Study what other copywriters do. Pay attention to award-winning work; there are reasons it was successful.

Be a good talker. Keep to the point. Be concise, pleasant, and always courteous. More importantly, however, be a good listener. When it comes to good advertising, the key to success is in finding out what's really important to your clients and their customers. This will be essential if you're to serve their needs successfully.

Learn to stay calm under pressure. Cultivate a sense of humor. Be a good team player. Be flexible, cooperative, and remember that clients are always right, even when they're being boneheaded about something. Find a tactful way to point them in the right direction if you want to continue to work on their accounts. And, for heaven's sake, learn when to push a little harder, when to back down, and when it's wise just to keep your mouth shut.

Finally, advertising is about image. Tend to yours. Be well-groomed and well-dressed. For most business-to-business clients, be stylish but not too trendy in your overall look.

FINDING A JOB

Positioning yourself to be perceived as a valuable prospective employee to an advertising agency or a marketing communications firm takes some thought and preparation. First, understand that many such companies, advertising agencies in particular, have a very narrow view of what a technical writer does. Knowing how to position yourself properly is essential to getting an interview and to getting hired.

In researching this chapter, I found quite often that the first response I got from advertising agencies was that they don't hire full-time technical writers—and if they need "that sort" of writing, they find a freelancer to work with them on the project. However, my personal experience in the field tells me this isn't entirely true, since I was recruited by a major regional advertising agency straight out of a master's degree program in technical communication. That agency wanted someone with advanced academic credentials in technical communication, who also had experience in basic industries, such as metals, plastics, and chemicals. They hired me to handle both account management and technical marketing copywriting for one of their largest accounts.

The answer, then, to the question of positioning yourself lies first in finding a firm that has made a substantial commitment to serving business-to-business, rather than consumer product, clients. It helps to know who an agency's major business-to-business clients are. Reading trade publications, such as *Advertising Age* and *Ad Week*, can often help you learn about which agencies represent what clients in the industry sectors in which you have technical expertise. These magazines regularly report on accounts which are up for agency review (which means the present agency could be out and a new one hired) and agencies which have just landed new accounts. New accounts often lead to hiring new staff, so knowing what's happening in the firms you're targeting for a job is very important. Call an advertising agency you're interested in and ask the receptionist who some of their biggest business-to-business clients are. If there's an industry you're particularly interested in, call the companies within that industry and ask them what agencies they use. Don't be afraid to pick up the phone.

Second, you'll need to make a case for the advantages you offer as a highly skilled writer. Your prospective employer may think that a technical writer's capabilities are confined to writing documentation, reference manuals, grant proposals, and similar communications. Your task is to make your resume, cover letter, and interview responses demonstrate that you are a very creative copywriter, who brings the added benefit of being able to handle technical concepts and vocabulary with ease, and who can transform technical information into creative, effective promotional copy. Prospective employers need to see a spark of creativity, some pizzazz, the proverbial "sizzle" in both your writing and your presentation of yourself . . . because that's what they're buying, and that's what they, in turn, are selling to their clients. These two basic principles hold true regardless of whether you're targeting an entry-level or advanced position in this field.

Finally, be persistent and don't lose heart. Even in a constrained economy, if you've got the flair for advertising copywriting, you've got the skill to sell yourself right into that job you've always dreamed about.

PROFESSIONAL PROFILES

The profiles which follow provide two views of technical communicators in the advertising field. The first, Chuck Stanwix's profile, is a view from within a traditional advertising agency. The second, Wendy Jameson's profile, gives the perspective of someone who developed her career within an agency environment, then moved successfully to freelancing.

Chuck Stanwix

Chuck Stanwix (a pseudonym) is a copy supervisor/senior copywriter in the Pittsburgh office of a large, national advertising agency. Chuck has been in his present position for four years. He came up through the ranks of the agency, starting as a junior copywriter, then moving to writer, then senior copywriter, before adding copy supervision duties to his job responsibilities four years ago. Before joining his current agency, Chuck was a senior copywriter at a smaller firm for nearly four years. Earlier in his career, Chuck worked for five years as a troubleshooter in an engineering firm, where he gained considerable hands-on experience with technical subjects and equipment.

Chuck's undergraduate degree is in medical anthropology, with minors in English and journalism from Penn State University. He is also certified as a Professional Engineer (P.E.) in mechanical engineering in New York.

As a senior copywriter, Chuck develops copy concepts for advertising and sales promotional materials for several of the agency's clients, then writes copy based on some or all of the approved concepts. In his role of copy supervisor, Chuck oversees concept development by junior writers and edits their copy. Chuck reports jointly to the creative director for his group and to the agency's executive creative director.

Meetings with clients to obtain input on projects are an integral part of Chuck's working day. He is also called upon frequently to present agency-developed creative concepts to clients for their consideration and to bring their responses back to the creative team for any rework that's necessary. Because Chuck is also a client liaison, he often schedules and coordinates the photographic sessions for the projects he manages.

According to Chuck, brevity is the soul of good ad copy; creativity and originality, its heart. He believes that the ability to reduce complex subjects to their essence is what makes technical communicators valuable to the advertising world.

Chuck has witnessed changes in the advertising industry, and, in his opinion, these changes have had a profound effect on communicators in the field. Technically oriented advertising and sales promotion writing have increased in volume, and he expects that trend to continue as client companies work towards reaching more specifically targeted audiences. He notes that, "We do far more work on a greater number of accounts than ever before."

Asked his sense of the importance of professional communicators to the advertising field, Chuck's response is, "They *are* the field." As to his feelings regarding his own future in the advertising industry, it was Chuck who said, "The future for an individual in this type of job is bounded only by his or her ability, mitigated aggressiveness, and blind fate." He also commented that technical advertising is a niche that he's "happy to occupy because there aren't too many people around with the skills mix to satisfy that niche." That pretty much leaves the door wide open to people with talent. Chuck's advice to you if you truly want to land a job in an advertising agency: "Call until they beat you away from the door with a stick."

Wendy Jameson

Wendy Jameson (also a pseudonym) is a successful freelance writer serving the business-to-business marketing community. One of Wendy's advertising agency clients in the Chicago area, whom I interviewed for this chapter, specifically mentioned her as a good role model for technical writers considering freelancing in the advertising industry.

Wendy earned a BS in communications (in advertising and journalism) and a minor in English from the University of Illinois. Interested in fiction writing as well, she then went on to earn a master's of fine arts degree (MFA) from the University of Iowa Writers' Workshop.

Wendy says she always knew she was a writer and that as an undergraduate she deliberately picked a profession that would allow her to write. Her first jobs were in large agencies—she asked that I not mention them by name, but you'd probably recognize them as major forces in the advertising industry. Wendy worked a lot in television advertising, especially on consumer goods. However, as she advanced in the agency world, her career path gradually led her towards becoming an executive, not a writer. And that's not what Wendy had in mind.

After successful stints with agencies in both Chicago and New York, she decided she wanted more freedom to balance her career in advertising writing with more time to pursue her fiction writing. Freelancing seemed an obvious, although financially risky, solution. She worked the contacts she'd built over the years and began to receive freelance writing assignments from agencies serving business-to-business and industrial clients. Wendy is certain that the reason freelancing has worked for her is because she "put in the time in the business working in heavy-hitting agencies" that gave her a solid track record and provided her with a large network of contacts from whom she now receives freelance assignments. Without those contacts, she says, "I would be sweating it a lot more and would have had to hustle really hard just to get started."

Wendy quickly built expertise in several specialized fields, among them health care and publishing. Her assignments come mostly from advertising agencies and not directly from business-to-business companies. Wendy is usually present at client meetings and is introduced as part of the agency's team. She receives a steady stream of work from these agencies, in part because they know she will not compete with them by approaching their business-to-business clients directly.

Wendy observed that most freelancers she knows "have personal reasons for wanting to freelance. They want the kind of increased flexibility in their schedule that freelancing can provide. They want to be able to fit the various priorities in their lives together better than is often possible in an agency environment."

She also stressed how important it is for freelancers to be good at balancing their level of effort with the fee they agreed to accept for the assignment. Since most freelance assignments are awarded on a fixed-fee basis, freelancers who do not master this business aspect of the profession may well end up with a net per hour that's far lower than their desired hourly rate.

According to Wendy, the demand for freelancers is both high and increasing because of the structural changes within the advertising industry and shifts in the economy. "A lot of agencies," she says, "are cutting back in their creative departments, yet still need the skills of writers who can handle technical ad copy. Smaller companies are looking for alternatives to putting writers on staff, especially the flexibility that freelancers provide to match specific skills with a specific client assignment." If you are not too scared of risks, Wendy says freelancing can be fun.

APPENDIX

FURTHER INFORMATION

Professional Organizations

If you've read this far and are still interested in pursuing a career in marketing communications and advertising, you could contact a number of professional associations to gather more information. Each has a different mission and focus. Some are trade associations; some are professional organizations. Each has information which could be useful to you in learning more about the structure of the business-to-business advertising industry, its agencies, and the nature of the work. Most have both a national (or international) headquarters as well as local chapters in cities throughout the United States. Unfortunately, no association that I'm aware of really focuses on technical communicators in advertising. We get lost in the cracks between the focal points of one organization and another. But if you're resourceful and persistent, you can build a network of contacts who can provide useful information and perhaps some job leads.

Here are some good places to start, in the membership ranks of the professional organizations listed below.

The Society for Technical Communication
901 North Stuart Street, Suite 904
Arlington, VA 22203-1854
(703) 522-4114
Fax: (703) 522-2075
www.clark.net/pub/stc/www

Public Relations Society of America
33 Irving Place
New York, NY 10003-2376
(212) 995-2230
Fax: (212) 995-0757
www.prsa.org/facts.html

Women in Communications.
1244 Richie Highway, Suite 6
Arnold, MD 21012-1887
(410) 544-7442
http://www.womcom.org

To find the addresses and phone numbers for the national headquarters of other organizations of interest to you, refer to the *Directory of Associations* in the reference section of your library. Then contact the national headquarters to find out where the nearest local chapter is and who the current local membership and programming officers are. The topics at monthly membership meetings are usually interesting, and attending is a good way to start networking. Many of these organizations have reduced rates for students. Often, some of the local chapters operate a job hotline or referral service for their members.

chapter 12

Freelancing or Consulting

David N. Dobrin
Freelance Technical Writer
Cambridge, Massachusetts

Jobs

Self-employed writer or editor; consultant; or writer or editor for a "job shop" or contract company (an organization that provides temporary or contract work for writers and editors).

Responsibilities

Writing and editing a variety of communications; being able to understand quickly the culture and needs of different organizations; being responsible for the entire document development process; managing your own business, including marketing, writing contracts, billing, and controlling your own finances and benefits.

Employment Outlook

Businesses are most likely to turn to a freelancer or consultant when they do not have the personnel to do a job in-house. However, the ability of an organization to do this kind of hiring is always dependent upon how good business is.

Salary Range

Anywhere from $18 to $75 an hour.

INTRODUCTION

This chapter differs from earlier ones, because it's more about the business of freelancing than it is about the work a freelancer does. Work for a freelancer is much the same as work for a writer employed in an organization, but business for a freelancer is quite different. As a full-time writer employed by a single company, you don't worry about finding new work (it will show up on your desk soon enough), and you don't worry about getting paid (the money will show up too). However, as a freelancer, you have to search for work actively, and you have to solicit payment, also actively. As a freelancer (or as a consultant), you are in a business, and if you don't learn how to deal with other businesses as a business, you won't eat.

If you haven't been a freelancer, you probably believe that freelancing is good because you make a lot of money and you get to work for yourself. I have been freelancing for 10 years, and I haven't found that either is necessarily true. Some years I did make a lot of money, but I would probably have made more as an employee. Other freelancers I know also make roughly what their employed counterparts do. If you want to know what you would make as a freelancer, look at the salary information in any other chapter of this book and extend the range. Drop the bottom down to $0.00, and put the top up about 50 percent) Being your own boss? The best thing about working for myself, I now think, is that I do better work than I would do if I had a less exacting boss.

Let me start you off with an exercise that will have to become second nature if you're going to survive as a freelancer. Imagine that you're a manager in a company that needs some work done. A brochure or a poster has to be produced; some press releases need to get out; your company needs a highly finished and professional proposal. It's a one-time-only project, and you don't want to commit your budget to a permanent employee. So you think about hiring a freelancer.

You would prefer to hire a permanent employee because a permanent employee is cheaper (in the long run). Also, a permanent employee is continuously available, has displayed commitment, and often adds to your managerial standing in the company. (Ironically, a freelancer takes away.)

But in this case, you feel that you must hire a freelancer. Maybe the job requires special expertise or has to be done immediately or must be done without management or is in an area where top management is not ready to make a commitment. Maybe the training time, the lead time, or the management time involved in getting an employee to do this job would be prohibitive. So, reluctantly, you conclude that you have to hire somebody from outside.

Now, switch hats. You want to be that somebody. How do you do it? Well, the outlines are easy. Somehow or other, you're going to have to make yourself known to that manager. You'll have to convince the manager that you can produce the document she wants. You'll have to charge an amount of money that the manager thinks is plausible. And you'll have to beat out any competition.

If you can do all that even once, you're a freelancer. Pretty easy, really; anybody can do it. I have had students who became freelancers right out of school, friends who moved back and forth between freelance work and employment all their working lives, colleagues who work only 25 or 30 days a year, because they're specialists. All have been able, somehow or other, to set themselves up in business, to find work, to do the work, and to get paid for it. How they did it (and how you can do it) are the subjects of this chapter.

SETTING YOURSELF UP IN BUSINESS

When I started, I had only one guiding principle. I didn't want to establish a separate office, so I set myself rules: Don't open an office; work out of my home. Never hire employees (broken once or twice). Never take up a project I can't do pretty much by myself. Never manage other people. However, a good friend started at much the same time. In two years, he had 20 employees.

So, you want to set yourself up in business. You can follow my model. For example, in my home town of Cambridge, Massachusetts, all you have to do is go to city hall, pay $10 for a license, give the officials the name of your company, and you're in business.

Don't worry too much about the name. Even if you think you must have something reliable, interesting, clever, illustrative, solid, and attractive, you'll do better if you worry more about the form of your business.

To see what I mean by the "form" of your business, put on the manager's hat again. You want to find a person for that temporary writing job? What do you do?

- Advertise. Fill the position with part-time or temporary employees, people who answer ads in the paper. However, this method is chancy and rarely the method of choice.
- Call around to friends for the names of freelancers. This method can be quite successful, but can be a lot of work.
- Call companies that are in the business of providing temporary labor or contract labor. These are commonly called "job shops." They make money by doing the work of searching for you.
- Call companies that will do the job. Sometimes these companies will be a freelancer with an assistant; sometimes they will be job shops who also do what is called "contract work." Contract companies make money both by finding the right people and by managing them.
- Look in trade journals or call universities for the names of recognized experts in the area (subject matter area or technical writing). These experts are also freelancers, but sometimes, because of their expertise or experience, they are called "consultants."

Back to your writer's hat again. If you want to find that temporary, fill-in work, you may not want to set yourself up in business at all. Just answer the ad or let your friends know you need a job. If you picture yourself in a small firm, you might want to join a job shop—or start one, in which case your first task might be to seek out resumes of people just like you. Or you might want to try for large writing contracts—say three or four person-years—and then hire people as those contracts come in. If you want to be an expert, start developing credentials.

If you want to be anything but a temporary fill-in, you will need appurtenances: a name, a place to work, telephone, stationery, business cards, and availability to potential clients during business hours. You'll need to spend some money, and you'll need to think about how you're going to behave toward the IRS. (This is too big a subject to cover here, but remember two things: The IRS has some nasty rules about deducting expenses for businesses run out of the home, and if you ever do get profitable, Keogh plans are a huge tax shelter.)

But more than anything else, you need clients. All of us who have set ourselves up in business have had the ugly feeling of looking at our clean desk, our crisp stationery, the sign on the door, and the telephone and wondering why it doesn't ring.

FINDING WORK

I was lucky. The first two companies to hire me fell over shortly after I left. This was financially problematic at the time, but it turned out well. You see, everybody who got to know me at those companies went off and found work at sounder companies. And they remembered me. The next time there was work, my name came up.

But even if you don't have this kind of good fortune, your telephone will ring. You'll get calls from office supply warehouses, prospective employees, fax machine salespeople, time-share condo organizations, and stockbrokers. But for a long time, you won't get calls out of the blue from people who want to hire you. Freelance writing is not like plumbing; few writing emergencies are so severe that someone will just look in the yellow pages and make a call. Instead, the vast majority of work is doled out by way of contacts.

In order for you to become one of those contacts, do the following: Buy a notebook in which to keep a record of every single person you meet professionally. Get their business cards, and put them in the book. At meetings of professional societies, keep records of the people who are mentioned. Look up their phone numbers; put them in the book (you've already got the cards of everybody you've met). If you come across a name in an article, write it down, get a number, put it in the book. When you get a wrong number, and it sounds interesting, put the name of the person who answered in the book. These people could become people who will think of you when the need for work comes up. The more contacts, the more likely a job will come your way.

Why contacts? Honestly, I'm not sure. For some reason, in American culture, most people are unwilling to hire anyone to do anything important unless that person is vouched for by someone they know. Need a doctor? Go to one a friend has already seen. Same with a lawyer or accountant. The college professor whom some of your friends took a course from is usually preferred to the unknown R. Smith, who might, of course, be far superior. It's exactly the same with freelance writing. People will always look first for somebody they've had some connection with, however tenuous that connection is. The problem for you, sitting at your new desk looking out the window, is how to become that friend of a friend that somebody will trust.

This chapter is not the place for a course in salesmanship, advertising, self-promotion, or entrepreneurship. But you will need to learn some basics of each of these in order to get into this business. Here are a few easy things that I know have worked.

- Call up your friends, acquaintances, former teachers, and cooking school buddies, and talk to them. Find out what they are doing, what kinds of businesses they are in. Everybody needs writing done at some point. Ask your friends how their companies hire writing. Ask them for the names of managers who do the hiring. Call those persons and ask what they look for and when they hire. Your aim is not to find a job, but to find out how jobs are gotten and to make it known that you are available.
- Talk to people who are already making money as freelance writers. With most people, their desire to help is stronger than any fear that they are nurturing competition. Besides, they are always looking for contacts, too.
- Go to business meetings, presentations, professional society meetings, conventions, and so on. Talk to people. This activity, often called "networking," is usually unproductive in its bald form; people don't, upon meeting you, offer you work. But every so often, it can produce a lead, and in any case, it can teach you a great deal about how people behave, and what they value.
- Be ingenious. A design firm I know of had good success in combing the papers for announcements of new marketing directors. (Marketing directors are the people who usually hire designers.) They figured that the new person wasn't already enmeshed in a network of commitments, so they would send out their brochure and make a follow-up call. Surprisingly often (five percent of the time), they

made a presentation. When I first heard about this strategy, I thought it was too obvious, but it did seem to work.

Your ways of getting contacts often depend on your personality. Two friends of mine come off poorly in person, but write authoritatively. Both have chosen to advertise themselves by writing freelance articles in journals their prospective clients are likely to see. The payoff was painfully slow and uncertain, but gradually, their names became known. Somebody, somewhere said, "I remember reading an article about that; maybe the person who wrote it can help."

Of course, all these activities are slow and uncertain. Nothing you do today along these lines is likely to produce work tomorrow. Some efforts might not pay off for years, and some will never pay off. But that's okay. Eventually, part of the work you do in setting up a network and making contacts will indeed create work in return.

"I CAN DO THAT" VS. "THIS IS WHAT I DO"

"Listen, we're looking for somebody who can write a tutorial for a DOS extender. I understand that your C skills are pretty good." " . . . Do you have any experience in analyzing service communications?" "I represent a large consumer products company . . . I hear you're an expert on XXX. Can you ghostwrite two articles on how our customers are using it?"

I was asked all of these questions, and at the time I didn't know C, service communications, or XXX. But I was considered for all of these jobs, took one, and got the job done.

At some point, somebody is going to get hold of you, describe a project, and say, "Can you do that?" Think before you answer.

If you're just starting out, especially if your basic talent is that you can write, your inclination is to say you can do anything. Publicity? Sure. Editing scientific prose? Why not. Indexing? Of course. Creating a brochure? Can do. Hiring a printer? Where are the Yellow Pages? Okay. But here's the problem: Most employers looking for writers are like smart tourists looking for restaurants. They avoid the ones with the big menus, because a good chef can't possibly do too many things well. When the menu has only five or six items, they can hope that each is done superbly.

Doing an index, you see, is much like cooking a souffle. There are tricks of the trade; it takes time and practice to learn them; and until you learn them, the product is likely to be flat. Yes, you can probably do a passable index. But professional indexers will do a much better job than you can do. Yes, you can probably write 500 words on trails in the

White Mountains for the travel section in your local newspaper, but you will skip things that an experienced travel writer would know to include, and your editor might return it to you three or four times.

So, is the trick to specialize? Not exactly. What every employer really wants is a person who has already done exactly what they need, but doesn't cost very much. No employer finds that; instead, they compromise. They find a generalist and swallow the cost of training and management, or they find a specialist and pay more than they really wanted to pay. So there's no reason, a priori, to specialize or to generalize. In either case, you will miss out on jobs, because the potential employer made the wrong decision (from your point of view).

Put the old manager's hat on again. What do you want? You want somebody who can walk in and be productive tomorrow. That person must know the computers, formatting programs, word processing programs, and illustration programs that are used at your company. Let's call such a person a specialist in the tools. That person must also know your company, its product, its market, its customers, the reasons for producing this document, and the readers. Let's call this person a technical specialist, using the word "technical" in a very broad sense. And finally, that person must know how to write the kinds of things you want that person to write. We'll call this person a genre specialist. As a manager, you want a tools, technical, and genre specialist all wrapped into one. Unfortunately, you are likely to be disappointed. Superperson is just not going to walk in; you're going to have to compromise.

For you, the freelancer, this means that at some point in the conversation, you may say, "I can do that," when you've never done it at all. "I can program in C." "I can use Corel Draw to do award-winning art." "I can write 10,000 words on the extinction of freebies."

But if "I can do that" comes out of your mouth too quickly, either you're going to get into trouble when you can't do that or you're going to drive off prospective employers who get suspicious. You have to have some abilities in a couple of specific areas, something you can rely on while you're going through the difficult process of learning the stuff you can't yet do. Thus you must develop an expertise and be able to say, "This is what I do."

I remember one time I said, "I can do that," when I shouldn't have. I was asked to do a business plan. I figured that it was a piece of persuasive writing, that I could persuade, and that I could always cheat by copying other plans. It didn't work. For a good business plan, you need a driving optimism and a willingness to overlook unpleasant facts, plus you need to know the form very well. A mediocre business plan is worthless, but that's what I produced. It was an easy lesson to learn; they didn't pay me for it.

PREPARATION

Of course, when you start out, you'll need a lot more of "I can do that." As you go along, however, you should get to know some subject matter or industry; you should get some practice producing some genre of prose; and you should be able to use certain tools handily and effectively. So you do these things, you specialize, and you're able to say "This is what I do."

Which specialization should you try to develop first: tools, technical speciality, or genres? For my money, the expertise in a subject or industry is the most important, but that's also my approach to life. I know one man who is a pure genre specialist. He can write a newsletter about anything, from trailer parks to video stores. And, particularly for lower-level jobs, many people I know advertise themselves as tools specialists—Pagemaker specialists or Microsoft Word specialists, for example. You can see why, if you think about it. Managers can tell fairly quickly whether you know how to use PageMaker, but they can't tell whether you can write. And if you already know Pagemaker, they won't have to take the time and money to teach you.

If you're in school, you may be able to develop your expertise in all three specialties—tools, technical specialties, and genres—by taking courses. You can learn about different genres by taking professional writing and editing courses, both introductory ones and more advanced courses that deal with specific kinds of communications—for example, courses in writing proposals, manuals, feature articles, or online documentation. You can develop your knowledge of tools by taking courses in computers and computer programming, especially courses that deal with computer applications such as desktop publishing and interactive and multimedia communications.

Becoming knowledgeable about a subject matter or industry is a little more difficult, but you can do that by taking courses, perhaps even a major or minor, in a specific area, such as biology, computer science, engineering, or accounting. Understanding a prospective employer's specific products, markets, or customers may require some actual experience working in the industry, but some well-chosen course work can provide a good foundation and can make developing that understanding easier.

You can get some of that valuable work experience through an internship or co-op assignment working as a technical writer or editor in industry. An internship can be a good opportunity not only to get some hands-on experience as a writer but also to learn more about how organizations in a particular industry operate, what types of communications they use, and what they expect of professionals in their field.

Whichever of the three specialties you choose, what you're eventually looking for is a niche, a place where you really are a specialist—ideally, the best person around. Once there, the network starts working for you, because you get to be known to everyone, and they start calling you when they have work. But the definition of a niche is a complex one. My niche, for a number of years, was high-quality manuals on difficult subject areas for small software companies. Those were the only kinds of jobs I had; I was good at it, and people would call me when they had that kind of work.

The choice of niche may be somewhat accidental (one of my first jobs was working on a database program, and now I do a lot in that area), but a wise choice of niche depends on a frank assessment of your strengths and desires. Follow your talent. It is much easier to do a task when you're good at it or when you enjoy it, and you do much better work. "I can do that" should have some element of truth to it.

If you're just starting out, you often think you have no specialization. "The only thing I like doing is reading Trollope." You'd be surprised. Maybe you're also a feminist and like rock-climbing on weekends; there's money to be made writing articles on women who climb. There's money to be made from manufacturers of climbing gear who need help with brochures. There are people who run climbing tours who need to advertise in the climbing magazines. Because you're interested in the subject, you will think of these things, and in all your writing, you can be far more ingenious and pointed than a more experienced writer who cares less.

To find your niche, you should probably rely more on common sense than on college. Writing well about something or using a tool well requires some life experience, some interest. Yes, majoring in technical writing or taking a course in Pagemaker may help you land a job. But it scarcely amounts to expertise. If you want to be hired because you have expertise in a subject or an activity, it's wise to pick a subject you are interested in or an activity you like doing.

CONTRACTS

Let us assume that you have succeeded; somebody wants you to do something for them. At this point, you must set up some expectations about what you will do, when you will do it, and how much you'll be paid for it. You need to set up a contract.

You'll remember at the beginning of this article I said that the big difference between freelance and regular work is the way it's managed and

paid for. The contract is what determines how management and payment happen.

When you're an employee, the rules about who is in charge, how work
is evaluated, and how you'll be paid are set by the state, by company
policy manuals, and by American culture's idea of how work is done. In
general, it's quite simple. You show up at work for regular hours; you do
what your boss tells you. If you do a really terrible job, you get fired, and
if you do a really good job, you might get a raise or even a promotion.

If you're a freelancer, though, you must establish the terms and conditions yourself. Even such simple things as where you will work and who
provides the tools are subject to negotiation. The boss doesn't just tell
you what to do; you have to agree on the scope of the work. In general,
you are not subject to a boss's whim in the same way that you are when
employed, because the boss's whim can end up costing you money. Say
you've promised to give the boss a brochure, and the boss decides, after
seeing it, that a different brochure is required. As an employee, you do a
new one. As a freelancer, you've got a problem. Do you redo it for free,
or does the boss have to pay for the new one?

The common law (and the IRS) establishes some rules about freelance
work which underscore this fact. Most important of these, psychologi-
cally, is that your boss (your "client" might be a better word) cannot dictate either your hours or the way you do your work. Technically
speaking, you do not report to anyone in the way you do as an
employee. Instead, you point to terms of the contract, announce that
they have been fulfilled, and submit a bill.

How do you write a contract? Two things are obviously true. One,
writing it badly can cause enormous amounts of grief, and two, there's
no best way of doing it. The best contract might be a simple verbal
agreement over the phone, or it might be a 100-page document drawn
up by a lawyer and haggled over for months.

All contracts set out an agreement about the scope of the work, the
schedule according to which it will be done, the fees you will charge, and
the terms for payment.

Scope of Work

In its simplest form, the scope of work is a statement that you will write
something that the company needs. As long as both you and the company have a very clear idea of what that is, that's all you need to say in
the contract. But very often, you and the company won't quite agree.

Let us say that you will write a user manual for a software product.
Does that user manual include a reference section? A tutorial? Installation instructions? Quick reference card? Does anyone know how long

(or short) the manual will be? Is there any documentation right now which you can use as a head start? If not, how easy is the software to learn? Is the software product finished, or will there be changes in it? Who will check the manual for errors, and what happens if there are any? In what form will your end product be? Do you do the formatting, design, and/or layout, or does someone else? What about diagrams? Do you produce them?

Believe me, I could add a couple of hundred extra questions along those lines, many of them discovered and answered at considerable personal cost. The cost, you see, is the issue. If you agree to provide the manual on disk, and you agree that you will do the formatting, then the company won't have to pay somebody else to put it on disk and format it. If you agree to do a quick reference card, they don't have to pay another expert to do it. The definition of the scope of work is precisely that, an agreement about how much work you'll do. The company wants to maximize that work (as long as they don't have to pay for it). You want, ideally, to minimize the work (as long as the pay's the same). The company has leverage because it knows what it wants, and it has the checkbook. You have leverage because you write the contract. It behooves you, therefore, to be very clear in that contract.

It is, however, just plain impossible to anticipate every disagreement about scope of work. To some extent, you have to count on good faith when problems come up, and to some extent, you have to write in procedures for dealing with out-of-scope issues. Even so, you may end up with disagreements about scope, and, if so, you'll end up losing some of them. My recommendation is to accept this fact and build it into your fee structure. Charge a little bit more for the work than you think it's worth because you figure you're going to end up doing more work anyway.

Schedule

In almost any contract you will be asked to provide a schedule, and in almost any contract, that commitment will really be no more than a guess. Can you, in fact, write this software manual in 90 days? That depends on factors it is currently impossible to estimate accurately—within 20% would be very good. For example, you don't really know within 50 pages how long the manual will be, but your normal rate of production is two pages a day. That's a month's worth of uncertainty.

Still, even though it was a guess, people will try to hold you to it: "You said you would finish this 500-page manual by June 1. It's May 15, and I only see 250 pages. Where are the other 250?" How can you satisfy this person? Well, deadlines concentrate the mind wonderfully;

you could try to write very fast. A more reasonable approach is to renegotiate the schedule.

There is a whole science to scheduling, but much of the science relies on being able to break up large tasks into subtasks and then estimate how long the subtasks will take. In a business where an ingenious alteration of an outline can eliminate subtasks in a stroke, where a paragraph can take a day to write and four pages, an hour, such estimates usually reveal themselves as fictions within the first few days of a project.

Many people pretend, however, that this isn't so, and such people tend to write fairly detailed schedules, which set out defined "deliverables" and delivery dates every week or so. If you do this, you will have to review this schedule regularly with your clients, and if it turns out to be fictitious, these reviews could turn painful rather rapidly. I prefer broader schedules, which are more flexible. However, one advantage of a specific, detailed schedule of deliverables is that it justifies a specific, detailed payment schedule. Of course, before you can draw up a payment schedule, you must establish your fees for the work you'll perform.

Fees

I have lost jobs by charging too much. I have lost money by charging too little for a job that took too long or was worth more. I have also lost money by charging less than I could have. I've found that I am best off if I don't negotiate very much. Those people who tried to get me cheaply usually didn't want me anyway. Those people who were willing to pay were also the ones who trusted me the most and got the best results out of me.

Most freelancers I know prefer to be paid by the hour; most employers I know prefer to pay by the job. Each, that is, prefers that the other party take the risk. If you get paid by the hour and a job doesn't get done on time (it almost never gets done early), you make more money. Most employers don't like this much. If you get paid by the job, then you get paid the same whether it takes a long time or a short time to do it. Occasionally, this turns out to be a good thing. (I have once or twice made hundreds of dollars an hour by churning out something that an employer was willing to pay a lot for.) But usually it means that you run the risk of putting lots of free hours in on a project when it took far more time than you estimated.

In this section, I know your basic question is, "How much should I charge?" But sheer dollar amount is often almost irrelevant in this business, because you have to factor in risk. Someone can offer you $10,000 to do a brochure, but if it turns out that you have to redo it six times and pay for the photography, that may turn out to be a pittance. Someone can offer you $200 an hour for advice on how to write a letter that staves off creditors, but you might be better off taking $10 an hour in advance.

Still, one way of starting is to figure out a base charge, usually an hourly base. Here's one way of doing it. Figure out what people usually get paid by the hour for equivalent work when they're employed. Add eight percent for Social Security tax (you pay more than an employed person does) and another 20 percent for benefits. This would be the cost to the employer for whatever it is you do; if you charged that rate an hour, it would be a bargain. Now, look at your cost of doing business. How much does your office cost you? How much does the equipment cost? (Don't forget that these overhead charges are tax-deductible.) How much time per year do you spend looking for work? Take the employer's cost and multiply it by about one-third to one-half. In other words, take the prevailing wage and add about 60 percent for taxes, benefits, and overhead. That should be your base charge per hour.

Now, start calling around and find out what people actually do charge. If your base charge is significantly less or significantly more, find out why. At this writing, I would find it hard to hire a low-level freelancer for less than $18 an hour, and I would rarely pay more than $75 an hour for a very good person. If you work for a job shop, you are probably paid about half that; the other half is the shop's overhead and profit. These charges will vary somewhat by region and by economic conditions.

For me, it was hard to get my fee out of my mouth the first time I said it. But for employers, too, the nominal amount is often not that important. They are willing to pay a large premium just to be sure that something will be done on time and with a high enough quality. They are willing to factor in the supervisory costs, and an $18 per hour person might really be very expensive if a $40 per hour supervisor has to spend half the day teaching and watching.

To some extent, they measure quality by your fee. One problem I had working with lawyers is that I was charging too little. They didn't think I could be an authority, given that I was charging what they charge for their secretary's time. I learned—and upped my fee.

Of course, as I said, most of the time, the hourly amount is not the basis for payment; the work is. Most employers want brochures to have a price tag, just as shampoo does. They have budgets, and they are risk-averse. They want to pay exactly this much and no more. It is probably not good policy in the long run to thwart this desire. Quote people a fixed price, if that's what they want, and live with it.

If you're going to live happily with it, however, your quote had better make you money. Take the overall expenses, including phone calls, photocopying, diskettes, special computer programs, and add to it the amount of time you think it will take times your hourly fee. That's the price you're willing to do it for. Add a bit more if you think they're willing to pay more, and add at least 10 percent more if their financial condition seems shaky or if you think they will be a lot of trouble to work with.

The crucial factor here is your estimate of how long it will take. Most people aren't very good at estimating. I'm by no means fabulous at it, but whenever I do it, I remember two of my favorite maxims from software engineering: "The last 10 percent takes 90 percent of the time" and "For any software project, ask the engineer to estimate the absolute maximum amount of time it will take, then double that estimate." The latter maxim is published in Frederick Brooks' *The Mythical Man-Month*, the best book there is on software project management (1975). In my experience, merely doubling is optimistic. The last project I worked on was a three-month project that was six months late.

What if your estimate looks like a great deal of money? I would be reluctant to get talked down. After the project has gone through five delays, that great deal is going to look fairly puny. I have had projects bid at a fixed price that I thought would be finished in two months and were actually finished in 12. I got other work and also renegotiated.

Do you need to worry about being undercut? Well, if somebody else takes a problem for less money, they will also have bought all the headaches. You're probably better off leaving it alone. However, if you are consistently being undercut, you should rethink your hourly rate or seek out a different kind of work. Your market value may have gone down.

Payment

Most contracts specify a payment schedule which is directly or indirectly based on the deliverables schedule. With a broad deliverables schedule, you might be paid at the beginning, in the middle, and at the end of the contract. Or you might specify a specific amount for each deliverable or a billing schedule based on the number of hours you work. Your choice of payment schedule is usually a sign of how much good faith you think there is in a contract.

If you and your employer are sure of each other, you might specify a simple 1/3-1/3-1/3, where you get paid the first third before you start and the last third after you finish. When your employer is unwilling to give you money up front, or when you are not sure of the employer's ability or willingness to pay, you might want to specify weekly payments or a deliverables schedule that effectively results in weekly payments.

If you don't trust a client, do not become vulnerable by having them owe you too much money. Let's say you get into an argument over whether the product fits the agreed-upon scope of the project. If you are owed most of the cost of the project, clients can essentially force you to work to their specifications by refusing to pay you. If you had been paid regularly up to that point, you would be able to walk away from onerous demands much more easily. Avoid the same level of vulnerability whenever you think the client is not doing well. If the business does hit hard times, the first person not to be paid will be you. If you insist that a shaky client pay you regularly, not only will you be less vulnerable, but you will also be able to tell more rapidly when the business is doing poorly.

Writing the Contract

How do you write up a contract? You can get a lawyer to do one for you, or you can get sample contracts from bookstores or libraries, friends, or professional colleagues. But don't just copy a contract. Talk to people about what their strategies are. The intent of a contract is to protect both parties, but in fact, the amount of protection afforded either of you is limited. If you don't deliver, there's rarely much they can do. And if they don't pay, there's almost nothing you can do. Therefore, it's essential that you write up a sensible contract, given the situation. You may even have an oral contract, if that's appropriate. Whatever you do, you can spend a lot of time working out penalties for either side, establishing methods for resolving disputes, setting out exacting standards of quality, and precisely specifying each deliverable. Sometimes that can really pay off. And other times, it can be a colossal waste of time. The contract is a bridge between you and the employer, but not one that too much weight can be put on.

For example, imagine that some troglodyte has stiffed you in some egregious way. You have two choices. You can make a pest of yourself, which rarely works. Or you can go to court, which doesn't work at all. You have to hire a lawyer (who makes three times your old hourly fee, so it's only worthwhile if the amount owed is huge). You have to wait around two years for your day in court. You have to prove in court that you did the work specified, when all the former client has to do is claim that the work wasn't up to generally accepted standards, and the judge doesn't have a clue. And then, if you win, you gain the rare privilege of being allowed to search for the stiff's assets, a search as foredoomed as

Lancelot's for the Holy Grail. Any company can hide its assets permanently just by changing bank accounts.

Contrariwise, let's say you just walk. They have the same problem.

WORKING

I rather like the first day, when I find a new parking place at a new building, and the people scramble around looking for a desk, a phone, a computer, and a chair for me. I like being able to work at home, and I like being able to finish a project and then take off for three weeks. I like meeting all the new people and figuring out their computer system and finding new places to have lunch. Hey, I'm easily pleased.

As a freelancer, your work is pretty much what it is as an employee. However, you'll have some special freelancer rules to learn; they mostly have to do with the fact that you have the right to set your own hours, and you evaluate your own progress. It is both courteous and practical to be at once clear about this right and clear about what you are doing. If you are not going to work the normal employee's hours, you should say so, and if you deviate occasionally, you should say that, too. Working at home is often a good idea, but if you do work at home, let the client know where you are and what you are doing. Most managers would prefer to keep an eye on you; don't cause them unnecessary grief. Even though you don't report to them, it's wise to set up regular sessions at which you talk about your progress.

If there are special rules, it's wise to set people straight about them. Say you're working two jobs at once, and you'll be getting phone calls from (or making phone calls to) the other client. Let your first client know and offer to pay for the phone calls.

At work, you should remember that you are a stranger and a high-priced non-employee. Spread sunshine. You never know who might be your reference later on, and if some of your coworkers prove difficult to get along with, well, you won't be there that long anyway. Also, in any organization, it's important to develop a network of contacts: the people who get supplies or who know the important gossip or who can fix your computer. As a freelancer, you have to develop this network quickly.

Even though you are a freelancer, or perhaps because of it, you will be drawn into the political battles fought in any organization. You can't avoid this, though it is often wise to try. Sometimes, after all, you are the result of some previous skirmish. In these battles, try to preserve your diplomatic skills. Listen more than you talk. Express decided opinions rarely. Form alliances judiciously.

There are two things about working as a freelancer that many people new to the business don't know, and I will close with them. First, it's an extremely good idea to study previous work in the area very closely. If you've been hired to write a brochure for a company, look at brochures of the company's competitors and the last brochure of the company that hired you. Study advertisements and collateral materials. Understand the buzzwords. If there's anything freelance work usually suffers from, it's that the writer doesn't really understand the organization.

Second, believe in your own expertise. You are hired, usually, because nobody at the company can do the job you are doing. If you think it should be done a certain way, say so. Remember, you're the expert. Too often, I've seen people do things just the way the company wanted, when in fact the company would have been open to alternatives, had they been suggested.

You might have noticed that the first piece of advice contradicts the second. Worry that you're not the expert, but be confident in your expertise. If contradictions don't bother you, welcome to freelancing.

PROFESSIONAL PROFILES

The following profiles will help to give you a better idea of the work that freelance and independent technical communicators do. Zeinab Schwen is a freelance medical writer in Cincinnati, Ohio, while Tom Collins, until recently, was President of the Oxford Associates, a technical communication consulting firm.

Zeinab Schwen

Zeinab Schwen is a freelance medical writer in Cincinnati, Ohio. However, she didn't start out as a professional writer. After receiving a bachelor's degree in zoology and chemistry from the University of Cairo in Egypt and a master's degree in pharmacology from the University of Minnesota, she began work in 1979 as a research associate for the pharmaceutical firm Richardson Merrell (later Marion Merrell Dow), investigating drug metabolism in animal research studies. After a few years, she became a clinical research associate and worked on the development of the anti-allergy drug, Seldane.

Thus, Zeinab did her first medical writing while preparing pharmaceutical research protocols and some of the many documents pharmaceutical companies submit to the U.S. Food and Drug Administration (FDA) to get approval to manufacture and sell new drugs. She also created an information center for Marion Merrell Dow to handle professional and consumer questions about both over-the-counter and prescription drugs.

However, in 1988, after failing to get a promotion she believed she'd earned, Zeinab left Marion Merrell Dow and launched her career as a freelance medical writer. At first working mostly as an independent contract writer for her old employer, she later sought out a more diverse clientele. Today, Zeinab manages her own consulting firm, ProMed Communications, in which she writes a variety of regulatory submissions, including New Drug Applications, Investigational New Drug Applications, Clinical Study Reports, Clinical Investigative Brochures, medical device regulatory submissions, and monographs. She also prepares scientific articles for researchers on topics in animal research, clinical research, and pharmacokinetic studies. In addition to Marion Merrell Dow, her clients include Abbott Laboratories, Alza Corporation, Excerpta Medica, Hillshire Farms, Hoechst Marion Rousell, Pro/Com International, Procter & Gamble, Sterling Winthrop, and Upjohn.

Until recently, Zeinab has operated ProMed Communications as a sole practitioner and says that for her, the most attractive features of the freelance writer's life are the ability to work on a variety of projects and on different topics; the freedom from office politics; and, most important, the freedom to follow your own schedule. The pay can be very good, she points out, if you're willing to work more than the traditional 40-hour week.

On the negative side, though, is the unpredictability of the independent writer's business, the ever-present fear that your business may run dry, and the requirement that you sometimes work on projects that don't demand much creativity. An additional drawback, Zeinab says, is that even though you may work very hard on a client's project, you almost never get credit as an author.

Zeinab echoes many another freelancer in pointing out that a consistent marketing effort is crucial to success as an independent writer. "You can't be complacent," she warns. It's important to "call people when you're most busy" to ask what projects they're working on that might need the talents of a writer or editor. This is because it often takes two to four months for writing jobs to "get through the pipeline" as contracting decisions are made, funding is sought and approved, and materials are sent out for you to review.

Although ProMed boasts a polished promotional packet that includes a brochure describing the company, Zeinab's resume, her client list, comments from satisfied clients, and descriptions of ProMed's services, Zeinab finds that mailing isn't nearly as effective as calling when you're seeking out clients. Also important is using professional meetings to network with other technical communicators and managers—not necessarily to ask for jobs, but just to get to know different sources for work and to let those people know who you are. She cites the American Medical Writers Association (AMWA), the Regulatory Affairs Professional Society, and the Drug Information Association as the most useful organizations for independent medical writers to join.

As for the qualities most important for a freelance writer, Zeinab emphasizes being customer-focused—being able to understand and meet your client's objectives—and being dependable. A client has to know that you'll get the project done on time and according to specifications. Asking for an extension, a common practice in school work, is the "kiss of death" to a freelance writer.

Zeinab wishes that freelance writers were recognized more consistently in the industries where they work for the complex tasks they perform. In fact, she prefers the term "medical communications consultant" to "freelance writer" since she doesn't just write for her clients, but researches, plans, writes, edits, and advises her clients on publications.

After nine years as a sole practitioner, Zeinab recently has added some coworkers to ProMed Communications: four writers, an editor, and an administrative assistant. She did this because having additional people to help her enables her to take on larger projects and to pursue more projects at one time. Doing this, though, has forced her to acquire new management skills. Zeinab says that ProMed's income dropped when she first expanded but has since grown steadily as she's become a more efficient manager of her staff and other resources.

Thomas Collins

In 1983, Tom Collins had been a writer for more than 13 years. He started out as a broadcast journalist, then worked for a Fortune 500 manufacturing company, did a stint in graduate school before joining the staff of Miami University, and next spent two years at a utility company. In each role, he gained valuable experience and new perspectives about the importance of clear, accessible writing in the workplace. He also developed his skills for doing various types of writing: news stories, documentary scripts, technical specifications, scientific reports, product instructions, courseware materials, procedural guides, and reference manuals.

So by the spring of 1983, when he began to be frustrated with the ineffectiveness of a bloated, bureaucratic workplace and tired of the long, tedious, daily commute, he decided to pursue his dream of independence. He abandoned the security of a steady paycheck and the potential of a climb up the corporate ladder to become a freelance writer.

Freelance. As in freedom! Freedom from endless meetings and weekly status reports. Freedom to work whatever hours suited him. Freedom to take on only those projects that were of particular interest. What could be more satisfying and fulfilling?

Well—not quite.

Endless cold-calling replaced the endless meetings, and client updates replaced departmental status reports. And while in the beginning he had enough work to keep going, he certainly didn't have enough to be picky. As for the flexible hours, he had the freedom to work any 14 hours a day he wanted. It was the only way he could both meet current deadlines and prospect for new assignments. When he received one assignment, he found there was little time for celebration before he needed to start looking for the next one.

And he discovered there were aspects to running a business that the old, bloated bureaucracy had handled amazingly well. Things such as tax reports, contracts, insurance, credit lines, invoicing, accounts payable, accounts receivable (especially accounts receivable!), purchasing, marketing, and more. It was difficult, sometimes impossible, to do justice to each aspect. Tom soon began to wonder whether independence was such a dream after all. So as more and more opportunities for projects came up, he decided to invite Neil Herbkersman, an old friend from graduate school, to join him in a partnership. They would form a company that would offer professional writing and education services. The company was called The Oxford Associates.

Soon after the two formed the company, the division of labor began to pay off. One could work on marketing while the other worked on billable assignments. Together, they designed systems so the new company could handle all the important peripheral activities. Tom devised accounting procedures and tools; he put together some algorithms for estimating work. They designed a methodology for planning and executing projects.

Gradually, whenever there was a lull in the billable projects, they worked at improving the planning, tracking, and execution of each area in the business. Finding outside support for the business became increasingly important as well. Tom spent considerable time doing research on suppliers who could provide graphics support, printing, typesetting, and so forth. And as the work load increased, he also began interviewing other freelance writers to work with the company from time to time.

Throughout this process, he also became more active in the Society for Technical Communication. He attended local chapter meetings and learned from presentations on subjects ranging from computer-based training to project management.

In the summer of 1986, Neil Herbkersman was offered a position as grants developer for a nearby community college. It was an opportunity he didn't want to pass up, so the two partners negotiated a buyout agreement. Tom was again a sole proprietor. He slowly began building a staff of full-time, salaried people. While he continued to rely on some freelance support, he felt building a staff of graphic artists and writers would give the company greater ability to respond rapidly to client needs. Over time, less and less of his work was related to turning out projects, while more and more was related to training his growing staff and managing the company.

Today, The Oxford Associates has a staff of 25 writers, artists, managers and support personnel. The company occupies a three-story building with an extensive computer and communications network. Shortly before this book went to press, Tom sold his interest in The Oxford Associates and now serves as a consultant to the company he helped to start.

APPENDIX

FURTHER INFORMATION

Professional Associations

The Society for Technical Communication (STC)
901 North Stuart Street, Suite 904
Arlington, VA 22203-1854
(703) 522-4114
http://www.stc.org

STC has a Consulting and Independent Contracting Professional Interest Committee (PIC), which publishes a quarterly newsletter, *The Independent Perspective.*

The National Association for the Self-Employed (NASE)
2328 Gravel Road
Fort Worth, TX 76118-6950
(800) 232-6273
http://selfemployed.nase.org/nase/

Publications

Bellman, G. M. (1990). *The consultant's calling: Bringing who you are to what you do.* San Francisco: Jossey-Bass.

Bly, R. W. (1990). *Secrets of a freelance writer: How to make $85,000 a year.* New York: Henry Holt.

Brooks, F. P. (1975). *The mythical man-month: Essays on software engineering.* Reading, MA: Addison-Wesley.

Caernarven-Smith. (1992). The workshop front: What we found out. *Technical Communication.* 39:1, 145–147.

Kelley, R. L. (1986). *The complete guide to a profitable career* (Rev. ed.). New York: Charles Scribner's Sons.

Kent, P. (1992). *Technical writer's freelancing guide.* New York: Sterling.

Lant, J. L. (1991). *The consutlant's kit: Establishing and operating your successful consulting business* (3rd ed.). Cambridge, MA: JLA Publications.

Laurance, R. (1988). *Going freelance: A guide for professionals.* New York: John Wiley & Sons.

National Writers Union guide to freelance rates and standard practice. (1995). New York: National Writers Union.

Shenson, H, & Nicholas, T. (1997). *Complete guide to consulting success* (3rd ed.). Chicago: Upstart.

Society for Technical Communication. *Marketing yourself as an independently-employed professional.* (1991). Arlington, VA: Society for Technical Communication.

REFERENCE

Brooks, F. P. (1975). *The mythical man-month: Essays on software engineering.* Reading, MA: Addison-Wesley.

About the Authors

This concluding section contains some information about each of the chapter authors. We think it's important that you hear what they say about themselves so that you can understand more fully the persons speaking to you in this book. We also think that you'll find their stories—about how they became involved in technical and scientific communication—as fascinating as the chapters themselves.

MARION G. BARCHILON, PhD
"WRITING FOR ENGINEERING FIELDS"

I am an Associate Professor in the Department of Industrial Technology at Arizona State University (ASU). Since I joined ASU's faculty in 1989, I have taught engineering and technical communication courses, published extensively, and served as a professional consultant for business and industry.

My applied research/sponsored projects, teaching, and service activities have focused on the changing role of technical communication in business and industry's workplace. To that end, I have published many articles in both the technical communication and engineering disciplines on this subject. My research has helped me to identify and then help solve communication problems in business and industry. For example, my work has led me to develop new ways to use project plans to help students (future employees) improve the logic of their business communication. My work also has led me to re-examine expensive and inefficient business meetings and to develop new technical communication models that help ensure meeting productivity. Recently, I designed a new, flexible resume model that improves the content of resumes to ensure their success in the downsized, re-engineered workplace.

How did I get here? I became interested in technical communication in the early 1980s when the computer industry was burgeoning in Massachusetts. I was an executive director of an art museum and gallery, and although I enjoyed my work very much, I was beginning to think of ways in which I could become a part of a new and exciting profession that involved high technology.

Because of my graduate work in museum education, I knew that I enjoyed helping people learn. Also, since I had been an undergraduate English major, I knew I had diverse interests and abilities. In my search for the perfect profession, I contacted faculty at Northeastern University to discuss their new technical communication program. Almost immediately, I became excited about the field and decided to return to school. In hindsight, it was the best decision I ever made.

While attending Northeastern University, I put my education to work in industry by serving as a management information specialist and then a senior systems accountant/analyst in the corporate controls area at a major health insurance company in Boston. Because of my background in technical communication, I analyzed, developed, and documented business and computer systems and processes in the controller's area. I was the project leader for major development projects, supervising a team of analysts, programmers, and documentation specialists. I also recommended control solutions for implementation by corporate management.

In 1986, I moved to Arizona and continued to work in industry as a systems analyst. For the next few years, I was actively publishing in the field and serving the Phoenix Chapter of the Society for Technical Communication (STC) as General Manager of the Southwest Communicators' Conference. Then, in 1989, I was invited to apply for a position as a technical communication professor in Arizona State University's College of Engineering and Applied Sciences.

Since joining ASU, I have worked closely with engineering and technology faculty to develop new programs and courses that integrate engineering and technical communication. For example, I was the principal investigator and founder of the Sun Devil Bridge Program, a joint project with South Mountain Community College. The program, which was funded by the National Science Foundation for three years, was designed to help under-represented minority students achieve success in engineering and technology. In 1993, I also initiated an innovative long-distance electronic communication project with engineering faculty at Temple University in Philadelphia. The project's purpose was to have students from ASU and Temple work together on teams to perform research and write proposals. The project has run successfully for three years now. Additionally, I have worked closely with ASU engineering faculty to develop and implement a new engineering core course that integrates engineering design and technical communication. It is the first ASU course that is team-taught by technical communication and engineering faculty.

In 1994, I coordinated a team of faculty in technical communication, interactive computer graphics, and graphic communication, who worked together to design a program in Computer Graphics, Imaging, and Technical Communication (CIT). The purpose of this proposed program is to integrate technology, communication, and management so that engineering graduates are prepared to face the interdisciplinary challenges demanded by communication experts in industry.

Today, I am planning a new phase of my career, which is to develop electronic courses in technical communication that meet the needs of academia, business, and industry. This new area of interest and my ability to explore it are what make the technical communication field so exciting for me. Because the future drives the field, I always find that new challenges and rewards lie ahead.

REBECCA O. BARCLAY
"WRITING IN THE AEROSPACE INDUSTRY"

Writing an autobiographical narrative that describes how I came to be a technical writer in the aerospace industry (the industry about which I contributed a chapter to this book) was perhaps the hardest part of fulfilling my obligation. First, I'm not a technical writer in the aerospace industry, nor is my co-author, Dr. Thomas E. Pinelli. Although I happen to have considerable knowledge of the workings of the aerospace industry, I work as a knowledge management consultant and publisher of an electronic journal.

For the past 10 years, I have also worked with Thom Pinelli and Dr. John M. Kennedy, Director of the Center for Survey Research at Indiana University in Bloomington, IN, on a research project called the NASA/DoD Aerospace Knowledge Diffusion Research Project. Our objective was to learn how knowledge is produced, transferred, and used within the aerospace community at the individual, organizational, national, and international levels. The long-term and very practical goal of the project was to develop information that could be applied in evaluating the effectiveness of the current federal system for transferring aerospace knowledge and making specific recommendations for improvement in systems and policies for knowledge transfer.

To better understand the processes and the people involved, we surveyed approximately 20,000 aerospace engineers and scientists, academicians and students, and librarians and scientific and technical information specialists in the United States and abroad. We studied their communications practices and needs, their use of information technology and specific information products and services, the kind and extent of technical communication training they had received and its value to them, and other issues. Our work is published pretty extensively; one contributor to this book has even referred to it as "have survey, will travel." The findings of our research were recently published in book form as *Knowledge Diffusion in the U.S. Aerospace Industry: Managing Knowledge for Competitive Advantage* (Ablex Publishing Corporation, 1997).

Currently I am president of Knowledge Management Associates, Inc., a firm that provides business consulting services designed to help organizations identify, manage, and apply their knowledge resources. I am also managing editor of *Knowledge at Work,* an online journal devoted to the practical aspects of knowledge management in business (http://www.knowledge-at-work.com). My KMA partner and I recently co-authored *The Practice of Knowledge Management,* a comprehensive market report that provides a look at the origins of knowledge management, in-depth case studies of knowledge management implementations in industry and government, a systematic evaluation of more than 30 commercial knowledge management applications, and a detailed analysis of current knowledge management practices within the Fortune 1000. In addition to providing knowledge management services, I have also consulted for government and industry on ISO and ANSI standards development and implementation. In 1994, I received the Society for Technical Communication's 1994 Best of Show award for a co-authored journal article, "The Impact of Language and Culture on Technical Communication in Japan."

I came to my present position on a convoluted path, having earned a bachelor's degree in theatre arts and a master's degree in Shakespeare studies, so my educational background emphasizes communication. In addition, I took extensive coursework in biology, chemistry, and physics to give me the background I needed to apply to medical school (although I was never accepted into a program). I completed coursework for a PhD in communication and rhetoric at Rensselaer because I anticipated that my career path would lead to teaching and, in fact, I taught for ten years at the college level, supplemented by consulting work in technical communication. However, cutbacks in education, a general lack of respect for technical communication that pervades many traditional college English departments, and a particularly rewarding consulting assignment for a major software developer convinced me that a much brighter and more stimulating future lay ahead in the business world.

In building that future, I worked as an independent consultant on a wide variety of assignments that included standards development, ISO 9000 documentation development, technical writing and editing for federal agencies, textbook editing, computer documentation, and marketing communication. I found that the written and oral communication skills I brought to each job were transferable, and I developed new skills—both technical and non-technical—with each new assignment.

R. JOHN BROCKMANN, D. A.
"WRITING FOR THE COMPUTER INDUSTRY"

It's funny how you can become very good at that which initially gives you the most problems. As a youngster, I was dyslexic and had many difficult times learning to read and write. But with a lot of parental encouragement and teachers whom I still remember fondly, I eventually learned how to write. Once I did, I had plenty of fun inventing stories and writing reports. The delight in writing nurtured in these elementary school days was nearly snuffed out in high school as the rules and regulations of grammar, punctuation, and spelling took precedence over creativity. Luckily, in high school I was able to write underground student newspapers, poetry, and 60s-type political tracts and thus kept my interest in writing growing and deepening.

With my continuing interest in writing, I also soon learned I was interested in teaching writing. I have taught writing in every grade from preschool Head Start programs to juvenile reformatories to tough neighborhood high schools. In each situation, I saw that I could conjure up the same delight I personally had by encouraging these kids, for example, to write fables about their experiences or to investigate real-life murder mysteries from the microfiche of nineteenth century newspapers. I remember seeing gang members, who previously would have nothing to do with school, sitting in the city's central library on a Saturday, ferreting out clues and suspects for their assigned murder writing assignments.

When I went to a University of Michigan doctoral program to work on further ways of encouraging this delight in writing, I wanted to be sure that I would not fit the adage: "Those who can't do, teach." Thus I volunteered to take an internship in a company that had some very new technology: small desktop terminals that could work with mainframe computers. In this internship, I discovered from a new source the same delight in investigating and writing—ferreting out the correct information from multiple sources, getting unique insights on how to organize material, and then packaging it in words and pictures so that I could convince others of my ideas. In short, I had stumbled into the world of computer documentation. And I just happened to stumble into the world of computers in the late 1970s when the whole revolution in microcomputers was about to happen.

The following decade of the 1980s was an incredible ride as desktop computers hit the market with spreadsheets, then with word processing, and then with desktop publishing. I was there, I was a writing teacher, and somebody was needed to teach the computer company employees how to write. As a professor, I taught computer documentation each semester to undergraduates at the University of Delaware, and on "vacations," I brought computer documentation techniques to working programmers and technical writers. Thus, I have been able to teach computer documentation on three continents, from Israel to Australia to Singapore, with some 50 American and Canadian companies and universities in between. I have also written far more books and articles on the subject of computer documentation and the teaching of writing than I would have ever dreamed in those years long ago when I was dyslexic. I was even elected chair of the oldest organization of writers of computer documentation, SIGDOC (Association of Computing Machinery's Special Interest Group on Computer Documentation), and served two terms. In each place, in each class, and in each role I have played in the world of computer documentation, I have tried to share my delight in investigating and writing. The ways we present the findings of our investigations to our audiences have perhaps left pen and paper and have reappeared on the computer screen in hypertext and multimedia, but the delight and fun are there all the same.

My advice to you is to get an internship in computer documentation as soon as you can so that you can begin to experience the fun of investigating and sharing your ideas with others in a field that can use all the help it can get!

WILLIAM BUCHHOLZ, PhD
"WRITING IN BUSINESS AND MANUFACTURING"

Like many people who find themselves in publishing, teaching, or the media, I've always been fascinated by words and pictures. One of my earliest memories about words and pictures involves going to the movies with my sister when I was three or four. Curious about the strange red letters glowing brightly just below the lower left of the big screen, I took a pencil and notebook to the theater and copied out (very roughly) the letters E-X-I-T. My mother told me what these strange letters meant and kindled my lifelong desire to "know what the letters mean."

I couldn't wait to learn to read so that I could decipher billboards and mail. And, probably like most of us, I always preferred books with pictures. I think that haunting early linkage of the "glowing" word and entertaining pictures in the movie theater has stayed with me. Early on, I realized that letters and words were the keys to a world I wanted very much to be a part of.

A little later, I got my first paying job with words as a radio announcer. Not quite 16 years old when I started, I soon fell completely in love with radio. I worked 20 hours a week throughout the school year and put in 40-hour weeks in the summer. I was a DJ; news, weather, and sports announcer; commercial reader; and program host. The program, called "Bill's Night Out," aired for three hours on Saturday nights. I didn't write any ad copy, by the way. The announcers often just ad libbed commercials, as we looked at an outline supplied by the advertiser or taken from the local newspaper. It was fun to make a 30-second spot come in on time right to the second. Remember, we did this live on the air, just making up the entire script as we went along. However, at the end of the summer, after graduating from high school, I had to leave radio and go off to college.

In college, I majored in English—for the noble reason that it was the only subject in which I got an A my first semester. But I guess that grade was an accurate indicator of my interest in English, because early in my junior year, I decided to pursue a PhD in English at Ohio University. I wanted to study Robert Browning there with the noted Browning scholar, Professor Roma King. That study was interrupted by service in the navy during the Vietnam War. I was in Communication (what else?) with the Naval Security Group and fortunate to serve tours in Washington, DC, and Rota, Spain. After the navy, I returned to college for my PhD—this time to the University of Illinois to study the poetry of John Keats with Professor Jack Stillinger.

I was a grad student with a young family (a wife and two boys), so I was a little worried about getting a job after the PhD. I decided to teach business and technical writing at Illinois, because it seemed like a good area to get into if I decided to go into business. Besides, I always liked the idea of applying my writing and speaking skills, and what better way to do this than in the College of Commerce at the University of Illinois? One semester, I remember, was a little schizophrenic. On Tuesdays and Thursdays, I taught business and technical writing, all dressed up in a jacket, slacks, white shirt, and tie. On Mondays, Wednesdays, and Fridays, I taught poetry, all "dressed down" in jeans and a turtleneck. What a balancing act. I've always felt that Keats would have appreciated this mix of the ideal and the real.

Attracted to the East after receiving my degree, my young family and I came to Bentley College in the mid-seventies, where we've been ever since. I've been drawn to teaching about Thoreau, Emerson, Hawthorne, and the Salem Witch Trials, as well as to courses in technical writing, public relations, and business communication. In my spare time, I've been engaged in professional consulting and in teaching business and technical communication seminars at various corporations in the Boston area and around the nation. So over the years, I've managed to keep both feet in two pretty different worlds.

I'm still waiting to get back to radio, though. Maybe that would be a good place to retire. On Saturday nights somewhere in the future, way up in northern Maine—where I couldn't do too much damage—you might pick me up on your crystal sets, wheezing faintly in the distance on "Old Bill's Night Out." Give me a call. I'd be more than happy to play your request.

PATRICIA L. CORNETT, PhD
"WRITING IN MEDICAL AND HEALTH
CARE ENVIRONMENTS"

When I got my PhD in English from the University of Michigan in 1975, after four years of teaching English literature and composition at Wayne State University in Detroit, Michigan, a career in medical communications was the farthest goal from my mind. Even if someone had suggested it to me, I wouldn't have been interested since I had never heard of medical writing. I wanted to teach college English, especially my hard-earned doctoral specialty—Renaissance drama and Shakespeare.

Yet three years later, I was a medical editor in the research department at Henry Ford Hospital in Detroit. Because the academic job market was dismal in the mid-1970s, I was forced to make an abrupt career change. Besides my PhD in English, my qualifications for the medical editor's job were my credentials as a college composition teacher (in my resume I wrote that I had "edited" hundreds of student compositions), some freelance copyediting experience (for the Wayne State University Press and the Bureau of Business Research in the University of Michigan Graduate Business School), and two undergraduate science courses—botany and geology. Hardly preparation for a career in medical communications! Since then, however, I have met other medical communicators whose academic backgrounds are remarkably similar to mine, not enough perhaps to consider this background a solid career

path to medical writing, but enough to encourage you if you are majoring in English rather than in science or medicine. My chapter discusses
the kind of academic background that will help prepare you for a career
in medical communications.

To say I learned on the job at Henry Ford Hospital is a gross under-
statement. It took me about a year, including the first three months, in
which I was sure I had made the biggest mistake of my life. But by the
end of the first year, I felt comfortable enough with the language of
medicine and the format of medical writing to consider making my
career change permanent instead of the temporary respite from academia I first envisioned. Also, my initiation into medical communications was eased by starting as a medical editor rather than as a medical
writer. Besides medical manuscript editing, I was also the managing editor of the hospital-sponsored medical journal. This job gave me an
invaluable opportunity to learn about all aspects of producing a publication, from layout and key lining to printing and distribution. By 1985, I
had gained enough confidence and experience in my second career to
start my own medical publications business. In it, I have developed additional experience as a pharmaceutical writer and producer of medical
and health care publications.

Shortly after I started at Henry Ford Hospital, I discovered the American Medical Writers Association (AMWA) and the many wonderful kin-
dred spirits who encouraged my efforts to become a competent medical
editor. If you are considering a career in this field, I strongly recommend that you join this organization and take advantage of everything it
has to offer. Thanks to AMWA's workshops, meetings, networking, and
friendships, I got a sound professional education in medical communications. Without this organization, I would never have succeeded in my
career as quickly or as well. To repay my debt, I became active in
AMWA, first as president of the Michigan chapter for two years. Then I
rose through the administrative ranks and became the National President of AMWA in 1988-89, just 10 years after I started a career in medical communications.

For a long time after I established my medical communications career,
I was not tempted to return to academic teaching, although I gave many
educational workshops at AMWA meetings through the 1980s and 90s
and at one point was the Director of AMWA's Education Department.
But in 1991 I returned to university teaching, this time to teach technical communication at Lawrence Technological University, a small engineering and architecture school in Southfield, Michigan. Now I combine
both careers, using my professional experience in medical writing to
teach technical communication.

I have other interests besides medical communications and teaching, such as food and cooking (especially culinary history), travel, Michigan history, and Shakespearean drama. But as I look back over where I have come in the last 20 years, I realize that all of my interests revolve around editing, writing, and publications. I love to eat and cook, but besides the endless hours I happily spend in the kitchen, I have turned my passion into several writing and editing projects, including a short freelance stint as a cookbook editor for a Chinese cookbook and several years as the editor of the newsletter for the Culinary Historians of Ann Arbor. I also love to travel and pursue the recreational delights of the Great Lakes and my adopted state of Michigan. Ten years ago, I worked with the Wayne State University Press to reprint a classic work on Michigan history. I adopted U. P. Hedrick's *The Land of the Crooked Tree*, his biography about growing up in northern Michigan at the end of the 19th century, promoted its reprinting, and wrote an introduction for the new edition. Most recently, I have managed to join two of my interests, Shakespeare and food, by presenting a paper on English cookery in Shakespeare's plays at an academic meeting.

Apart from providing me with a satisfying livelihood for the last 15 years, my career in medical communications has allowed me to develop my writing skills in ways I could never have imagined when I got my PhD. I did not go to college to become a medical writer. Like many other medical communicators of my generation, I fell into the field almost by accident, borne of a need to find respectable employment that would make use of my academic training. In retrospect, however, that fall was serendipitous. Because of my career in medical communications, I have become a professional writer and editor, sharing ideas and information through the medium of publication. Whether I am reviewing a new technology, such as laser surgery to dissolve kidney stones; writing about drugs to help retard the ravages of Alzheimer's disease; or researching the complex pharmacological interactions between drugs, gender, and ethnicity, I am always learning something new, often on the cutting edge of modern medicine. For diversity and challenge, a career in medical communications cannot be surpassed.

DAVID N. DOBRIN, PhD
"FREELANCING OR CONSULTING"

I got my first job in technical writing only because there were no qualified applicants, and I have continued to mow down the competition ever since. A Bachelor of Science in math and a PhD in English literature, I taught technical writing for two years at Miami University and five years at Massachusetts Institute of Technology—where, for several years, I was the lowest paid person on the faculty.

After I parted company with M.I.T., I wrote for a living, documenting financial software, developing training materials for workmen's compensation departments in several states, and writing manuals on DOS extender software and the use of TCP/IP protocols. I also published frequently on graphic design.

After several years of this, I landed a job developing documentation and training material for a manufacturing software firm in California. I am now a consultant in manufacturing processes and business re-engineering in Cambridge, Massachusetts.

JOAN STRAWSON DOLLARHIDE
"WRITING IN HAZARDOUS WASTE MANAGEMENT"

My mission is to promote environmental protection and preserve natural resources with a multidisciplinary approach, using my knowledge of science, law, and communication. I want to help others solve environmental problems and learn about environmental protection. However, I have come to this point by a roundabout route.

A college summer job at the National Cancer Institute convinced me that I wanted a career investigating the health effects of chemicals that are contaminating the environment. So I headed off to graduate school at the University of Kentucky, completing a master's degree in toxicology in 1986. During my years as a graduate student, however, I learned two very important things about myself. First, I hate killing mice (it's hard to believe, I know)—something toxicologists are expected to do regularly. Second, I enjoyed telling people about science more than I enjoyed doing science.

The second phase of my professional life started when I completed a master's degree in technical and scientific communication in 1988. For several years, I have worked in jobs where I communicated about the effects of environmental contaminants. The most rewarding was as Director of the U.S. EPA's Superfund Health Risk Technical Support Center, where I worked with other scientists to explain the health effects of chemicals found at Superfund sites and with the public to help them understand how scientific information was used to make decisions about how to clean up Superfund sites.

Over the years, I have come to realize that environmental problems cannot be solved with science alone, because many problems arise out of legal rather than scientific issues. To round out my knowledge, I attended law school and finished my degree in May 1997. I have also started work with a nonprofit organization, Toxicology Excellence for Risk Assessment (TERA), as director of Education and Public Involvement. Working for a nonprofit provides me with a neutral, nonbiased arena in which to carry out my mission.

In my spare time (a foreign concept!), I enjoy riding my horses, Tucker and Hasufel, and helping my husband remodel our farmhouse. I also try to fit a good novel in when time allows.

KAREN LEVINE
"TECHNICAL AND SCIENTIFIC
COMMUNICATORS IN ADVERTISING"

Daughter of two physicians, I recall dinner table conversations from my childhood that were exercises in technical and scientific communication. Patiently and precisely, my parents would explain complex medical terms and procedures in words my brother and I could understand. My mother, an amateur poet, also taught me to love the nuances and rhythms of the English language. My father, intellectually driven and extremely focused, taught me to respect its razor-sharp precision.

Yet I had no clue what a cornerstone strong communication skills would be to my professional development. Unlike many people who enter college with a career in mind, I studied philosophy without a thought to how I might earn a living. In retrospect, some career counseling might have streamlined the route I took to arrive at my present career. As it was, my language ability, coupled with the disciplined approach to problem-solving I'd learned studying philosophy, probably landed me my first job after college—conducting nonferrous metals market research and producing commodity forecasts for a major, international minerals corporation headquartered in New York.

I spent eight years in the metals industry, the last three with Exxon. When a major restructuring eliminated my job, my communications skills probably saved me from the unemployment line. I was reassigned to a project development department as a technical editor. In so doing, Exxon unwittingly launched my career in technical communication.

One long, snowy winter in a small town in northern Wisconsin, as I worked with an Exxon project team to prepare an environmental impact report for submission to the state Department of Natural Resources, I made several discoveries. Working in a large corporation felt, surprisingly, very limiting to me. I felt pigeon-holed, and I wanted more diversity and autonomy than a career in a large corporation seemed likely to provide. I also wanted to change industries. At the time, the metals business was run by a male fraternity, to which I, for obvious reasons, would never belong.

I realized, too, that native intelligence alone would not foster career growth. I would need a specialist's credentials, a "label" that companies would find familiar, in order to be marketable. It was only then, approaching thirtysomething, that I recognized I could make a career out of one of the things I do best: communicating clearly. And while working as a technical editor, I'd discovered that the ability to communicate was in short supply in industry.

Everything fast forwards from there. Finally, I had a career path in mind: to marry marketing expertise and communication ability to help companies promote technical products and services effectively and with some pizzazz. I resigned from Exxon, and completed a master's degree in technical and scientific communication. A midsize, midwestern advertising agency with a high concentration of business-to-business clients recruited me out of graduate school to develop a technical marketing communications function within the agency, starting with one of their Fortune 500 clients. Today, I am Director of Communications for a corporate identity consulting firm, responsible for the communications services we provide clients. Our clients are in a diverse group of industries: banking and finance, plastics and specialty chemicals, health care, construction, real estate development, high technology, basic materials, energy, higher education, professional services, retail, and the performing arts.

Variety has been a hallmark of both my life and my work as a communicator. To date, I've lived and worked in eight cities—everything from the fast track of New York to a quiet little community of just a few thousand. I've worked for the largest corporation on the Fortune 500 list and now for a consulting firm of 20. I've created communications concepts and materials for clients in over eighteen different industries.

I know now that I do what I do for a living largely because it's who I have always been at heart—a communicator, a problem-solver, and a promoter. Over the years, I've named products and written and produced countless marketing and technical brochures, annual reports, data sheets, print and broadcast ads, direct mail programs, trade show and special events plans, public relations programs, press releases, and more.

You won't see my name, though. These materials never carry a byline. So if you choose a career in advertising, you must be prepared to get your satisfaction from the challenges of the work and from seeing your clients succeed, because it will not come from seeing your name in print.

RICKI LEWIS, PhD
"SCIENCE WRITING"

I never consciously set out to become a science writer. My career goal, from my earliest memories of dragging home creatures dead or alive, was to be a biologist. When I discovered fossils, that shifted to paleontology for awhile, then back to the living. Throughout school, I wrote constantly, even won essay contests, but still always thought I would be a scientist. Special English classes in high school taught me much of what I know about writing—I received credit for all required college English while still in high school. I was not to take a formal course in journalism until I was very close to earning my PhD in genetics.

That course, science journalism at Indiana University, convinced me that writing was what I was meant to do. By that time, I'd had a chance to fully experience "doing" science and was finding that concentrating on one problem—flies with legs growing out of their heads—16 hours a day, year after year, was a bit too narrow for me. I thrived on the diversity journalism offered and liked the camaraderie compared to the cutthroat competition of science. Through the journalism course, I made the contacts necessary to begin writing for the school and then the local newspaper—the best possible training.

So after earning my PhD, I built a dual career, freelance writing for magazines (starting with the then-brand-new *Self* and a few others) and being a zoology professor. I met with several publishers and began my career as a college textbook author, although it would be a decade before my first text was published. After moving to upstate New York in 1982, I embarked on two other careers—motherhood and genetic counseling. Today, I've had three textbooks and more than a thousand magazine/journal articles published. I haven't the time for university teaching anymore, but I still do quite a bit of genetic counseling. The clinical experience finds its way into much of my writing.

My science background has opened many doors for me. If you want to be a science writer, my advice is to do science for a time—a summer program is perfect. If you can think like a scientist, yet maintain a journalist's objectivity and curiosity, you will make a great science writer.

SANDRA J. LOBBESTAEL
"PHARMACEUTICAL WRITING"

My career started in the basic sciences; today I own AZTECH Communications, a consultant firm for writing, editing, conducting research, and preparing documents using desktop publishing. As I look back, some markers along the way remain clear, and others have become clouded with the passage of time. One thing has been constant, however, and that is my interest in words and what they can do, either alone or together. The following describes a few highlights enroute to where I am today.

My education dates back to a time of one-room country schools with one teacher for 10-20 students in kindergarten through eighth grades. Spare time was filled with reading books from the "library," a collection of books in cupboards that spanned the back wall of the schoolroom. By the time Fowler School closed, I had completed seventh grade and had very few books yet to read. This experience had opened new worlds, the most intriguing of which was science. Throughout my life, science has continued to challenge me, and words to captivate me.

I studied chemistry, math, and physics during undergraduate training and then earned a master's degree in organic chemistry. English and communications courses were inserted into my curriculum to give me the traditional liberal arts training. My first full-time job after college was as a research chemist in the pharmaceutical industry, where I designed and synthesized novel compounds for testing as potential drugs in several therapeutic areas. I started working at the end of the golden era of the pharmaceutical industry. Hoffmann-LaRoche had just marketed Librium® and Valium®; Parke-Davis was a giant with its anti-biotic, Chloromycetin®. And scientists around the world were busy looking for new drugs. It was very exciting.

And with the surge of research in the scientific community, there was an increase in the number of scientific journals and publications. However, at this time, original work used as a basis for patent applications was not allowed to be published until much later, as doing so could compromise the future of the drug. Indeed, much of my work appeared in scientific publications and patents much later than when I had done the work. Much of my work remains locked in laboratory notebooks that I carefully maintained throughout those days.

While employed as an organic chemist, I completed MBA studies. Later, complications from a broken back forced a career change, as I was no longer able to perform the physical tasks required for lab work. I could design, but not perform, the experiments. Some thought I should claim long-term disability and go on permanent leave; others avoided discussing the situation, hoping it would go away. I, of course, had other thoughts and requested that I be allowed to prepare manuscripts for publication of my research results. I did this temporarily and then had an opportunity to move to the medical writing department, where I prepared documents to support the registration of new drugs.

The first year was extremely challenging. I was given a desk with a computer in an office shared with another writer, a style manual that described the format by which all my documents were to be prepared, and two handbooks of policies and procedures I needed to follow. These handbooks did not include the many guidelines and regulations the Federal Food and Drug Administration (FDA) had issued, nor did they include the special requirements for each of the many types of reports I would prepare. All that would be covered later—on my own time—under the heading "on-the-job training." Also, they neglected to tell me that the environment was so dynamic that the information in the handbooks was outdated. That, too, I discovered on my own, when a vice president initialed and returned my draft report without providing review comments. I thought that strange, and I asked about it. His answer was simple—he only saw the final copy for his signature. The procedure had changed, but the department had not revised their procedures accordingly. Of course, he thought I had not given him the final draft.

Every project was a major undertaking; I had to research everything. It was time-consuming, and time was not in abundance. Reports seemed always to be due yesterday. And if they didn't issue on schedule, the whole world knew. Such challenges were exhilarating, albeit draining. I learned quickly, and later, as a manager, I coordinated the work of other writers as they completed major projects that culminated in many regulatory submissions.

During this time, I participated on interdepartmental teams and continued my education through on-the-job training as well as by completing job-related courses for clinical research, computers, regulatory affairs, and writing. I received dual certification in medical communication with multidisciplinary and regulatory affairs specialties through education programs sponsored by the American Medical Writers Association, of which I am a member.

Writing and editing remain an integral part of my life, despite my having moved from medical writing into other areas of specialization within the pharmaceutical industry. In fact, I continue to write reports for submission of safety data to regulatory authorities worldwide, including the FDA. And in my spare time, I write fiction, participate on panels, lecture, and conduct workshops.

I have met many challenges and had many opportunities over the years. I look forward to many more.

THOMAS E. PINELLI
"WRITING IN THE AEROSPACE INDUSTRY"

I am currently a co-principal investigator of the NASA/DoD Aerospace Knowledge Diffusion Project and the instructional technology and distance learning officer in the Office of Education at the NASA Langely

Research Center (Mail Stop 400, Hampton, VA 23681; e-mail: t.e.pinelli@larc.nasa.gov). From 1992 to 1996, I was the Head of the Visual Imaging Branch, Research INformation and Applications Division. I received my MSLS from Catholic University and my PhD from Indiana University, Bloomington, in 1990. My research interests include technology policy, technological innovation, and knowledge diffusion. I am co-author of "The Impact of Language and Culture on Technical Communication in Japan," which won Technical Communication's Outstanding Article Award for 1994. My professional appointments include Associate Editor (for research) of *Technical Communication*, 1983–1996 and member of the ASIS Public Information Policy Committee, the SLA Research Committee, and the American Institute of Aeronautics and Astronautics (AIAA) Technical Information Committee. I also chaired NISO standard Z39.18, Scientific and Technical Reports: Elements, Organizations, and Design in 1985 and 1994, and have authored or co-authored 150 conference papers, journal articles, technical reports, book chapters, and book reviews.

MELINDA THIESSEN SPENCER
"WRITING FOR THE ENVIRONMENTAL SCIENCES"

I have worked in the environmental communications field for 10 years, gaining experience in many of the disciplines described in my chapter. After graduating with a master's degree in technical and scientific communication, I began my career as a technical editor for an environmental consulting firm, reviewing all types of documents related to regulatory compliance and prevention of environmental degradation. As my knowledge of these subjects increased, I began researching and writing sections of reports, especially those related to health risk assessment and environmental impacts on biological resources, using knowledge gained from my undergraduate degree in biological sciences. After two years with this firm, I became the manager of the technical communications group for the Sacramento, California, office. I also began applying my skills in the new discipline of community relations (prompted by the Superfund Amendments and Reauthorization Act of 1986).

As a community relations specialist, I was a liaison among industry, government agencies, special interest groups, and the public. I translated technical information so various audiences could readily understand and participate in discussions about environmental problems, and I opened the lines of communication between groups with conflicting perspectives about environmental issues. My community relations work required me to travel to communities across the country.

My most memorable adventure in community relations took me to a very remote part of Alaska by bush plane. My job was to open up communications between people affected by environmental contamination at a remote airfield and air force officials in Anchorage. It was gratifying to work one-on-one with people, to hear their concerns, and to relay those concerns to people who could provide answers. If people hadn't had access to accurate and understandable information, they could easily have felt victimized by the agency or industry that caused the pollution. In general, people who have information can feel armed and can have a voice in decisions that affect their environment.

After six years in environmental consulting, I took two years off to earn a master of philosophy degree in peace studies from Trinity College in Dublin, Ireland. My work in environmental community relations prompted me to take a broader look at causes of conflict. I'd focused on science and communications in my first degree, and I wanted to round out my education by learning about the political, ethical, religious, and economic causes of conflict. Expanding my knowledge helped me return to my career with renewed energy and a much broader perspective.

Currently, I work as a scientific communications consultant in Seattle, Washington, where my focus remains on community relations activities and freelance writing. I contributed four chapters to the text *Biosphere 2000: Protecting Our Global Environment*, (Donald G. Kaufman and Cecilia M. Franz, New York: HarperCollins College Publishers, 1993), and am currently working on a novel.

LISA MEEDER TURNBULL
"WRITING FOR GOVERNMENT AND NONPROFIT
SOCIAL SERVICE AGENCIES"

I became a technical writer because my undergraduate mentor thought I would be good at it. After completing a bachelor of arts in foreign language and international studies, I chose to pursue a master's degree in technical and scientific communication. The latter offered the perfect opportunity to build on previous academic work and internship experience while developing my interest in stakeholder relations in the government and nonprofit sectors.

For the first six years of my career, I served as Program Manager and later Assistant to the Director, Development and Stakeholder Relations, in the Center for Chemical Education at Miami University, Middletown, Ohio. This organization's mission is to enhance science education through professional development for teachers and enrichment opportunities for students. My role was to develop new programming, identify and pursue sources of funding, and maintain communication with the Center's various constituent groups. Because I joined the organization as it was becoming established, I had a unique opportunity to develop a career path that offered a broad range of experience in several stakeholder relations functions.

In August 1995, I became the development officer for the Institute for Biospheric Studies at Yale University, a position I held for two years. It was during this period that I developed an outside research interest in nonprofit management, with a particular focus on churches as organizations. In June 1996, I received a graduate-level Certificate in Nonprofit Management from Case Western Reserve University. While earning this degree, I gained consulting experience in strategic planning for nonprofit organizations and learned how to conduct related research in financial management and strategic financial analysis, analysis of organizational structure and culture, and human resources management with an emphasis on conflict/resolution analysis. My practicum was hosted by the First Congregational Church of Greenwich, Old Greenwich, Connecticut. I intend for this study to form the basis of future academic undertakings.

In June 1997, I became Director of Graduate and External Relations at the Yale Divinity School. I am directly responsible for three functional areas of the School's administration: I manage all aspects of alumni relations; I am responsible for the School's alumni magazine and other publications; and I am the School's publicist, handling both proactive and reactive media relations, as well as selecting and purchasing advertising media for the School. In addition to the work for which I am directly responsible, I also serve as an in-house consultant to other administrative offices within the Divinity School in the areas of alumni relations, publications, and publicity and media relations. The daily activities of the position require both technical competence and interpersonal skills; in addition, I must have the vision to see the role of the office and its functions in the broader scheme of the School's future and be sufficiently comfortable in a managerial position to supervise a small staff and maintain a departmental budget.

I entered the technical communication profession on faith, and it turned out to be a great decision. To help give you a formal introduction to the profession, or lack thereof, was my primary motivation in accepting the challenge to contribute the chapter "Writing for Government and Nonprofit Social Service Agencies." I hope this chapter will be informative to those of you who will become my future colleagues, all of whom I wish the best of luck.

CHRISTOPHER VELOTTA
"WRITING FOR THE COMPUTER INDUSTRY"

I sometimes wonder if my interest in technical communication has anything to do with my childhood experiences watching my father struggle valiantly to put things together and hearing him grumble about those "lousy instructions." I'm sure those experiences contributed, but I'd attribute most of my interest to my love of writing, which grew from my love of reading.

From an early age, I read whatever I could find. I often marveled at how my favorite authors could create whole new, incredibly detailed worlds and how they could communicate their ideas as if they were talking directly to me. Slowly, I began to build confidence in my own writing ability as I gravitated toward English and literature courses in school.

However, I also had a strong interest in technical subjects, especially in anything having to do with the sea. This seemingly odd combination of interests led me to major in creative writing and to minor in marine biology as an undergraduate at Bowling Green State University (BGSU). When I finally learned about the field of technical communication in my junior year, I knew that I had found a way to combine my interests while pursuing a career.

I then took as many technical communication courses as I could in my remaining time at BGSU. However, I knew that there was much more to learn and experience before I was prepared to enter the job market, so I enrolled in the master's program in technical communication at Oklahoma State University. While there, I completed a two–month internship, taught two technical communication courses per semester, presented papers at professional conferences, wrote until my fingers ached, and took courses in editing, grammar, cognitive psychology, management, and advanced technical communication, among others. During this time, I also developed a strong interest in computers. I learned everything I could about them as tools during my internship and wrote programs on the computer I purchased for my schoolwork. This experience taught me that I could learn unfamiliar, technical subjects on my own, and I found the achievement to be very rewarding.

The confidence I gained in my communication ability and in my technical aptitude helped me land my first job with the NCR Corporation. I started out developing information products for computer subsystems, peripherals, and networks and was even able to teach an internal engineering class on one of our products in my first year.

After a few years, I took a position in a corporate staff organization, providing support for our information products departments company-wide. We provided assistance in process development, university relations, quality improvement, and tools and technology. From there, I moved to my current position on a re-engineering project, charged with creating new processes and software applications to support our company's sales and fulfillment functions.

Each assignment has broadened my exposure to the company and stretched the limits of what I believe I can accomplish. That's what keeps the job interesting, and as you embark on your career, I hope you'll find what interests you and continue to take chances and expand your horizons.

Author Index